getting the
bugs out

getting the bugs out

The rise, fall, and comeback
of Volkswagen in America

DAVID KILEY

John Wiley & Sons, Inc.

Published by John Wiley & Sons, Inc., New York.
Published simultaneously in Canada.

All photographs courtesy of Volkswagen of America

This publication is designed to provide accurate and authoritative information in regard to the subject matter covered. It is sold with the understanding that the publisher is not engaged in rendering professional services. If professional advice or other expert assistance is required, the services of a competent professional person should be sought.

Library of Congress Cataloging-in-Publication Data

Kiley, David.
    Getting the bugs out : the rise, fall, and comeback of Volkswagen of America / David Kiley.
       p. cm.
    Includes bibliographical references and index.
    ISBN 0-471-40393-8 (cloth : alk. paper)
    1. Volkswagen of America, inc.   2. Automobile industry and trade—United States.   3. Corporations, German—United States.   4. Corporate turnarounds—United States.   I. Title.

HD9710.U54 V655 2001
338.7'6292'0973—dc21   2001046543

Printed in the United States of America.

10 9 8 7 6 5 4 3 2 1

This book is dedicated to the memory of my father, Charles Kiley, who inspired me to appreciate a good story. And to my mother, Billee, who still inspires me to love life and the things that are worth writing about.

Contents

Acknowledgments

It's difficult to know where to start when thanking people for the help they provided in a project like this. I would have been lost without the help of many good friends and loved ones.

First on my list is Daniel Forbes, both a treasured friend and talented writer who lent his time, counsel, and sharp pencil to my efforts. Every writer should have a friend and fellow writer who is as generous with his time and good nature as Dan. My wife, Amy, who helped me research and implement Dan's many useful suggestions, was invaluable as well. Amy also supported me in ways that are difficult to detail here, picking up the slack in our lives when I had to spend so many weekends and evenings writing and editing. Thanks also to my sister, Anne Kiley, whose keen eyes I drew upon for photo selection. Thanks to Jessica Noyes at John Wiley & Sons for her help and patience.

I offer thanks to the people at Volkswagen of America who could not have been more helpful to me. Dr. Jens Neumann was generous with his time and approvals for others to help. Steve Keyes, Tony Fouladpour, and Chris Drouin gave me access to the company's archives and provided much help in fact checking. They are tops in the business.

Arnold Communications has been building something special in the field of advertising. This does not surprise me, as it is a company made up of lovely and talented people who were very generous with their time. Special thanks to Jon Castle and Ben Muldrew, who were my go-to people and frequent e-mail recipients on matters of advertising.

Clive Warrilow, Steve Wilhite, Dave Huyett, and Bill Young gave me invaluable interviews. Without their help, there would have been no book.

John Slaven, though not around to enjoy the book, gave me vital help over the years and encouraged me to write this book. I daresay the results would have been even better had he been around to kibitz. I am grateful to him and to his son, Drew Slaven, who was helpful in assembling research material.

Andrew Jaffe has helped me in my career more than a few times. It was he who supported the project with John Wiley & Sons, and I thank him for his efforts.

A writer could not ask for a more delightful, supportive, and helpful editor than Airié Dekidjiev. She has the vital skill that every editor needs: the ability to make a good writer look better than he is. Thank you.

Introduction

Volkswagen of America has experienced huge success and bitter failure. From just two deliveries in 1949, the brand rose to capture 5 percent of the auto market in 1970. It then plummeted to less than 1 percent in 1990. In 1975 Volkswagen lost its position as the leading import brand in the United States to Toyota. The Japanese combination of value for the money and high quality could not be matched by either the Germans or the Big Three. Though Volkswagen was the first import to build a U.S. assembly plant when it began building Rabbits in Pennsylvania in 1978, just a decade later the plant was shuttered. Beset by its own arrogance throughout the 1980s, Volkswagen was with an inattentive mother company in Germany, had currency disadvantages, and an unwillingness to recognize the special needs of the U.S. market apart from its home market of Western Europe and the developing markets like Brazil and Eastern Europe.

Volkswagen reached its nadir in 1993 when it held less than a 0.5 percent market share. Unable to supply its dealers with product from its Mexican plant, which was experiencing severe quality problems, Volkswagen actually paid dealers to stay in business. By 1996, though, sales had trended upward; a decision to bring back the legendary Beetle was made, and fears that VW would leave the U.S. market evaporated. The result is a remarkable story of how a company blazed a path, lost its way, and then found itself again.

———

It is difficult to pinpoint when the idea for this book first arose. I wrote my first Volkswagen piece in 1989 for a magazine called *Adweek's Marketing Week,* later renamed *Brandweek.*[1] Entitled "Can VW Survive?", it prompted me to think of a book that might be called *Bugged: The Fall of Volkswagen in America.* I was intrigued by the brand that had played such an amazing role to a generation of Americans. This brand, an icon, had been loved and had meaning. Volkswagen was a leading player in a cultural revolution in the United States. It had brand equity that companies spend hundreds of millions of dollars to craft and nurture. Disney made the Beetle a movie star! Yet, in 1988 the company was caving in. It was on its knees. The U.S. management, who was all I had access to at the time, seemed extraordinarily patient for a company that had gone from selling over one-half million cars in 1970 to less than 200,000 in 1988.

I recall asking then Volkswagen of America Executive Vice President Bill Young about the possibility of bringing the Beetle back to juice things up again. His response: "That's not going to happen, and for a lot of very good reasons." Young, a long-time respected Volkswagen executive, who had recently returned to the company after a six-year hiatus, spoke of an outmoded design that the company had discontinued for good reason. In fact, Young was right. Volkswagen had stopped making the Beetle for sound business reasons. The company had made so many mistakes regarding the U.S. market in the mid-1970s and 1980s that the lack of a Beetle was hardly the biggest problem.

When the last Beetle Cabrio was delivered to a U.S. dealership for sale in 1980, sales of the Bug were less than 5,000. It was not quite the great value that it once had been, compared with the Japanese cars that were arriving in the United States at the time. In addition, it certainly did not meet Washington's toughening safety standards. Volkswagen AG in Germany, full of proud and talented designers and engineers, had every reason to believe that the Golf, to be sold in the United States as the Rabbit when it was introduced in 1975, would do just fine in maintaining the brand's sales volume and market share. In fact, the company was sure that business would grow. It built a factory in Pennsylvania to crank out cars and was planning a second plant in Michigan by 1980.

———

What took Volkswagen a decade to understand, from 1980 to 1990, was how vital the Beetle was to the Volkswagen brand in the United States. It was the soul of the brand in North America, a fact lost on the Germans. They were all too ready to move on to the next big thing. In fact, the company that had done so much to revolutionize advertising through the 1960s and 1970s (and not just car advertising) appeared to have lost its brand management skills entirely. It's unimaginitive, dishwater advertising reflected what the public at large had come to view as the bland, pedestrian products—the Golf, Scirocco, Quantum, and Jetta. They were as successful in Europe as the Beetle had been. In the United States, however, these cars had neither the quality nor the personality that VW lovers had come to cherish in the 1960s and 1970s with the Beetle, Karmann Ghia, Microbus, and Squareback wagon. And the spotty quality of the newer products, as contrasted with the Japanese companies' exacting standards, became a bigger issue in the United States than Germany was willing to comprehend.

At bottom, though, the company underestimated how critical an ingredient the Beetle was to its recipe for success in the United States. Other companies, like Honda and Toyota, had scooped up Volkswagen customers with cars that were dependable, fuel-efficient, and peppy. A generation of advertising copywriters had gone to school on the work Doyle Dane Bernbach did for Volkswagen, and they injected personality into the advertising of Honda, Subaru, and later, Saturn.

Japanese quality surpassed Volkswagen's, as well as the U.S. Big Three, by a wide margin. From a personality standpoint, Honda, Subaru, and Saturn became the spiritual successors to Volkswagen. They married quality with that essential, quirky lovability.

———

Like many others, I have a personal relationship to the Beetle. I'm not sure that I would have latched on to the VW story in the way that I did if it were not for a purchase that I made in the spring of 1982, when I took a year off from college halfway through my freshman year to "find myself." I began the journey by buying a 1964 white Volkswagen Beetle from my neighbor. Margaret Wolf, a friend of our family, lived across the street and was the widow of a craggy, cigar-chewing German, Karl, who bought the Beetle new and maintained it himself. The car cost me $250 to drive across the street to my driveway, and this included the book, *Fix Your Volkswagen,* by Jud Purvis, which still had Karl's oily fingerprints on the pages. Even with 100,000 miles on it, the car seemed like a deal for the price. It would eventually cost me (and my father) another $1,500 in repairs over the next 18 months before it gave up the ghost after too many trips on the New Jersey Turnpike between Westfield, New Jersey, and Fordham University in the Bronx where I finished my schooling. That year of finding myself took me to a frigid dock on the west side of Manhattan where I loaded and unloaded trucks of copier paper, and to the broiling loading bay of Channel Home Center in Springfield, New Jersey, where I unloaded trucks of two-by-fours and fiberglass insulation. Those experiences were enough to lead me back to the classroom. My Bug saw me through it all.

———

After taking possession of my Beetle's keys, I immediately discovered something that is shared by almost everyone who owns one of the original Beetles: The car is not so much a mode of transportation; rather, it is a medium—a canvas. The car's simplicity and its lightweight and eggish shape made it more an extension of its owner than any car I have ever driven or even encountered. In no time I had pried off the rusting running boards and replaced them with lacquered oak. On the floor I installed green, and later, brown indoor-outdoor carpeting filched from Channel Home Center. My dear and tireless mother custom-fit imitation sheepskin seat covers. I replaced the AM radio with a Kraco AM/FM cassette player, and I mounted speakers in the well behind the rear seat on a wooden shelf. It took me all day to discover that I couldn't match a 12-volt stereo to a 6-volt battery. It is the only time in my life when I ever tinkered with the dashboard in a car, but I did so because the Beetle's rear-mounted engine made access a breeze. In fact, more opportunities for repair on that car seemed within my limited mechanical reach than any other car I've owned. The only time that I really crossed the line between ability and ineptitude was when I thought I could paint the car emerald green with a half-dozen cans of spray paint from the parts store. I only got as far as making a mess of the hood before I broke down and repainted it a version of white that was close, but not an exact match, to the rest of the car.

I have always had a subconscious love for the Beetle, I think, because three of my favorite teachers drove them.

1. Miss Jane Sterling, who taught me in second grade, drove a yellow Cabrio Beetle. She may still be driving it, for all I know.
2. Karin Ninesling, my eighth-grade English teacher, drove a yellow Beetle in which she gave me many rides to school as she saw me walking on North Avenue in Westfield toward Roosevelt Junior High.
3. The late Richard Veit, my seventh-grade geography teacher, too, drove a Beetle, as did many wise, if underpaid, teachers.

By 1996 and 1997, I was glad not to have undertaken the book that I envisioned in 1988, because I would look pretty foolish today. Under the leadership of Ferdinand Piëch (the grandson of Beetle originator Ferdinand Porsche) and helped by talented people at Volkswagen of America and an ad agency (Arnold Communications), the company came to its senses and reincarnated the Beetle as the New Beetle.

Volkswagen's recovery has been enormously helped by the New Beetle. The redoing of the Bug, however, is not the whole story. Yes, the New Beetle has certainly been a rallying point for the company, its followers, and its dealers; however, excellent remakes of the Passat, Golf, and Jetta have also driven success. Piëch is a product man first and last, and it shows in perhaps the most fun-to-drive vehicles in the industry. We will never know if the stunning recovery of Volkswagen in the United States, which continues into 2001 when the company expects to sell close to 400,000 vehicles, would have been possible without the New Beetle. The company well might have recovered anyway, given the brilliant restyling of the other cars. It seems certain, though, that recovery would not have taken place as quickly, nor would the people responsible have had nearly as much fun.

———

Volkswagen had already embarked on a car that would become the New Beetle before it fired its longtime ad agency, DDB Needham, and hired Arnold Communications. The work that Arnold did, though, to reposition the Volkswagen brand in advance of the New Beetle's arrival has a great deal to do with the company's turnaround. The brilliant work that it did with the launch of the New Beetle—the classic though still original homage to Volkswagen's world-beating advertising of the 1960s and 1970s—deserved the many awards that followed.

———

One of my first interviews for that initial story on Volkswagen was with John "Jake" Slaven, at that time the former director of advertising for Volkswagen, whom I had come to know as an executive at the ad agency Scali, McCabe, Sloves. Slaven, though he had moved on to another car brand, Volvo, never lost his affection for VW, and continued to consult for the company into the 1990s after his tumultuous agency days were behind him. It was Slaven who fostered my interest in writing a book about the brand. He remarked more than once that the Volkswagen brand would come back, "Because it's so much bigger than the people who come and go at the company and the agency and seem to have an infinite capacity for screwing it up." After that first story ran in 1988, Slaven also told me to keep my notes on the subsequent Volkswagen stories I would write, "Because there's a book about this brand to be written." Slaven said from time to time that he might write it, but he doubted that he would because he continued to earn part of his living from VW right up until his untimely death in 1999. I thank him for encouraging me to save my notes.

———

The objective of this book is not to capture all of Volkswagen's complex history in one volume. Reporters and historians have produced some wonderful scholarship on Volkswagen's early years of the 1930s and 1940s, as well as its U.S. growth in the 1950s and 1960s. Many of the people whom those reporters interviewed are now gone, and I would be foolish to try to surpass them.

I hope that I have included enough historical information and insight to give readers a sense of Volkswagen's story. My goals are to provide a sketch of Volkswagen's history, going back to the 1930s so readers can appreciate the brand's importance throughout most of the twentieth century, and to chronicle the remarkable comeback of the company in the 1990s, especially in the United States.

As someone who has worked in the advertising business and seen some of the most inept marketing and advertising ever foisted on the U.S. media landscape, I hope that people who are trying to figure out how to fix a brand will learn a few things about how to do it—and how not to do it. The story of Volkswagen is a good teacher—and it's a good story.

The Unveiling

ONE

The proving ground for Concept 1, a reincarnation of the legendary Volkswagen Beetle, was the 1994 North American International Auto Show in Detroit. This was a brave choice for Volkswagen, like taking a show straight to Broadway with no Hartford tryout.

In the early 1990s the Detroit show became the most important one after many years of also-ran status. It's held in the backyard of the Big Three U.S. automakers—General Motors, Ford, and Chrysler—as well as VW's own North American headquarters. By the early 1990s, the international press had turned the Detroit show into a media circus. In the past, reporters could count on leisurely buttonholing auto executives at each company's press stand. By 1992, the throng of international reporters was so thick, reporters had to skillfully jockey for appointments in order to get key interviews. If Concept 1 lacked credibility, or failed to impress, VW would be embarrassed in front of a large, jaded, international gallery of reporters. Sales of Volkswagens in the United States had fallen below 50,000 in 1993, down from a half-million 20 years earlier. The auto press was already throwing shovels of dirt onto Volkswagen's future in the United States.

It would have been safer for VW to unveil Concept 1 at the Los Angeles Auto Show, just a week after the 1994 Detroit show. The Los Angeles show would have allowed the company to do an outdoor publicity stunt, like dragging reporters to the Santa Monica Pier or Venice Beach for the unveiling—an impossibility in Detroit's cruel January. A smaller, regional show drawing fewer reporters was another cautious option.

Nonetheless, VW decided to float Concept 1 on a big stage; Chrysler had seen to it. By 1994, Chrysler was the court jester of the auto shows, staging theatrical stunts at the Detroit show to jazz reporters' interest in the company and its cars. One year, Chrysler President Bob Lutz drove a car through a glass window to introduce it. Another year, the company introduced the Dodge Ram pickup by dropping it from a platform 15 feet off the ground. At the 1994 Detroit show, Chrysler was introducing its Cirrus and Stratus sedans with a *Mission Impossible* theme, complete with actor Peter Graves (Mr. Phelps in the TV series) as press conference host. Chrysler was also showing the Neon, a cuddly little economy sedan priced under $9,000. Priced with college students and underpaid teachers in mind, the Neon was launched with an ad campaign that had been described as reminiscent of the classic VW ads of the 1960s and early 1970s. Ads for Neon simply said, "Hi." Some people in the car business thought the Neon could, in fact, be the spiritual successor to the Beetle. That notion seems ridiculous now: Since the launch of the New Beetle, the Neon is scratching for a toehold against its Korean rivals amid mismanagement of the Dodge brand by parent Daimler-Chrysler.

Volkswagen's public relations staff was steeped in secrecy over Concept 1. Public Relations Director Maria Leonhauser hid the press kits at her own house. Freeman Thomas, one of the two lead designers of Concept 1, drove the car to Detroit's Cobo Hall in a ridiculous disguise: The car was clad in foam blocks to conceal the Beetle's familiar eggish profile.

Usually, the auto press knows for weeks, if not a few months, what to expect at the auto shows. This allows time to prepare coverage, which is particularly important for the monthly buff magazines like *Automobile* and *Car & Driver*. There are few surprises. Those products and product plans that *are* pulled from a hat are usually greeted with skepticism by the press. Particularly frowned upon have been the concept cars, which rarely end up looking much like the show car when they are produced and eventually hit the showroom.

There were two inescapable facts weighing heavily on the people connected to Concept 1. First, not everyone at VW wanted Concept 1 to succeed, which created huge internal political ramifications for the whole project. Second, those itching for success knew that if it failed, it could mean the beginning of the real end of the brand in the United States. The headlines running in business magazines spelling out the demise of Volkswagen in America might well come true.

What Volkswagen and Concept 1 had going for them was that the United States was beginning a love affair with retro culture. The cable TV station Nick at Night started resurrecting TV series from the 1960s and 1970s with sensational ratings in prime time. Movies based on those series were in development. Teenagers were wearing bell-bottom trousers and platform shoes. So-called futurists said that baby boomers were turning to their past, looking for what they perceived as simpler times as a refuge from broken marriages and the overconnected madness of computers, pagers, and cell phones. Just a year before, Porsche, a kin company of Volkswagen's, introduced the Boxster concept, a dazzling retro sports car styled to remind people of the classic 550 Spyder that James Dean made famous both in life and in his death behind the wheel.

Volkswagen's management, namely, VW Group Chairman Ferdinand Piëch (the grandson of the original Beetle's inventor/designer, Ferdinand Porsche) and Dr. Jens Neumann (who was in charge of Volkswagen's North American business), had an idea that a new Beetle would jump-start U.S. interest in the Volkswagen brand. However, they didn't know for sure if people would still care that much about a new Beetle, or if the idea would prompt the press to view the company as desperate. If Concept 1 wasn't liked, or not taken seriously, it would be a terrible blow to VW's hopes for a comeback.

Concept 1 was freighted with much change from the original Beetle. It was a front-wheel-drive car with its engine mounted up front, instead of the rear-mounted engine and rear-wheel drive of the original. The engine would be liquid cooled instead of air cooled. It was a three-door hatchback, unlike the two-door original. Finally, it wouldn't be the simple car that so many owners had fixed on the side of the road. Modern auto technology, full of computers and sensors, made do-it-yourself repairs an impossibility. Concept 1 would have a sophisticated microchip-controlled engine. The question loomed: Would the complex necessities of modern engineering and safety technology obliterate what made the original Beetle lovable? Would Concept 1 end up a niched retro oddity like the Plymouth Prowler, a modern homage to street rods of yore, which sold just a few thousand units a year? If Concept 1 were to become the new Beetle, VW had to have some real indication that it could sell at least 75,000 in the United States and Canada. Otherwise, production wouldn't make economic sense.

To understand how close the New Beetle came to never being built, one must understand the mentality of the German engineer. The only car worth working on, worth developing, is the *next* car—one representing design and engineering advances, not a retreat to the past. It was this mentality of always moving forward, never looking back, that erroneously convinced those German designers and engineers that Americans in the mid-1970s would gobble up Rabbits, the U.S. version of the Golf, just as they had Beetles, Karmann Ghias, and Squareback wagons. Going backward is nothing more than weakness, and that's how VW had long viewed any ideas about reintroducing the Beetle.

However, a new Beetle was not really a new idea. Reporters and customers had been badgering VW's U.S. management for years about a new Beetle. That is what gave Neumann some inkling that a comeback would work.

Some VW executives, on the other hand, had little faith that the press would embrace Concept 1. They prepared for the worst by having three pieces of so-called news for the January 5 press conference, the date scheduled for the release of Concept 1. Volkswagen executives would talk up the third-generation Golf and Jetta, which would hit showrooms later in the year, but had already been introduced in Europe, and a new hybrid diesel/electric engine designed to meet future fuel economy and emissions standards. If the press jeered Concept 1, VW still had two other news items it could use to play down the significance of Concept 1. Volkswagen was prepared to call Concept 1 "just something we brought to the show . . . not significant . . . a design exercise for an electric vehicle." That Concept 1 was an electric design, in fact, had been the cover story that designers Freeman Thomas and J Mays used in their Simi Valley, California, studio to put off inquiring eyes and wagging tongues.

Tom Shaver, then VW's American sales and marketing chief, was selected to introduce the new Jetta and Golf, and Ullie Seiffert was tapped to introduce Concept 1. Seiffert, the VW board member from Germany in charge of technical development, was an ironic choice for this task because he was among the Germans who were decidedly against Concept 1. Not only had Seiffert led VW's battles in Washington, D.C., during the 1970s on safety and emissions standards that ended up killing the original Beetle, he also played a key role in developing the Golf/Rabbit that replaced it. Also, he was among those Germans eternally frustrated with the peculiarity of the U.S. market, like the importance buyers placed on trivial items such as high-fidelity stereo systems and cup holders. The Germans believed a car was for driving, not for concerts or picnics.

What transpired next makes those who witnessed it grin and chuckle even now. From the start of the press program, Seiffert was really being set up for an ambush. Although he knew how the press conference was planned, he couldn't, in all his cynicism for the idea, anticipate the crush of attention that would follow.

Thomas and Mays had produced a video summarizing why Concept 1 should be built and why the time was right to reintroduce the Beetle to the U.S. car-buying public. The video opened with the dial of an old, black rotary phone, as if the past was about to be dialed up.

Then, a shot of a 1950s-era tailfin and a 45-rpm record on a turntable followed.

———

"It's funny the things we remember," the video began. "The things we hang onto. The first day of school. A first dance. A first kiss. Our first car. Some things are simply unforgettable." Text was set against background photos and film footage of original Beetles. "One little thing can bring it all rushing back. A song on the radio. The smell of suntan lotion. Seeing an old friend at the beach. The friend you could always depend on. Everything was a little less complicated then. Tennis shoes didn't cost $200.00. A jukebox played your favorite song. And a car was a part of the family. Right from the start."

The tempo and beat of the music then transitioned to be faster and more contemporary. Then, shots of Concept 1 appeared on the big screen.

What if quality never went out of style? What if originality still meant something original? What if simplicity, honesty, and reliability came back again? Imagine a new Volkswagen. A concept that defines the automotive icon. Imagine a vision of high technology and advanced engineering. An expression of innovation, safety, and performance. Imagine the descendant of an enduring original. Different, unmistakable, yet true to its heritage in style and spirit. Every line, every curve, every memory. Not just the evolution of a cherished classic, but the continuation of a worldwide love affair that began 21 million cars ago. Innovation embodied in tradition. A new Volkswagen concept. One look, and it all comes back. But then, it never really left. The legend reborn. A friendship rekindled.

The response from the press gallery was over the top. You could hear gulps in throats and people catching their breath. Typically gritty auto writers gushed. Helen Fogel of the *Detroit News* reported that some were wiping tears away. *Autoweek* named it "Best in Show." Just about every newspaper in the country covering the show, along with many that just picked up the wire stories, put a picture of the car on their front pages. The *New York Times,* the *Wall Street Journal,* the *Los Angeles Times,* and *USA Today* all gave Concept 1 prime real estate in its pages. All three network newscasts in the United States ran pieces, as did most of the local newscasts around the country. A month or so later, the *Chicago Tribune's* Jim Mateja wrote an open letter to VW Chairman Dr. Ferdinand Piëch that began[1]:

Dear Dr. Piëch, What are you waiting for, Doc, Bring back the Beetle. And hurry. In case you hadn't noticed, VW has been in the latrine since you stopped selling the Beetle in the U.S.

In retrospect, it seems incredible that, despite the reaction from the press gallery, Seiffert told reporters, "We can never bring the Beetle back, but we would like to go back to our roots with an honest, reliable, timeless, and youthful design on an affordable car." Hedging? The press stand was going nuts, and he was still hedging. The emotion was palpable.

Also incredible was the reaction of Volkswagen Club of America President Shell Tomlin. "We all know those modern things cost money . . . The Concept 1 is not a Beetle. I think people are going to be disappointed in it. I don't know if I would even have one."[2]

Made in America

For good reason, Germans tend to be wary of history. Whenever the Beetle is mentioned as "Hitler's car" (referring to the fact that the Beetle was a car commissioned by Hitler), and a German VW executive is present, the unease is so palpable it can be cut with a knife. Too few Germans appreciated the romance and, ironically, innocence that Americans associate with the Beetle. Germans view it as a car that had its time and ran its course. To Americans who owned one, however, it was a pet, a child, a canvas. It became an icon for a time when young Americans felt more in touch with their lives' dreams and aspirations, and when life seemed simpler, less connected to technology. People had relationships with their Beetles like no other car before or since.

Not surprisingly, it took two American baby boom designers to light a flame under the New Beetle: J Mays and Freeman Thomas. Mays, in his early forties when he began thinking about a new Beetle, was from Oklahoma and studied at the Art Center College of Design in Pasadena, California. He was recruited by Volkswagen from his job at BMW in Germany to work at its Audi division. In 1991, he was named head of VW's new North American design studio in Simi Valley, California. Thomas, born and raised in California, also attended the Art Center College, and initially worked for Porsche's design studio in Germany. When he was hired by VW, Thomas first worked in Germany and then moved to the design studio in Simi Valley.

Growing up, Thomas's family owned a succession of Beetles in the 1950s and 1960s. He drove Beetles of all kinds, from the basic model to one tricked out with the legendary Baja dune-buggy packaging. He drove a Beetle while attending Art Center College. "In my neighborhoods in Southern California, Cypress and Huntington Beach, the culture was and is very different than Detroit," said Thomas. "California is like Switzerland. We don't care what the rest of the country is doing. My neighborhood was a combination of Mustangs, Beetles, the newer Japanese cars, older Detroit Pontiacs and Chevys that had been preserved, Jeeps."

Mays worked on an important design for Audi, the Avus concept car, which would become the hit of the 1991 Tokyo Auto Show. It was a beautiful design—a midengine, all-aluminum-body supercar that was inspired by the German Auto Union show cars and racers of the 1930s. It was an important experience for Mays, and it provided an important lesson to Thomas as well. Like VW, Audi had been driven to its knees in the United States. The company chose to unveil the Avus at the Tokyo Auto Show—for symbolic reasons. Japanese companies like Honda and Toyota won many of the customers that both VW and Audi lost in the 1980s. Therefore, Audi wanted to make a splash by introducing the Avus in its rivals' backyard. Mays said the lesson of the Avus, which energized the organization and stirred interest in the Audi brand with the press, was that a design was "an important piece of brand communication." Inspired by the Auto Union race cars of the 1930s, it also showed his German colleagues the value equity that is inherent in historic designs.

As a designer, Mays was no more interested in lifting a design from times past than any of his peers. There were, however, "lines and proportions" that remain timeless, Mays said. "You can take a design, if it was beautiful and enduring, and let it establish a tone. It would never be right to take an old design and just make it again." Though the Avus was a retro design appealing to people's emotions, it was packed with cutting-edge technology.

Mays recalls a lunch that he had with VW Designer Peter Schreyer, who was on assignment from Germany to the California studio. Both men were despondent over the sagging fortunes of VW in the United States, and they discussed the frustrating, long shadow that the Beetle cast over the company. The subject often came up with people they knew outside of the company, especially previous Volkswagen owners. Discussions inevitably concluded with the sentiment, "You guys should never have gotten rid of the Beetle." Bill Young, president of Volkswagen of America at the time, concurred: "Every interview I did at that time would touch on the Beetle, and why didn't we bring it back somehow."

Mays really started to think about possibly doing a new Beetle design. He reasoned that VW in Germany failed to grasp the importance of the Beetle as a symbol of the company and the Volkswagen brand. What was missing in Volkswagen, as far as Americans were concerned, was the very heart of the brand: the Beetle.

In fact, very few marketing experts could understand why VW wouldn't give serious consideration to a new Beetle. "VW left an awful lot on the table when they stopped the Beetle in the late 1970s," says Donny Deutsch, whose ad agency pitched for the VW business in 1995. "There are all sorts of economic reasons why you do or don't build a car. It has to make a profit. You have to be able to sell enough to make it worthwhile. But this car was so much bigger than what a balance sheet would show. It was the heart of the brand in America.

Volkswagen's problem throughout the 1980s was they operated too much like a global company. Every big company is global, but there is a danger in acting too globally. Markets like America, Europe, Australia, [and] Japan are individual. It's not one global market. They have to be thought about as individuals."

When Mays floated the idea of a new Beetle to Thomas, he immediately understood its importance. However, one potentially polarizing issue, recalls Thomas, was the varying viewpoints around the design studio regarding retro designs versus something new and forward-looking. Full of ego and pride, most designers hate the idea of resuscitating an old classic. They're certainly inspired by past designs, but at first no one beyond Mays and Thomas could conceive how to bring back a Beetle, with its totally unique shape, without stepping full-shoe into the footprints of designer Ferdinand Porsche. The other problem was that both men were technically working for Audi at the time when they started to conceive the New Beetle. It was also the last decade before the new millennium—no small importance. Designs were already in progress for Volkswagen and Audi that would keep the engineers busy for the last decade of the century. Few wanted to commit to making one of those designs the reincarnation of a 50-year-old idea.

Thomas is fond of the phrase *coconspirator* to describe himself and Mays as they set about making a case for a new Beetle. Both were skilled enough to know it would not be that difficult to actually conjure a design. The template was there. Doubtless, any reinterpretation of the original Beetle certainly had to capture the unique geometry of the original form. The real challenge, they knew, was lining up the right allies within the organization to support and fund the idea. A new Beetle had been so controversial within VW's ranks that they had to make their initial forays with care before the idea finally reached Dr. Piëch. The designers needed open-minded friends in high places at VW who could recognize the concept's value.

Dave Huyett, VW marketing director in 1992, first became aware of the secret Beetle project when design studio administrator Mike Toser confessed that a Beetle design was on the boards. "I thought it was a fantastic idea, especially with the guys at Simi Valley working on it," said Huyett. "If it could work, that was the place to do it, not in Germany." Toser asked Huyett for all the archival information and material he could lay his hands on about the importance of the Beetle in North America.

In early 1993, Huyett asked Charlie Waterhouse from Volkswagen AG's marketing staff to come to the United States. Huyett and Waterhouse, plus VW Brand Chief Tom Shaver and Sales Director Steve Wilhite went to Simi Valley to meet with Mays, Thomas, and Toser. The designers wanted some advice from Huyett and the other executives from Volkswagen of America about selling the idea upstream to the Volkswagen organization in Germany.

Most companies have executives with power and influence, known by staffers as go-to people for approving risky projects. In this case, Mays and Thomas knew they had to get Dr. Helmut Warkuss on board. Design director at Audi when the idea for the Concept 1 emerged, Warkuss liked the sketches that Mays and Thomas sent him. He told the designers that Piëch would soon be named head of Volkswagen AG, and he would follow Piëch as design chief of the company. In addition, everyone would have to endure the dramatic changes and restructuring of the company that Warkuss anticipated under Piëch before a design so controversial could advance. Their concept had an angel, though, and it would be shown to Piëch when the time was right.

Warkuss knew Piëch's mantra—more than just a shibboleth—Piëch truly believed it: Change comes from great product, not the other way around. Warkuss had some idea about the importance of the Beetle in North America, and he knew that Piëch didn't want to cut the cord in North America. Nor did Piëch want his legacy to be "The Man Who Pulled Volkswagen from America." Warkuss shrewdly figured that two young U.S. designers working in California were just the right people to plant the seeds for a new Beetle, and that Piëch could warm to the idea. Not least among his enthusiasms for the project: The sketches were great.

Warkuss approved the idea with the following parameters: Keep the project secret, keep working on designs, and refine the concept.

"We had to keep the idea to ourselves, because at that time we couldn't sell it. If we had, it would have been killed before it got off our sketchpad," recalled Thomas.

Indeed, the fall of 1991 was not the time for go-aheads on controversial projects. Piëch, not yet in the job of running Volkswagen AG, had a lot on his plate. There were many long-time executives who would soon fall to Piëch's knife. The entire company was awash in runaway losses and product problems. Volkswagen's horrible condition in the United States, though, was a double-edged sword. Sometimes great ideas come from companies when their backs are to the wall. However, a long sales descent had also created a shortage of funds for product development.

The New Beetle would have to wait—and for more than financial reasons. In 1992, Thomas temporarily moved back to Germany to work on an Audi project. However, the idea for the New Beetle was never far away. He continued to work on the designs in his room in Ingolstadt and occasionally spoke with Mays about it by phone.

Thomas returned to the California studio in the fall of 1992, and he and Mays sought out Warkuss to see if the timing was right for the New Beetle to move forward. Warkuss, still wary of the timing, gave them the go-ahead to build two quarter-scale models of their designs. But he warned them to do it in private, someplace where other designers in the studio could not see what they were up to—that, or generate some sort of cover story. If the idea was worth selling to Piëch, Warkuss would need something tangible to sell to the old man.

Oddly enough, Thomas and Mays got help from California regulators in getting the project moving without the heavy burden of total secrecy. California had mandated that 2 percent of an automaker's in-state sales be zero-emission vehicles by 1998. So the designers shrouded the project under the guise of creating an electric car to meet state regulations. Companies working on electrics found designs of scant importance because of the small volume and experimental nature of the cars. Ultimately, no one placed much value on electrics at the time, so a design reminiscent of an old Beetle would only be seen as a gimmick to get an electric car noticed. The project was christened "Lightning Bug."

For Thomas and Mays, understanding the geometry of the original car was crucial to the design of the New Beetle. Though the old Beetle was unique from every angle—something the two realized had to inform their interpretation—the side view was critical to the Beetle's iconic qualities: the roundness, the egglike qualities of the roofline, and the four separate fenders. Another designer in the California studio, Craig Durfey, worked up a design that integrated the fenders into the rest of the body, as is the case with most modern car designs. However, it was eliminated from consideration early on because it lacked the multiangle quality that is critical to the original Bug's design and that is so vital to the new design. Thomas explains that looking at the New Beetle from the side, the car comprises three cylinders: (1) the front end, (2) the rear end, and (3) the passenger compartment. The front and rear views look alike, more so than in other cars. A critical design element identified on the original Beetle was the roofline. The overall profile created the illusion of an arch but actually the roofline was flattened and lengthened a bit. The New Beetle's roofline, however, is a genuine arch, giving a great deal of headroom to the driver and passenger in the front seat. The backseat is much more practical for a couple of eight-year-olds than for two linebackers. It is as classic and perfect a design, says Thomas, as Mickey Mouse's head.

Back to the Future Bug

At Audi, the single strongest design influence is from the Bauhaus School. Mays's designs for Audi drew heavily from Bauhaus principles, and the New Beetle was no exception. Bauhaus was a school of design in Germany in the 1920s that taught there should be a correlation between creativity and modern industry and science. It marked the beginning of truly creative industrial design. Art Deco, for example, sprang from the Bauhaus School. Thomas cut his teeth at Porsche, where there is more cultural emphasis on emotive design. After all, no one buys a Porsche for rational reasons. The two men came from different directions, but the sum of their perspectives proved just right. Both took a very similar approach with the basic shape, and the two kept sharing drawings and ideas. As they did, one would take elements of the other's design and incorporate them. Thomas gets credit for some of what Mays calls the "warm and fuzzies"—windows with eased, rounded corners. Mays's design had windows with sharp square corners and called for a flat front end. Thomas's front end had a real nose in order to support a front bumper.

As any Bug devotee knows, the interior of the original was just as important to the car's lovability and character as the exterior. The interior of the original Beetle had a simple metal painted surface, with the paint matching the exterior color of the car. The only instruments were the speedometer and the gas gauge. Both Thomas's and Mays's dash designs called for a single, large, round bezel behind the steering wheel in homage to the original. The rest of the new interior would have large fascias and panels colored to match the exterior. The familiar grab handle on the passenger's side would be in the new version. Both men agreed on an original touch that recalled the heyday of the first Beetle: a dashboard-mounted bud vase to hold a flower. Think "Flower Power!" Later, the bud vase became a huge debate in the studio and among German executives, who thought it silly. This was a German executive body that had continued to scoff at Americans and their cupholders, and even at their wanting automatic transmissions right into the mid-1990s.

Because the personality of the Beetle was why it remained such a powerful icon, both designers put much thought and energy into what each calls the "face" of the car. It was important that, like the original, the New Beetle "smile" at the world, an effect created by the round headlights and fenders, which sit above the eyeball lights like actual brows.

After endless tinkering with the quarter-scale models, Mays and Thomas decided to photograph them. Of course, they wanted natural bright light for that—sunlight—no shortage of that in California.

They really wanted to take the model to the beach to shoot the pictures despite the lack of secrecy there. Passersby at Malibu Beach noticed the bright yellow and pale blue models, gawked, and asked, "Are those some new kind of Beetles?" Thomas put off the boardwalk denizens by saying they were college students just photographing an art project.

By early 1993, the two designers felt ready to take the idea to the next level, a full-scale model. That, however, would require Warkuss to cough up some funds. Usually, designers who are looking for approval simply show off their models, bring the boss into the studio, and walk him through the project. Mays and Thomas took another path. At Mays's invitation, Warkuss arrived in Simi Valley with two assistants, expecting to be taken to the studio. Instead, he was shown to a small conference room for a multimedia presentation (what an advertising agency might put together to sell a campaign strategy). A video started rolling, set to a soundtrack from the movie *Grand Canyon*. It chronicled the rise and fall of Volkswagen in the United States, from selling just two in 1949 to one-half million in the early 1970s, back down to less than 50,000 in 1992.

This, of course, was familiar and distressing territory to Warkuss. As the design chief began to wonder why he was being led into this dismal abyss, the music turned upbeat. Slides of the models appeared on the screen juxtaposed with images of the optimistic 1950s and 1960s. The presentation detailed a rebirth of a cultural attitude during the U.S. love affair with the positive vibes of past eras. Then the slides outlined the potential in the U.S. market for a true Beetle. Mays and Thomas presented four words that described their designs: (1) *honest,* (2) *simple,* (3) *reliable,* and (4) *original.* These words not only defined what the Beetle was, but what it could be and what differentiated the Volkswagen brand from all others.

After the presentation, Warkuss rose to his feet and, with his assistants, began rapping the conference table with his knuckles, the German version of a standing ovation. "It was not a usual approach for us, but this was a very special project, a special idea, that required special handling," says Thomas.

Rudiger Folten, who headed the design team in Germany that would take the Concept 1 design and make it into the New Beetle, gives much credit to the California studio. Folten has stated in interviews that it could never have originated in Germany, because the Beetle hasn't been sold there for more than 20 years, and not many remain in active use. The Beetle just wasn't part of the German market. In sunny California, far kinder to older cars than cold, wet, rust-inducing climes of Germany, Beetles still populate the roads, primary transportation for thousands who nurse their beloved antique Bugs from one year to the next.

Warkuss went back to Wolfsburg to plot strategy, knowing he had a huge battle to wage if Lightning Bug was ever to reach production. In the meantime, Mays and Thomas were certain of only one thing: If the U.S. public ever got a gander at a new Beetle, it would be harder for VW *not* to build it than to build it. They knew that they had tapped into something special. The ideas they had for paying emotional homage to the original Beetle, while eliminating its annoying, if endearing, shortcomings (rattly ride, deficient heater, insufficient crash safety), should produce a hit for VW. The designers were so sure of success that they began to work out the details for a full-scale production model immediately after Warkuss left to go back to Germany: the specs and calibrations for the headlights, mirrors, dashboard, seat sizes, bumpers, windows—the works.

Just as Freeman Thomas had suspected, a split developed in the Simi Valley studio once it became obvious to the rest of the design staff what was being worked on. Some were against a new Beetle. Contrary to the normal collegial atmosphere, the naysayers wouldn't even look at the designs or models. "There was tension within the studio to be sure," says Thomas. "The VW people were confused. Most of them were just taking existing product and doing splash graphics and the like. What we were after was a true reflection of the Volkswagen brand, but with modernity. Warkuss understood and appreciated this."

By the middle of 1993, Warkuss had shown the scale models to Piëch at a place in Wolfsburg the company calls "Valhalla," the mythological hall of the Norse gods. This was where VW's original chairman, Heinz Nordhoff, reviewed proposed changes and improvements to the Beetle, Transporter, and Karmann Ghia, most of which never made it into the product driven by millions. "We were like young children waiting by the phone," says Thomas. Piëch loved what he saw. Not a man to waste words, his response was "In Ordnung," which is German for "Consider it ordered." He was willing to show it at the Detroit show, which would come in less than 6 months.

Mays, Thomas, and Toser turned to Dave Huyett for advice for how to get all the right people from Volkswagen AG on board in order to get the car shown properly in Detroit. It was a tall order because Volkswagen had not previously made a big deal of the Detroit show. The display they had in the United States was not very good, and Volkswagen of America had no money to rush-order something built. The project was going to need help from Germany. "We were still lepers," said Huyett. "The German executives really wanted little do with us . . . and we didn't have a Godfather in Wolfsburg to fight for us." Just because Piëch ordered the car shown didn't mean he was personally going to write a check to make it happen. Concept 1's supporters would have to work the system.

The designer's video, produced for Warkuss, needed to be shown to Dr. Werner Schmidt, head of marketing at Volkswagen AG, to see if he would fund some of the show. Huyett advised the meeting should take place in Valhalla where Piëch had approved the project. Says Huyett, "It's where God comes for meetings." The auto show organizers at Volkswagen AG were invited, as was Worldwide Marketing Chief Dieter Dahlhoff. Technical Development Chief Ullie Seiffert would be invited, too. Seiffert was a hard sell as he was strongly against, in his mind, throwing good money after bad in the United States, and especially on a reincarnated Beetle.

The presentation was made in both English and German. Mays presented in German and distributed a brochure on the Concept 1, produced by the same creative firm that helped him produce the video that sold Warkuss and Piëch. Huyett brought coffee mugs with the slogan, "The Most Loved Cars In The World," Volkswagen of America's then advertising tagline. "The Germans love gifts . . . even three-dollar coffee mugs, and it helps to drive a cause through," says Huyett. The designers' Herculean task going forward was to lobby the Germans to do something they had never done before: Build a car specifically for the United States. To this point, all of Volkswagen's cars were built for world markets, including the original Beetle. A new Beetle was clearly something for the United States first, and for other markets such as Europe and Japan second.

Dahlhoff was convinced that Concept 1 was worth pursuing and agreed to help fund some of the expense of getting the car to the Detroit show, a major coup for the project. However, Shaver and Volkswagen of America President John Kerr, who had not made the trip, had little enthusiasm for the New Beetle project, especially for committing half of the money required to get into the Detroit show with all the necessary accoutrements. So, in a move to save money, the auto show group from Auburn Hills was dispatched to Wolfsburg to ferret around the basement of Volkswagen AG, scrounging what they could from the European show stand materials.

This process tells volumes about the workings of VW and shows what a unique company it is. Despite the fact that Kerr and Shaver didn't champion the New Beetle idea, they had no problem with their head of marketing, Dave Huyett, working with the designers and going to Wolfsburg alone to pull the project together. This was reality at VW. Shaver recognized Huyett, with more than 20 years at VW, had better relationships in Wolfsburg than he did. "It's a unique company in that these dynamics could go on in this way," says Huyett. "There are not a lot of companies where this process could have progressed the way it did. There might not be any."

After the Show

With the Detroit Auto Show behind them and the reception of Concept 1 a huge success, Volkswagen had to go about the work of seeing if it could afford to put it into production. It was not a guarantee, though Thomas's belief that it would be harder for Volkswagen not to build it was true.

For those working on turning Concept 1 into a viable production model, the actual size of Concept 1 became a serious issue. For the New Beetle to be built, it would have to utilize one of VW's existing platforms (i.e., the actual mechanicals under the exterior—the bone structure and guts of the car). In the 1990s, VW became the world leader at building the most models off the fewest platforms. The strategy was criticized by rival car executives as undercutting the integrity of VW's designs. It was partially responsible, however, for the company's economies of scale and return to profitability. Mays and Thomas thought the New Beetle could be built off of VW's smallest platform, the one under the Polo, a car sold outside of America. Indeed, the Concept 1 show car *was* based on the Polo.

As German engineers began developing plans for the New Beetle, though, they realized that the Polo would be too small and costly to certify for U.S. crash safety requirements. The engineers suggested the A platform, used for the Golf and Jetta. This was ironic because the need arose for the New Beetle precisely because neither the Golf nor the Jetta adequately captured the hearts or pocketbooks of the U.S. consumer.

Moving up to the A platform would require substantial changes to the Concept 1 prototype that was so warmly greeted in Detroit. The wheelbase would expand from 92.1 to 98.9 inches. The car would grow almost a foot longer and nearly double in curb weight, from 1,430 to 2,712 pounds. The larger platform would have another major effect. Those championing the Beetle's cause thought the car could hit the market priced at around $12,000 or $13,000—considered economical, like the original. Building the car on the A platform would certainly push the sticker price to the $15,000 to $20,000 neighborhood of the Golf and Jetta. At that price the Beetle would be a competitor to the Golf and Jetta, slicing up a single price segment three ways instead of two.

The economic viability of the New Beetle depended on selling 100,000 cars worldwide, at least half of that in North America. In 1994, VW had only just resumed selling Golfs and Jettas in the United States after production was restored, after almost a year of painful and costly delays at the Pueblo, Mexico, plant. No one wanted to cannibalize Golf and Jetta sales for the sake of the New Beetle. Despite the overwhelming response to Concept 1 at the Detroit Auto Show, Germany had yet to fully accept the importance of a new Beetle to the rebirth of the VW brand in United States. Piëch had approved the Concept 1 show car, which would continue to be shown at auto shows, but he was still short of approving the car for study as a full-blown production model.

Indeed, the reaction of Volkswagen's German management was tepid at best to the United States' enthusiastic response to Concept 1 at the 1994 Detroit Auto Show. It would be 11 months before VW issued a press release to announce the company was moving ahead with the development of Concept 1 for production.

WOLFSBURG, GERMANY: Volkswagen's popular Concept 1 automobile, a design study car that created public and media sensation upon its unveiling at the 1994 North American International Auto Show in Detroit, Michigan, will be produced and on the market before the year 2000, Volkswagen confirmed.

The Volkswagen AG Board of Management gave its approval in November 1994 for the development of Concept 1. The decision came in response to appeals from enthusiasts all over the world who embraced the design concept.

Volkswagen AG said the United States will be one of the main markets for the new car.[3]

Not exactly a statement filled with excitement and anticipation.

———

So ambivalent was Volkswagen's German management that it would not sacrifice its own in-house engineers to develop the prototype. The staff was busy developing the next-generation Golf. The Golf was small beer in the United States, but VW sold 700,000 worldwide in 1994. Given that volume, it's easy to understand why the German engineers weren't bowled over by the reaction to the Beetle prototype in the United States. Everyone else in the world was content with the Golf and was willing to let the Beetle nostalgically fade away.

"The Beetle was a kind of stepchild," admitted Piëch. He consigned the building of the prototype to Volcke, an outside production firm in Germany, arranging for a Volcke team to work with product planners from VW of North America. This was similar to the arrangement Volkswagen had with German coachbuilder Karmann, which had turned Beetle platforms into Karmann Ghia coupes, and still transforms Volkswagen's Golfs into convertibles, or Cabrios. Despite Mays and Thomas's optimism and the efforts of the North American management, there was still uncertainty in 1994 that the car would make it into production. Even after the press release was issued, the bottom line was that no one in Germany had yet taken symbolic ownership of the idea. At a company like VW, if no one on the board embraces an idea or champions it in the face of all the competing demands, the idea is unlikely to be funded. Most important, Piëch still had reservations.

In late 1994, not even Dr. Jens Neumann, head of VW's North American business, was ready to champion Concept 1's completion. Neumann, who had been a German high school exchange student in Baltimore in the early 1960s, believed the New Beetle should be built. He knew how beloved the Beetle was from his time in America. However, people who work for Dr. Piëch learn not to promote a plan unless they are 99.9 percent sure that he will be supportive. It was enough during the development process that Piëch remained neutral. (A neutral Piëch means that he still needs to be convinced—but keep working on it.)

Ferdinand Piëch first got behind the wheel of a new Beetle prototype in 1995 at the company's test track at Ehra Lessien, not far from Wolfsburg headquarters. Piëch is a serious car man from a serious car family, not a finance type who happened to rise to the top. He hated what he was driving. The handling was weak and sloppy. The car had drum brakes rather than state-of-the-art disk brakes, an attempt to keep the cost down. Volkswagen engineers didn't build the car, so it didn't reflect Piëch's standards. Failure to impress Piëch, Neumann, or anyone at Wolfsburg should have ended the car's short life. The poor showing, though, actually gave the car a much-needed boost.

———

"When we actually got to drive it and see it, I was pushed forward in the belief that it should be built, but, yes, we were so disappointed in this prototype that we resolved that a better version must be built inside our own facilities," says Dr. Neumann. "Dr. Piëch wasn't all the way convinced."

If the New Beetle was going to be built, it was not going to be a niche oddity that would sit outside the family of Volkswagen vehicles. Piëch did not want the New Beetle to be the equivalent of the Chevrolet Corvette, a showpiece with a cult following that had no connection to the rest of Chevy's product line.

After Neumann was disappointed by driving the prototype, he and Volkswagen Design Director Warkuss joined forces to champion the production of the car inside Volkswagen. They began to pester Martin Winterkorn, the VW board member in charge of technical development, asserting that the right version of the car could turn dismal U.S. sales around in a hurry. They convinced Winterkorn to overhaul the car in-house and got him to pitch his support of the project to Piëch. To be successful, both Piëch and Winterkorn felt that the car had to be thoroughly a Volkswagen. It had to be a serious car, meeting not only every U.S. safety standard, but also Piëch's own, more stringent standards for handling and performance. "Certainly, the car had to feel every inch like a Volkswagen, or I never would have given approval for it to be built," said Piëch.[4]

Piëch ordered a team to be broken off from the Golf development team to work on the Beetle on a parallel course. The more the design and engineering team made the car a Golf in Beetle's clothes, the more it became a product they could support. Under Winterkorn, the New Beetle, in comparison with Concept 1, became a totally new car with a longer hood and roof and bigger bumpers. Concept 1 was toy-like on the scale of the smaller Polo platform. Concept 1, now being called "New Beetle," was a substantial automobile on the level of a Honda Civic, Toyota Corolla, or the Golf itself. Other changes followed, especially in the interior. This is not unusual in the auto busi-

ness. The cars presented at auto shows, put together by studio designers, are meant to impress. Show cars, however, aren't fine-tuned with
actual consumers in mind, nor do they reflect decisions made prior to
production to keep the costs of the car in line. What seems pretty on
a designer's drafting table or in a clay model is often far from what
consumers want to live with day after day; these designs are also
beyond what most companies can profitably manufacture.

The process of finding the right mix of design and engineering for
the New Beetle on the Golf platform was not as easy as it might have
been had it been built as an entirely new car. The designers and engineers were caught between an adaptation of a legendary design and a
platform that was designed to support an entirely different car.
Thomas, Mays, and now Folten were only too aware that they were
tinkering with a legend, a piece of Americana. In a way, it was like a
film director trying to remake a classic film like *Casablanca* or *The Wiz-
ard of Oz*. Now in the hands of the Germans (who weren't enamored
of the idea to begin with), the project had to evolve in order to make
the car practical and economical to build, while staying faithful to the
design that was bowling over crowds at the auto shows.

Rumors and press leaks of how Concept 1 was evolving into the
New Beetle were rampant, with enterprising car magazines, such as
Auto Motor und Sport, running unofficial artists' renderings of some
awful-looking Beetles. To quell the negative and even silly speculations
about the New Beetle, a prototype based on the Golf platform was
readied for the fall of 1995, to be shown at the Tokyo Auto Show.

Some of Concept 1's features, taken directly from the original Beetle, were dropped by Winterkorn's German crew out of necessity.
Besides being larger now, vents beneath the rear windows and twin
air intakes in the front of the car were scrapped. Folten's team had to
balance the nostalgia of the Beetle with the responsibility of creating
a truly new design. The last thing anyone wanted was a joke on
wheels.

Piëch was adamant about the addition of four-wheel disk brakes,
rather than the drum brakes used on the car throughout the design
process as a cost-cutting measure. Ironically, the brakes created a stir

during the development of the original Beetle in the 1930s. Hitler wanted to keep the cost of the "people's car" low, demanding a peasant price scoffed at by the German car manufacturers. Engineers designed a version of the original Beetle car with mechanical brakes to hold down costs, not then-new state-of-the-art drum brakes. In the end, however, Ferdinand Porsche insisted that drum brakes be included, just like his grandson insisted on disk brakes. Cost be damned.

New Beetle was greeted with cheers at the Tokyo show. The original Beetle has a large enthusiast following in Japan, and both the press and public were pleased to see that some of the drawings that had been published by the motor press were false. A few months after the Tokyo show in March 1996, the design of the New Beetle was complete and the prototype was unveiled at the Geneva Auto Show. Eighty percent of the vehicle under the car's exterior was the same as the Golf, leading analysts and reporters to fret that the car would have to be priced around $20,000, which was thought to be too high to meet the sales volume targets.

The Big Show

Volkswagen launched the New Beetle on 5 January 1998 at the North American International Auto Show at Detroit's Cobo Hall, 4 years after Concept 1 had been driven by Freeman Thomas to Cobo Hall adorned with foam panels to disguise its bulbous profile.

Volkswagen was now serious about the Beetle. The years since Concept 1's debut had been good for VW in the United States. After years of inconsistent and muddled advertising, the old magic seemed to have returned with a new advertising agency in Boston whose work was being compared with the classic VW advertising of the 1960s, created by Doyle Dane Bernbach. The 1997 launch of the all-new Passat was a huge success. Sales were on the upswing for VW, as well as the recently moribund Audi division. The New Beetle didn't have to be a savior. It was going to act more like a supercharger laid onto an already fine-tuned engine.

It was evident that VW, both in the United States and Germany, had come to understand what a successful New Beetle could mean to the whole brand and to the fortunes of the whole North American operation and its employees. Using nearly 30,000 square feet of Detroit's Cobo Hall, VW constructed a special multilevel stand in a remote area of the car show. To get to the space, reporters, dealers, and other attendees had to leave the main arena and take an escalator down to a space large enough for more than one manufacturer. Yes, the Golf, Jetta, and Passat were there. But there was a special level of the stand reserved for the New Beetle, which was the main attraction. The car drew thousands of people, including many executives from other car companies who couldn't deny their curiosity. This was a far cry from 1994 when auto show planners at VW had to scrounge props and display stands from the Wolfsburg cellars.

Called "New Beetle World," the space showcased six New Beetles, including one to be autographed by showgoers and sent to the Volkswagen museum in Wolfsburg. People thronged to see the car in numbers unprecedented for the Detroit show. During the busiest times, people waited an hour to snake their way into the New Beetle display. No other cars came close to generating such interest that year. No single car had the celebrity of the New Beetle.

The New Beetles were painted with heat-sensitive paint. Like a mood ring from the early 1970s, the color changed when a visitor touched the car. The original Beetle was known as the most huggable car ever, and visitors were encouraged to hug the car. The show planners were prophetic. People couldn't keep their hands off the cars.

Piëch spoke: "Four years ago, VW presented the Concept 1 here in Detroit. At that time, we certainly did not expect such a favorable reaction from the public, our dealers, and the press. We were overwhelmed. From the very first moment, it seemed we were almost forced by the customer's voice to make a real car out of the concept." Exactly what Thomas and Mays had known 5 years earlier.

Piëch took advantage of the occasion and the overflow of positive emotion in the room to talk about the fortunes of VW as a whole and some of his plans for it. He boasted of the company's global results, which in 1997 included 4.3 million vehicles sold, an increase of 7.4 percent. This made VW the number one car company in Europe for the 13th consecutive year. He also discussed boosting the company's vehicle lineup from 41 to 51 models by 2000. And he stated emphatically that VW "would never again be the one-car car company."

How ironic that VW had to produce a New Beetle to escape the shadow of the original. The original Beetle had become an enemy to VW's recovery. There is a timeworn military strategy of partnering with one's enemy to save oneself. This was not lost on Piëch. Dr. Jens Neumann is less political in his assessment. "People still want this car to make them feel good about themselves, to share a smile with others. To have fun together. The New Beetle is an inspiration to live, or, you could say, the New Beetle is optimism on wheels." He was right. The marketing clinics conducted by VW's North American staff showed that the New Beetle crossed all boundaries—ethnic, age, gender, and income. (See Chapter 7.)

Neumann is an ebullient fellow, and much quicker to an earnest smile than Piëch. His enthusiasm could not be contained in Detroit. He had a ball at the unveiling in Detroit, more fun than at any other car show he could remember. Neumann was aware of the concern that was building over the anticipated price of the car. Therefore, he worked price into his remarks at the show and began to look like the cat that ate the canary: "Of course, this dream with a sound system is not for free, but we think it's not expensive either." The price of the New Beetle was going to be half the appeal, it was thought. Neumann's remarks were greeted with a hush not unlike an NBA or NFL draft lottery, the onlookers waiting to see which team gets the privilege of signing the prize player. "The base price will be nineteen thousand nine hundred and forty . . . (pause, smile) . . . Canadian dollars . . . or fifteen thousand two hundred U.S. dollars." The audience not only applauded, but cheered! The cynical press gallery was cocksure that VW couldn't sell the New Beetle for less than $18,000, modest options pushing it to $20,000. "The pricing was as huge as the design itself," says Paul Eisenstein, editor of thecarconnection.com, an automotive news website.

For a car show, the atmosphere was almost surreal. No other car in memory had stirred the public, let alone reporters, to this degree.

Cheering at a pricing announcement was unheard of. The reaction went far beyond that displayed for other sentimental favorites of the press core, like the Mazda Miata or Porsche Boxster.

Beetle Buzz

Reporters who drive brand new cars early in their release get used to the inquiring public. Go to the supermarket, a gas station, or on a trip with a brand new model and, like it or not, he or she becomes a spokesperson for the company. The New Beetle broke all records; once it was available to the press and in short supply to dealers, reporters were inundated with questions from onlookers. There were endless requests from strangers to "just sit in it for a second." People honked, waved, and gave double thumbs-up as they passed the car on the highway. One reporter gave no less than 10 speeches about the car in one day of driving on Cape Cod. Two guys offered him money to let them drive it. The same stories ricocheted around the press corps in all parts of the country for months after the debut of the New Beetle.

The remarkable genius of the New Beetle is that it reflects a perfect amalgam of the fancy of two U.S. designers and a modern sensibility and appeal built into it by the German engineers. The decision to base the car on the Golf was a smart move. Although some fretted that the car would not be different enough from the Golf—and too different from the original Beetle—to cause the necessary buzz, such experts couldn't have been more wrong. Piëch never imagined the New Beetle, mechanically speaking, would be anything more than a Golf "with a different hat on," as he touts his strategy of putting different car models on the same mechanical platform. And to the VW-devoted public, that's been just fine.

———

Volkswagen's payoff from the New Beetle has been shattering. The sheer public relations value of the New Beetle is hard to peg. However, if the company had to purchase the media that have been devoted to the New Beetle from its introduction as Concept 1 in 1994 to the production of the New Beetle in 1998, VW would have had to spend, conservatively, more than $500 million. Public relations value is notoriously hard to quantify. More liberal estimates of the Beetle's value are closer to $1 billion.

Piëch's insistence that the New Beetle be every inch a modern Volkswagen with cutting-edge technology paid off in terms of credibility. In May 1998, the Insurance Institute of Highway Safety reported that the New Beetle scored highest among 16 small cars that had been tested in crash tests performed at 40 miles per hour. This was a big coup for Volkswagen. Not only had tighter safety regulations doomed the original Beetle, but by 1998, the positive public relations generated by such high safety scores was worth as much as $30 million or more in free and positive advertising. If the New Beetle had scored subpar in the crash tests, its ovoid shape, critical to the success of the design, would have been seen as problematic. *USA Today*, which had put the New Beetle on the cover of its newspaper twice, and wields almost as much influence on consumer safety subjects as *Consumer Reports*, would probably have headlined a poor crash test result for the New Beetle with something like, "New Beetle: Cute, Yes, But Is It Safe?" The result would have been disastrous.

The Insurance folks reported that the New Beetle was the only one of the 16 cars tested to earn an overall safety evaluation of "good," and a "best-pick designation," beating out competitors such as the Honda Civic, Mazda Protégé, Dodge Neon, and Ford Escort. The large arc of the Beetle helps stiffen the body structure so much that the car even bested its template, the Golf, in front-crash tests. When Piëch learned of the Golf's poor score, he halted production and had changes made to the Golf so it matched the New Beetle's safety performance.

———

Has the New Beetle really served as the brand magnet it was intended to be? J. D. Power and Associates, an automotive research firm that is arguably the last word in rating cars for customer satisfaction and quality, notes that the New Beetle has earned some of the highest scores for styling of any model the firm has studied. In 1998, the New Beetle delivered best-in-segment performance on just about all measures of Power's Automotive Performance, Execution and Layout study (APEAL), which looks at what consumers like about their cars after 90 days of ownership. No car priced under $25,000 scored higher. Car companies should note that Power, when talking about the New Beetle, stated that buyers will respond enthusiastically to a vehicle based on styling and curb appeal even when it does not rate high on manufacturing quality. In other words, exciting design can make a huge difference with consumers, even if manufacturing quality isn't as bulletproof as what the Japanese companies produce. In 1999, VW triumphed again, especially with young consumers. Volkswagen led four of the seven categories in the APEAL study. New Beetle topped the list of compact cars, with Golf placing second. The redesigned Jetta dominated the entry midsized segment. GTI topped sporty cars, and Passat led premium midsized cars for the second year in a row.

"The New Beetle has done everything we could have asked of it," says PR Manager Tony Fouladpour. "The really important thing about the New Beetle is the way it has drawn people back to the showroom. In a lot of cases, people come in the dealership to check out the New Beetle, but they wind up test-driving the Golf or Jetta, which in many ways are more practical cars than the New Beetle. The pricing is not terribly far apart, and they wind up driving a Golf or Jetta away instead of a New Beetle. When we can sell them one car, and make them feel, maybe, a little wistful that they didn't buy another one of our cars, that's, to coin a cliché, win-win."

Even though the New Beetle was no longer new in 2001, says Freeman Thomas, who moved on to DaimlerChrysler, the car is a moving billboard for the brand. "It is, by itself, a vital piece of brand communication."

The New Beetle is not the original. Mechanically, it is a much different car. However, the Beetle was never just the sum of its nuts, bolts, bushings, and gears. The original Beetle had a unique birth at a very strange and violent time in our world's history. It emerged from a time and place, Nazi Germany, that was full of suffering and evil to be perhaps the most loved car of the century. The original Beetle after World War II was a lifeline to thousands of displaced and suffering people. Fifty years later, the New Beetle came along at a time when the people in North America who had earned their livings off VW were being threatened with having it all taken away as the American company was nearly out of business. Both Beetles have achieved much. Both are lovable in their own way.

The New Beetle more than met sales expectations in the United States in its first 3 years on sale. In 1998, with sales running only between May and December, sales hit 56,000. In 1999 and 2000, two very robust years for the auto industry, sales reached 83,000 and 81,000, respectively. In spring 2001, while the industry was slowing by 1 million units from the year before, New Beetle, which had hardly received a dime of advertising money in almost a year, was experiencing sales that were slipping and news articles that were surfacing doubting the staying power of the car. The New Beetle was expected to sell about 60,000 per year. Therefore, even at a rate of 70,000 per year in 2001, it is above the company's expectations.

———

No longer a novelty, New Beetle now seems downright ubiquitous at the mall and grocery store parking lots. And the car had not attracted as many under-40 customers as VW had hoped. Does all this mean it was a bad idea? Hardly. In true VW fashion, the company has not acted fast enough to freshen either the product or advertising. The Cabrio New Beetle won't arrive until 2002. Not enough has been done with special colors that might have nudged new interest. Three years after the launch, VW had already started to take the car for granted. Additionally, it didn't help that a good deal of the retro buzz was off the New Beetle and on Chrysler's PT Cruiser. The PT is a vehicle that encompasses aspects of a car and sport utility vehicle, a so-called crossover, or hybrid, vehicle. However, its designers were inspired by the old police cruisers of the 1930s and early 1940s, and the car has sparked more emotion and nostalgia in people than Chrysler ever imagined. The company in 1999 anticipated that it might sell some 60,000 or 70,000 PT Cruisers, using the New Beetle as a sales benchmark. In 2001, Chrysler was scrambling to mount annual production in excess of 200,000 PTs a year to meet the enormous demand.

More competition is on the way for New Beetle in 2002. BMW will launch its redesigned Cooper Mini, a vestige of its ill-fated acquisition of British carmaker Rover. By the time Mini comes out, BMW will have sold Rover, but it held onto the Mini in which it had invested hundreds of millions of dollars. The Mini has been more than just well-received at the auto shows, and at around $20,000, will attract a lot of would-be New Beetle prospects, around 30,000 of them a year in the United States.

All of this in no way suggests that New Beetle was a mistake. The time to worry will be if annual sales dip below 50,000 a year in the United States. At that level, it starts to be a worrisome business proposition. Smart marketing, which VW seems to know how to do now, though, should keep its arched roof above water. Nothing can take away the vital role played by New Beetle in VW's total recovery in the United States.

After neglecting the New Beetle for about a year, from spring 2000 to spring 2001, VW launched a new campaign for its brand magnet that played off actual product features than warm and fuzzy imagery.

Rather than the launch advertising, which pointed up the Beetle's personality and power to infuse its owners with hope and ethusiasm, the newer effort focused on the practical design elements, such as the headroom and safety benefits of the arc shape. In one of the two TV spots, for example, the timelessness and strength of the Beetle's shape is compared with the arch supports that have kept ancient Roman aqueducts standing. The "Drivers wanted" tagline that still accompanies all VW ads was augmented with the line, "Round for a reason."

The strategy is a natural evolution of the campaign, which eventually needed to talk about actual product attributes. In fact, the ads are worthy legacies of the Beetle advertising of the 1960s that so cleverly played up one significant attribute per ad. Indeed, the ads provide a clinic to most other car companies who most often achieve disconnect between a product information ad and a brand ad. Far from seeing the campaign as a sign of desperate effort on the part of VW and Arnold to prop up the car in its third year, the ads perhaps assert better than the original launch campaign that the New Beetle is a serious piece of timeless design. That message is directed at both current owners, who are still the best ambassadors of the vehicle and to people, especially men, who tend to view the New Beetle as a toy.

New Beetle Timeline

January 1991	Volkswagen/Audi design studio opens up in Simi Valley.
May 1992	Work begins on design for concept car that can use an alternative propulsion system.
September 1992	German and American planners realize that the Beetle legend remains strong, so they consider reviving it.
September 1993	Volkswagen AG design chief Dr. Helmut Warkuss presents the first scale models to Dr. Ferdinand Piëch, chairman of VW AG. They order a full-scale model for the 1994 Detroit Auto Show.
December 1993	First full-size model is finished.
January 1994	Response to Concept 1 at the 1994 Detroit Auto Show surpasses all expectations, and dealers soon ask for a production version.
March 1994	Convertible version appears at Geneva Auto Show. Piëch promises that Concept 1 need not remain a mere vision. Planners elect to put the New Beetle on the Golf platform.
November 1994	Volkswagen Board of Management approves development of New Beetle.

October 1995	Vehicle named New Beetle appears at Tokyo Motor Show, in form that is virtually ready for production. Some 20,000 buyers place orders.
November 1995	Design is finalized.
March 1996	Another version of the New Beetle appears in Geneva with sliding glass roof. Volkswagen uses the Internet to help promote this configuration.
January 1998	Production model premieres at Detroit show.
April 1998	New Beetle goes on sale as a 1998 model, with gasoline and diesel engine. Early examples fetch prices well above sticker.
February 1999	Turbocharged engine available in 1999 New Beetle.

Sins of the Fathers

TWO

If Henry Ford had envisioned its lucrative future, today Volkswagen might be a part of Ford Motor Company. In 1948, after the allies' victory in World War II, Ford was offered the VW factory in what would later be named Wolfsburg, Germany. However, Ernest Breech, then Ford Motor executive vice president and close advisor to the Ford founder and Henry Ford II, said that he didn't think it was "worth a damn."[1]

Socialist Tools

It was at the 1933 Auto Show in Berlin that Adolf Hitler addressed Germany's industrial leaders in his first public forum after being named chancellor by German President Paul von Hindenburg. Though Hitler was not much of a driver himself (he, in fact, never had a driver's license), he loved automobiles and what they were coming to represent—a symbol of national pride and technological prowess. A nation, Hitler ranted, is not judged by other nations by its railroads, but by its miles of paved motorways. He told the assembled industrialists that he intended to construct a vast network of such motorways, *autobahns,* and would champion the growth of auto racing, a vital ingredient, he believed, to national pride in the age of the automobile.

While the heads of Daimler-Benz, United Steel Works, Krups, the Adam Opel Company, and others were wary of the man with the little mustache, strident voice, and seemingly limitless ambition, as well as his propaganda chief Joseph Goebbels, they couldn't help but be intrigued by the first politician they had encountered to appreciate the importance of the automobile. Of course, with the 1933 election just a month away, everything Hitler said had to be taken with a carburetor-sized grain of salt. Within Hitler's booming speech on German nationalism and industrial pride lay a charge to the men present: that they must build not just glorious motor coaches for the rich, but also a cheap, small car "for the people." To the businesspeople present, this point of the speech seemed like electioneering claptrap to engage voters, not a blueprint for policy.

Though the idea was new to the rich industrialists, it was not some fleeting idea of Hitler's. In Walter Henry Nelson's book, *Small Wonder,* he notes that Hitler had discussed the idea with Jakob Werlin, a Munich-based Mercedes-Benz salesman whom Hitler had prodded to relay his notion of a people's car to his superiors at Daimler-Benz.[2]

A people's car had long been on Ferdinand Porsche's mind, too. Since the turn of the century, Porsche, Germany's most renowned auto designer, had believed that people of modest means should enjoy the freedom that a motor car could provide. This differed markedly with the prevailing opinion at Daimler and Opel, companies that believed common folk should be able to get along on bicycles and motorcycles, leaving expensive automobiles to the rich.

———

Porsche was a self-taught student of electricity, and surprised his father in the 1890s by electrifying their house with lights, a doorbell, and an intercom system. He didn't much like metalworking, but relished electricity. Porsche had designed electric cars at the turn of the century, as well as a hybrid gas/electric car that had battery-powered motors to drive each wheel. The gas engine on board recharged the battery. It is remarkable that it took almost 100 years after Porsche's designs for Toyota and Honda to put similar technology into production cars.

Porsche worked at a Czech car company, Tatra, and began work on a people's car there. He left Tatra, where growth was constrained by the company's limited financial resource, and moved to Austro-Daimler. When World War I broke out, Porsche used his knowledge of gas/electric hybrid technology to design task-oriented army vehicles. For example, he used the hybrid design to build a tractor that could move a 20-ton cannon that shot 1-ton shells. In the aftermath of World War I, Europe, especially Germany, was in a shambles. Porsche again turned his mind toward a people's car, despite the fact that Daimler was again interested only in building big, fast cars for the wealthy. Porsche saw the advantage to the debilitated German postwar commoner having motorized transportation. He believed most cars of the day were too tall and not as aerodynamic as they should be. He also believed that air-cooled engines were the way to go. The technology was simpler and more robust. He designed a *Volksauto* for NSU that was, as the company dictated, water-cooled; however, it was a dismal failure. (At the turn of the 19th century, the small factory town of Neckarsulm in southern Germany was home to a company that made automatic knitting machines as well as bicycles. It was known as Neckarsulm Strickmaschinen Union. It later became known simply as NSU and got into the manufacture of motorbikes and cars.) When NSU entered into an alliance with the Italian carmaker Fiat, the agreement resulted in NSU being restricted to making only motorcycles. Porsche would have to move on again. All the while, though Porsche was designing amazing, state-of-the-art race cars that were winning races for Austro-Daimler, he never gave up on his idea of the people's car, though.

Unquestionably, Hitler's interest in the automobile, especially a people's car, both technologically and symbolically, was forged during his 1923 imprisonment. It was at that time that the fledgling demagogue wrote *Mein Kampf* and read a biography of Henry Ford, a man whom he would come to call "the greatest American" for both his industrial ingenuity and his infamous anti-Semitism.[3]

Ferdinand Porsche would recall his first meeting with Hitler in 1933 when the head of Auto Union, an auto company recently formed from the merger of three others, took him to meet Hitler and convince the new chancellor to grant Auto Union government subsidies for racing cars and engines. Hitler, however, would recall the first meeting between the two as taking place much earlier, at an auto race in 1924 when Hitler was a fairly insignificant regional government official.

When Hitler spoke at the 1934 Berlin Auto Show, his rhetoric was even more forceful about the importance of a people's car than it had been the year before. "It is with bitter feelings that we see millions of honest, hardworking, and capable men whose opportunities in life are already limited, cut off from the use of a vehicle which would be a special source of yet-unknown happiness to them, particularly on Sundays and holidays. One must have the courage to grasp this problem in a decided and comprehensive manner. What will not be possible in one year will, perhaps, prove to be commonplace ten years from now."[4]

Porsche and Hitler met again in May 1934 to discuss Porsche's design ideas for such an inexpensive car and Hitler's political ones. Porsche, by all accounts, was apolitical, at least at this point. The politics he understood were more corporate than national, and he showed as much hatred for the former as disinterest in the latter. To Porsche, Hitler was nothing more than a means of getting his design produced. If Porsche was in sympathy with Hitler's post-WWI mission to reclench Germany's geopolitical fist, he didn't talk about it.

Porsche's notion was a car with a 26-horsepower power plant, weighing around 1,400 pounds, and capable of reaching 100 kilometers an hour. Hitler was encouraging and thought, given the high cost of fuel in Europe, the car should get the equivalent to about 40 miles per gallon. Hitler also thought the car should be air-cooled and seat a family of four. The production cost, as calculated by Porsche, was $620 per car, or roughly what Ford's Tin Lizzy cost.

Hitler envisioned a dirt-cheap people's car costing a mere $320. Porsche thought that ridiculous and was on the verge of excusing himself from the whole project, thinking it was madness to even try for Hitler's price. Prototypes, however, were under way by mid-1935, and Hitler was giddy during the preceding months when he discussed the progress. Said Hitler in 1934: "I am happy that due to the abilities of the superb designer Herr Porsche and his staff we have succeeded in completing preliminary designs for a German people's car, so that the first models will finally be tested by the middle of this year. It must be possible to make the German people a gift of a motor vehicle which will not cost them more than they have heretofore been accustomed to paying for a medium priced motorcycle and whose gas consumption will be low."[5] The auto manufacturers were cool to the notion of a people's car, but Hitler cowed them into participating and supporting Porsche's efforts.

The State Association of Motor Manufacturers (Reichsverband der Automobilindustrie, or RDA) offered to take over the development of the people's car as a measure to curry favor with the new chancellor. To please Hitler, the RDA and Porsche's company signed a contract to codevelop the car. The contract read, in part: "to co-operate in promoting the supply of motor cars to the German people making the utmost use of the German automobile industry's facilities and making every effort for the good of the German Reich."

In 1936, the United States had 70 percent of the world's more than 40 million automobiles, or one car for every 4.5 Americans. By comparison, with less than one-half the population of the United States, Germany had just one automobile for every 49 citizens.

If Porsche was going to design a car that might be built for so little money, he decided he must travel to Detroit to see how the Americans managed mass production. No assembly-line facility like Ford's had been built in Europe. In October 1936 Porsche and his nephew, Ghislaine Kaess, set out for Detroit. When they arrived, Porsche toured Ford's River Rouge complex plus the factory that made Lincolns, as well as facilities at General Motors, Packard, and Fisher Body. Porsche purchased a six-cylinder Packard for $1,000 and drove to Niagara Falls and then to New York City, where he and Kaess boarded the *Queen Mary* with notebooks full of jottings, sketches, and ideas to take back to Germany. Not only had the two taken note of how cars were made on Ford's mass-production lines, but also they'd seen skyscrapers for the first time. They also made detailed notes about U.S. life: the behavior and demeanor of U.S. drivers, workers, social customs, and the like. What impressed them most, according to Walter Henry Nelson's interviews with Kaess for *Small Wonder,*[6] was the prosperity of the U.S. worker. They made notes about what different workers earned, how long their vacations were, where they went, how they bought things, and the availability and utilization of personal credit. On their way back to Germany, despite the fact that animosity was building between Germany and England, they visited the Austin factory where, in contrast with their visit to Detroit, they were very unimpressed. The Austin factory was small and inefficient. The British were professionals when it came to building cars by hand, but efficient line production came slowly. That difference between British and American car building would hold true right into the 1990s when the last of Britain's auto producers, Jaguar, Rover, and Rolls-Royce were acquired by Ford, BMW, and Volkswagen, respectively.

Development problems in 1935 plagued Porsche's progress with the *Volksauto,* and he was further hampered by the foot-dragging support that he got from the RDA, Hitler's Nazi government arm funding Porsche's project. In fact, during the spring of 1935, Porsche was not enthusiastic about his chances of pulling off Hitler's miracle. A turning point in Porsche's own attitude, though, happened when Wilhelm von Opel, director of the Adam Opel Company, by this time owned by General Motors, said to Porsche, "A wonderful contract, Herr Porsche. You're going to work on this project for ten months, get well paid for it, and then you'll find out that you are facing an impossible proposition; whereupon you'll merely have to submit a laconic report to the powers that be."[7] Porsche reportedly gave Opel an earful, not being one to bow to people of position, especially when he knew he was working for Hitler. Additionally, Opel clearly was living in the past and didn't yet realize the seriousness with which Hitler viewed the project for political reasons, nor how seriously Porsche took the creative challenge. In truth, Porsche still felt the car could not be delivered to the people at the price Hitler imagined. He hoped Hitler would eventually realize this and approve a realistic, if more expensive, car that would be preferable to a fictitious propaganda car.

By late 1936, the deadline for producing a working prototype was already 18 months past. Not only was building a car at all in these prewar days a tough order, but to do so for the exasperating price of less than $400 was something that not only the engineers thought impossible, but the prospect failed to rouse any enthusiasm in German industry. Daimler-Benz, Opel, and the rest viewed the people's car idea as a threat, not a boon. They rightfully feared that the low-cost car, if it could be produced, would compete with their own larger, more profitable cars.

By the 1937 Berlin Auto Show, Hitler's power and drive had only intensified. His fierce determination to produce a *Volksauto* was clearer than ever. As he told the show: "It is my irrevocable decision to make the German automobile industry one of our greatest industries, independent of the insecurity of international importations, and place it on a solid and sure basis. And let there be no doubt: So-called private business is either capable of solving this problem or it is not capable of continuing as private business. The National Socialist state will under no circumstances capitulate before either the convenience, the limitations, or the ill will of individual Germans."[8] It was chillingly clear. Hitler was saying, "Either build my car, or the Army will show you how."

Hitler was not just intent on having a small people's car. He was intent on having the car *he* wanted, the car that he had godfathered along with Ferdinand Porsche. Hitler's wishes were demonstrated by his reported fury at the 1937 Berlin Auto Show when he saw a small car designed by the Adam Opel Company—the P-4. It was touted as "The automobile for the little man: 1450 D-marks." Hitler was enraged that a company would usurp his intentions and attempt to bring to market a small affordable car without his direct involvement. He wasn't going to be deprived of the credit he was after with the German people, and he made it difficult for Opel to obtain raw materials to build any cars at all, let alone a small one.

Not only was it not the car Hitler wanted, it was not at the price he'd ordered. Von Opel, thinking he had done something to please Hitler, exclaimed to the chancellor, "And this, my Fuhrer, is *our Volkswagen.*"[9] It didn't take von Opel long to realize he committed a mistake as Hitler turned on his heel and stomped away, red-faced and biting his lip. When he returned to the Chancellery, Hitler summoned advisor Jakob Werlin and Labor Front Chief Robert Ley and asked them if they would start a great motorworks to build his car. It wasn't really a request. Von Opel, without intending to, had given both Porsche and Hitler, on two separate occasions, all the goading they needed to put aside whatever apprehensions or doubts they had about the feasibility of the *Volksauto* project. Apparently clueless to the bigger picture, von Opel failed to recognize the impossibility of an American-owned company, as Opel was, snatching away the single biggest public relations lift the Nazis had up their sleeve.

In May 1937, the Nazis formed the Volkswagen Development Company. Hitler was set on the government producing the car, and he started the funding with almost one-half million marks. By 1939, the company would be funded with 150 million marks. The car had the funds of the Nazi party behind it because the Volkswagen was becoming an important tool of the party. By 1939, it was apparent that no one would lose by building a factory that was capable of producing automobiles. Even if few *Volksautos* were produced, which ultimately was the case, tooling was tooling and machinery was machinery. The war machine could, and would, make extensive use of the factory.

The RDA by 1939 was no longer much of a participant in the Volkswagen project, and Porsche got what he needed directly from the Nazis in the way of capital, facilities, and even staffing. More than 200 SS men became the drivers for the test cars. More money was poured into prototypes and testing than any auto manufacturer of the day would have approved or thought necessary. However, the extensive research and development was necessary precisely because Porsche's design was breaking all the rules of auto design. Answerable to Hitler's political will rather than the economic sense of a balance sheet, the vast resources committed to the *Volksauto* concept produced a car that even the people working on it couldn't fully appreciate. It turned out to be a highly durable, low-cost, relatively easy-to-repair car that would stand the test of time for the next 40 years. As a mechanical engineer hell-bent on constant improvement and innovation, Porsche had no idea that the design would prove so durable. In the late 1930s, technological advances happened so quickly that no one would have imagined a design that could hold up for 40 years, let alone one that would be killed and then be brought back by popular demand.

In 1937 and 1938, the United States was still ambivalent about Hitler, especially those in U.S. business. No less a U.S. hero than Charles Lindbergh had toured Germany, received a decoration, and then returned to the United States to front for America First, a right-wing political organization pushing an isolationist policy for the United States, and preach the folly of the United States siding against Hitler and Germany. Its military, especially its air power, was far superior to either the United States' or Great Britain's, Lindbergh argued. Still, the United States had know-how that remained foreign to Germany, because Porsche's trip to the United States in 1935 had convinced him that the only way to produce the *Volksauto* at the mandated cost was with a Ford-style mass-production line. The only trouble was that no German auto companies had adopted these processes yet, and no German workers were experienced in assembly-line production. Porsche figured that in order to get the project up and running, he would have to coax U.S. workers to come to Germany.

Porsche traveled to the United States again, this time with an entourage that included Kaess, the nephew who had accompanied him on the first trip, as well as Porsche's son "Ferry," his son-in-law Dr. Anton Piëch (father of today's VW chairman), and other Volkswagen Development Company senior executives. Before he left, Porsche was also named "Reich Auto Designer" by Hitler, the equivalent of "Court Engineer" or "Engineer Laureate." The group went to visit Henry

Ford, a man of great stature and reputation in Germany, as well as in the United States. The men asked Ford to share his ideas and know-how. Despite the tense political climate, Ford did not object to the visit. Indeed, he relished it, even though Ford Motor was already operating in Germany, and the car that Hitler proposed building would compete head-to-head with Ford. Nor did Hitler's worsening reputation give the legendary industrialist pause. Ford reportedly said at the meeting, "If anyone can build a car better or cheaper than I can, that serves me right." (By the 1960s, his children would remember that statement with bitter frustration as the Beetle captured the imagination of a generation of buyers, knocking Ford and General Motors back on their heels in the small, entry-level car market.)

At that meeting, Mr. Ford rejected an invitation from Porsche to visit Germany to see what *they* were up to. It was a polite gesture, but one that Ford spurned for very good reason. He told the visiting Germans matter-of-factly that he believed war was coming soon, which shocked and horrified Porsche. Despite his curiosity *and* anti-Semitism, Ford had seen how his friend, Lindbergh, was lynched in the press for both his visit and subsequent statements. Ford wanted no part of any visit to Germany that could be viewed in any way as sympathetic to Hitler's regime. Ford, like Lindbergh, also received a decoration from Hitler. In 1938, he was presented with the Supreme Order of the German Eagle, the highest honor the Third Reich bestowed on non-Germans, in recognition of his trailblazing endeavors in the field of automobile manufacturing and mass production.

Neither Ferdinand Porsche nor his family were thought to be ideological Nazis, though they were clearly Nazis in name, given their status with Hitler. This is supported by the vast majority of historical and journalistic accounts of those present during the development of the car and familiar with Porsche. The Porsche family unquestionably benefited by the Nazi regime, as many German industrialists did. Nelson and other journalists and scholars draw the same conclusion: Porsche was apolitical and interested only in seeing his designs brought to fruition with the least amount of interference from those who might oppose him. Porsche was the most admired auto designer and engineer of his day, responsible for toppling the French and Italian dominance of the racing circuit. There is little evidence that Porsche took any meaningful note of the Holocaust that was happening in Germany and Eastern Europe from 1936 into the early 1940s. Only when underfed and mistreated slave labor was assigned to work at the Volksauto factory did Porsche act benevolently, or in a manner that showed he took even an hour to think beyond his drafting table. Porsche fought for better food and care for the slave labor at the VW factory when it became obvious to him that starved, poorly dressed, and abused refugees couldn't produce much in the way of quality work.

Porsche's alarm at Henry Ford's discussion of a likely war indicates either remarkable naivete or an unfeeling blindness. Or it indicates a disingenuous response perhaps appropriate to the moment. He was, after all, visiting the greatest industrialist of the day in the city where a good many tanks, Jeeps, and half-tracks would be manufactured if the United States went to war.

Porsche's delegation met with the German consuls in New York, Chicago, Detroit, Philadelphia, and a few other cities asking for help in finding German nationals working at auto and airplane plants, as well as Americans of German descent. Twenty would ultimately be re-cruited to go back to Germany to work on the *Volksauto* project.

Finishing the development of the *Volksauto* and building a factory that could produce it in the volume envisioned was not going to be a simple matter even with party-supplied funds, imported workers, and Hitler's political muscle behind it. There was agreement, certainly, but the war machine was also draining vast amounts of capital. Hitler therefore turned to a time-tested funding technique: Soak the poor. He established the German Labor Front as a political apparatus to keep workers in line and help stamp out communism. It prohibited strikes and demonstrations and reaffirmed the role of the employer as master and caretaker of the workers' well-being. For these rather illu-sory benefits, the workers were forced to pay dues. Of the monies collected, 10 percent went to the German Labor Front unit named *Kraft durch Freude,* or Strength through Joy. It would become known simply as KdF. Its purpose was to organize recreation, sports, and leisure activities of all kinds and to provide discounted tickets to sports and cultural events, as well as bargain travel tickets. The *Volksauto* would be built through the KdF. Through the KdF, the Front could market a subscription to the cars. Based on the prototype and some propaganda brochures, the *Volksauto* was marketed to the workers, who previously had no illusions of affording an automobile of their own, so the prospect of owning one was tantalizing. Workers were sold on giving up 5 marks a week into layaway accounts that would eventually pay for their *Volksauto.*

By 1938, the planned price of the *Volksauto* was set at 990 marks, or almost $400, up from Hitler's original target. However, this would also cover insurance, maintenance, and garage costs for the first 2 years. It was all rubbish, of course, and the low prices cited by the Third Reich were sheer public relations; the figures had no basis in reality. The scheme called for workers to pay into this subscription until the illusive purchase price was reached. The money went into non-interest-bearing accounts, like a bank Christmas club account of years ago, which were nontransferable and nonrefundable. If a worker became disinterested, disabled, or died, no money was returned. The car's actual price was never fixed in writing, so the Reich could boost the cost endlessly if it saw fit. All the subscription promised was that the money would go toward the purchase of a *Volksauto,* and when the purchase price was reached, it would be delivered to the subscriber. No timeline. No fixed price. Just hand over 5 marks a week and some-day a car will be delivered. In the meantime, here's a picture to put up. Indeed, many Germans actually framed pictures of the imaginary cars and hung them in their living rooms. Almost 350,000 Germans contributed the equivalent of $67 million before the Reich fell in 1945, many pressured by superiors and Party regulars to make the contributions toward their *Volksauto.*

Though some wonder whether the Reich set out to defraud the German people in this regard, it seems unlikely that the notion of

actual fraud can be attached to the *Volksauto* enterprise. No one following Hitler's stance since 1933 could doubt that he had every inten-
tion of building this car. In fact, the $67 million was in a special fund in
the Bank of German Labor when Germany surrendered to the Allies.
However, the money was not refunded to depositors due to looting by
the invading Russian army. That the subscription scheme was so heavily weighted in the Nazis' favor and was so ill-conceived is a function of
the madness rife in Berlin, not of outright fraud.

"A People's Town for the People's Car"

To build the car, the Nazis first had to build a factory. Finding a location for a plant designed to stretch a mile long was no easy task. It
would, of course, need to be located somewhere that could accom-
modate tens of thousands of workers and receive ton upon ton of raw
materials every week. After much surveying, Dr. Bodo Lafferentz, a
KdF aide charged with site selection, settled on what many at the time
thought an odd choice. It was an expanse of open land north of Hannover, a thinly populated area of ancient villages and undesirable
swampland in Lower Saxony. To the consternation of Count Werner
von der Schulenberg, it was also on land granted to the Count's ances-
tors in the twelfth century. The location was chosen for its open space
(the project called for 10,000 acres) as well as its proximity to both the
railway and the Mittelland Canal. Responsibility for building the plant
fell to none other than Albert Speer, Hitler's minister of armament
and war production, who later served a 20-year prison term as a war
criminal. Speer in turn enlisted a prize-winning architect of the day,
Peter Koller, to design both the plant and city of 90,000 workers, their
families, and others needed to support the plant. For a young architect
like Koller, it was a stupendous commission. This was the first time a
town was designed and built to support a factory of this magnitude.
As envisioned, the town was a far cry from spare worker barracks. It
was to be a cultural center, with streets of small homes and apartments, theaters, shops, parks, schools, and hotels. It was intended to
be a testament to what National Socialism could create. The plant's

dedication and laying of its cornerstone took place on 26 May 1938 near the town of Fallersleben.

Naming the new town was a challenge given the many opinions and preferences floating around. Names considered by administrators were Neu Fallersleben and Porschestadt. Anton Piëch contributed Volkswagenstadt. Hitler had his own, if tone-deaf, idea. The town was named Stadt des KdF-Wagens after the Strength through Joy movement. KdF-Stadt became the acceptable, clumsy, shorthand name for the town.

Hitler spoke at the laying of the cornerstone. "When I came to power in 1933, I saw one problem that had to be tackled at once: the problem of motorization. In this sphere, Germany was behind everyone else. The output of private cars in Germany had reached the laughable figure of forty-six thousand a year. And the first step toward putting an end to this was to do away with the idea that a motorcar is a luxury. What I want is not a car for two hundred thousand or three hundred thousand persons who can afford it, but a car which six million or seven million persons can afford."[10]

Porsche's Idea

Porsche was the only independent engineer of any standing with his own design studio in 1933. He'd gone to work for Daimler Motor Company in 1923 as an engineering director. The company merged with Benz and Cie in 1926 and became Daimler-Benz. Porsche left in 1926 after several run-ins with the new management over product planning and decision making; basically, they didn't give him the creative freedom he demanded. Instead of hopping over to one of the other carmakers, such as the new Auto Union or BMW, Porsche struck out on his own, worked on his designs, and sought companies that were interested or took a commission.

Hitler's idea of a people's car bore no resemblance to what the other auto companies had in mind for a cheap vehicle—likely a three-wheeled car sprung from motorcycle designs. From the start, his was to be a four-wheel rear-drive car with a three-cylinder, air-cooled engine. Hitler initially thought the engine should be front mounted, unaware of Porsche's ideas for the rear-mounted engine. Hitler from the start envisioned a vehicle that could be adapted for military use.

In his earliest writings about the Beetle, Porsche said the car should be one of normal dimensions, "but of relatively low weight, which is to be achieved through fundamentally new techniques."[11] The car should be built "as foolproof as possible" to keep the repairs easy and cheap. He also knew the Fuhrer. So he determined the car should not be designed for a narrow and limited market. "Rather, through a simple change of its bodywork, it should be suitable not only as a passenger car but also a delivery vehicle and for certain designated military purposes." Porsche was thinking in terms of mass production on a scale unknown in Germany, emulating one of his primary inspirations, if not his hero, Henry Ford.

Porsche initially thought Hitler's intended price tag of 1,000 marks was sheer madness. He therefore left himself a bit of room, citing 1,550 marks as a price he could achieve. Germany had only 522,000 cars in use in 1933, half as many as Britain or France. Its total vehicle output in 1934 was 147,000 (127,000 of them cars). Britain produced 257,000 vehicles the same year. When discussion of 200,000 to 300,000 Volkswagens a year was bandied about in 1934, it was a terribly ambitious target. It was especially galling to Hitler that the GM-owned Opel was accounting for about half of Germany's automotive exports and a quarter of its total production.

Executives at Adam Opel thought a car priced near 1,300 marks was achievable; however, that was for a three-wheel car based on a motorcycle platform that wouldn't compete with any of Opel's existing models. The German carmakers were not interested in building a car that even middle-class Germans might opt for at 1,000 marks instead of a more substantial and profitable car at 2,500 marks and up. Another real concern was that suppliers, in an attempt to please Hitler and to help meet the discounted price of the Volkswagen, would then hike prices of materials and parts they were selling to the private companies for their more expensive cars.

Auto Union, Daimler-Benz, BMW, and Opel were part of a commission that the RDA formed to study the project in 1934. Ford, of course, was not included. Participation by GM-owned Opel would not last long, either.

Porsche had a studio but no real shop, so the VW prototype was hatched in Porsche's family garage after a drill press, milling machine, and lathes were installed. The first VW prototypes were delivered in 1936, built with the help of Daimler-Benz. Two of the three models had wood-framed bodies, while the third had an all-steel body.

While Porsche gets credit for bringing his own vision to fruition, Karl Rabe is often omitted from the story. Rabe was Porsche's chief engineer, and his job was to figure a way to make the designer's vision a reality—literally, how to build the vision along practical lines. Then as now, the trick in bringing a car to market was to build the car at the right price while preserving the design.

Details of the Volkswagen were finally released at the 1939 Berlin Auto Show when two models were unveiled. The year 1939 also saw the release of postage stamps picturing Germany's cars. The original Benz and Daimler cars were on the 6-pfennig stamp; the Auto Union and Mercedes-Benz racing cars were on the 17-pfennig stamp; the new KdF-Wagen, zipping along the Autobahn, was on the 25-pfennig stamp. Some enterprising businessman also created a board game to pay homage not only to the KdF-Wagen itself, but also to the process through which workers would acquire one. With illustrations of the KdF factory, Porsche's design facility, and the KdF town, the game took players through the stages of saving for and finally taking ownership of a new car, including the saving of stamps, passing a driving test, getting the car at the factory, and then driving the new car home.

Though Hitler conceived of the car for the poorest German workers—those making 25 marks a week—only about 5 percent of those who subscribed to the plan came from that bottom economic rung. This is not surprising, because 5 marks a week amounted to a fat 20 percent of their take-home pay. Most of the KdF savers earned from 80 to 100 marks a week. To the dismay of the private auto producers, one-third of the savers were already car owners saving for a second set of wheels.

Production of the KdF-Wagen was set to begin in 1939 at 20,000 units, with 100,000 to follow in 1940, 200,000 in 1941, and 450,000 annually thereafter. It was expected that a workforce of 17,500 would work two shifts on the car. The sprawling new plant was to be expanded in stages as materials became available and demand rose. The master plan ultimately called for the plant to put 30,000 people to work building from 800,000 to 1 million cars annually. No single North American plant, even today, produces 1 million vehicles a year.

Indeed, in the 1930s, Ford, the biggest producer, built 1.3 million cars a year worldwide in all of its plants. Chevy was producing about 1 million; Plymouth was building 500,000; and Dodge about 300,000.

Wartime Diversions

Work on the KdF plant and KdF-Stadt progressed in 1940 despite the War. With manpower short, though, Italian laborers were imported to Germany thanks to Hitler's alliance with Mussolini.

Ferdinand Porsche, according to his son Ferry, was one of the few men in Germany who could speak his mind to Hitler. The younger Porsche wrote that the elder Porsche was a kind of father figure to Hitler. He had latitude with the Fuhrer and could work the relationship to his advantage.[12]

Once the War started to rage in Europe and priorities shifted, it was Porsche's early experiences with political infighting at Daimler-Benz that worked to his advantage, perhaps even more than his relationship with Hitler. Despite turning his back on the corporate life to become an independent designer, Porsche remained politically savvy in the corporate sense. Although it was Porsche's desire to build cars at KdF-Stadt, he was well aware that the rapacious war machine would continue to divert precious raw materials needed to advance construction. As far back as 1938, Porsche realized that to keep his factory moving there needed to be military utility built into the KdF-Wagen platform. Beginning in 1940, the factory took on orders and commissions for gas tanks and other parts for fighter planes, torpedo hulls, land mines, and portable heaters for Germany's ever-marching infantry. All of the materials thus pouring in allowed some to be diverted to the plant's infrastructure. It was Porsche's strategy to keep the building of the plant going, so that when the War ended, it could quickly be converted to producing his Volksautos. If the factory languished during the War, there was no telling what might happen to it. If it never got completed or was only partially completed, any number of things could happen to prevent it from being finished. However, once a plant is built, its owners tend not to want to tear it down. Porsche had seen enough in his lifetime to know how to work the system.

This concept, however, cut both ways. A plant producing munitions and ordnance became an Allied bombing target. If it languished as an incomplete car factory, it stood a good chance of being left alone. Indeed, bombs began falling on the plant in 1940 and went right on falling through 1944. A disabled British Lancaster actually crashed into a plant building with its bomb load in tact. Allied attention to the KdF plant increased in 1944 when intelligence gathering revealed the plant was being used to make the particularly savage V-1 buzz bomb, also known as the Doodlebug. It was an unmanned, midwing flying machine with a guidance system that delivered a 1-ton bomb to its target up to 150 miles away.

The lofty sales targets set for the KdF-Wagen would prove totally unreachable once war started. In reality, though, they'd been set more for propaganda purposes than as reasonable production targets. The first KdF-Wagen built at the KdF plant for the military in Fallersleben rolled off the line in July 1941. It wasn't the vehicle that the world would come to know as the Beetle, but it was the first car to be produced on the production line. Up to that point, a few dozen had been hand-built at Daimler-Benz's factory for public relations and testing purposes, as well as to give to some of the Nazi elite. Between 1941 and 1944, just 630 KdF-Wagens (Beetles) were made for civilian sale. All of them went to the elite, not to the workers for whom they were intended. One was sent to Emperor Hirohito of Japan, and Mussolini received several as well—tokens of goodwill from one fascist dictator to another—and to thank him for supplying Italian compulsory labor.

Porsche and Rabe developed a military vehicle from the KdF-Wagen, known as the Type 82, or Kubelwagen. With rigorous attention to keeping the weight of the vehicle down, and designing some ingenious elements for traction in the snow and ice, the car proved a huge hit with most military leaders after they had initially scoffed at it. Ferry Porsche wrote in 1940:[13]

In the prevailing slippery ground conditions in the mountains . . . our four-wheel drive Types 86 and 87 cars without snow chains were vastly superior to the Army Uniform Personnel Car. For example, our Type 87 climbed the approximately 25-degree slope of the Hungerberg without trouble, while the wheels of the Uniform car began to skid after a stretch of about 30 meters.

The cover of the KdF magazine in May 1941 showed a Type 82 in front of an Italian temple ruin with an inset photo of a KdF-Wagen. The headline: "He too drives against England."[14] The captions read:

Mr. Churchill would certainly never have dreamed that so soon he would again meet the KdF-Wagen, which his radio broadcasts long ago consigned to the graveyard. With unshakable confidence in their KdF-Wagen, hundreds of thousands of citizens continue saving, hoping to receive them soon after the war ends victoriously.

Kubelwagens began to gain in popularity with the military personnel who relied on them in 1941. On the bitter cold Russian front in mid-1941, when the first Kubelwagens made their way to the battle line, Porsche's car performed much better than the Horch Uniform car then in use. The Horch was simply not equal to either the Russian winter or roads and suffered frequent breakdowns. In contrast, the tough Kubelwagen proved its mettle by standing up to the difficult weather and terrain, and was easy to fix when something did go wrong. It almost seemed that the car performed better in harsh conditions—a sure way to win the hearts of professional soldiers. In addition, the Kubelwagen's fuel efficiency made Porsche a legion of fans, for fuel was ever at a premium during the War.

The car was tested in the brutal heat and sand of Northern Africa and was unbeatable. This was due to the air-cooled Porsche engine that kept the oil from overheating, a feature previously found only in first-class sports cars. The Horch, BMW, and Tatra cross-country vehicles wouldn't start in General Erwin Rommel's desert, but the Porsche engine kicked over after a few turns. Some 350 Kubelwagens left behind in 1942 after the British and Americans drove General Erwin Rommel from North Africa were still running a decade later, used by the locals who had appropriated them as their own.

Rommel told Porsche during one of their wartime meetings that the old man saved his life. Hitler's favorite general discovered by accident one day that the Kubelwagen was tough, yet so light that it could be driven across a minefield without setting off the ordinance. A heavier command car built by Horch driving in the same field in the same tracks had been blown to smithereens.[15] In 1942, 5,000 Kublewagens were shipped from Fallesleben to the German military.

Bridges in the German and French countryside were a frequent target of Allied bombs, and wrecked bridges severely hampered Nazi troop movement. Perhaps Porsche's greatest adaptation of his car for wartime purposes was the Schwimmenwagen, a car that could literally be driven from the road straight into the water and converted into a boat without the occupants having to get out or attach any special gear. Porsche fitted watertight seals to the axles and added an engine-driven propeller at the rear of the car. The front wheels acted as rudders. The mechanical brakes were covered with a watertight material. Swimming Kubelwagens proved a great asset. In 1941, Heinrich Himmler was persuaded that the Schwimmenwagen, which also exhibited superior off-road performance, was a sensible replacement for the motorcycles and sidecars then employed by mobile units. Motorcycles were proving to be of limited use, especially in North

Africa and Eastern Europe where roads ranged from poor to nonexistent. The Schwimmenwagen was actually cheaper to produce than BMW's motorcycles. There were more than 14,000 Schwimmenwagens built during the War.

Porsche kept fiddling with the basic car, trying to develop new configurations with military application. He designed one with double rear wheels to behave better in the deep snows of Russia. He designed one with metal wheels that could be driven on railroad tracks. One vehicle was designed with wheels in the front and a half-track in the rear, also for snowy and muddy terrain. Porsche later admitted that he knew that many of these iterations had limited real-world applications. He had the money to keep innovating for the military, though, and had no orders to tinker for civilian applications. So adaptable was the Kubelwagen that officers in the field even did their own occasional improvization, such as attaching a wooden tanklike structure to the top, and having the cars run among tanks to mislead the Allies about the strength of tank brigades crossing the countryside.

While finding new applications for the car, Porsche also was compelled to keep working on the engine to make it more adaptable. The military was keenly interested in an engine that could be easily transferred from the Kubelwagen to a tractor and even a field-kitchen generator. Remarkably, the flat-four Kubelwagen engine became adaptable for generators, compressors, winches, a tank engine starter, and even a light aircraft engine.

The output of Kubelwagens (in all their versions) from the Fallersleben plant totaled 50,435. It was Germany's most abundant light military vehicle, ahead of Mercedes-Benz production. However, to put this in perspective, Detroit produced 650,000 Jeeps during the War.

———

The workforce at Fallersleben was composed largely of Italians, Russians, Poles, and French, virtually all held against their will as slave labor. Only one worker in eight was German, and they produced only the most sensitive material such as the V-1 bomb. In 1940, the first year that non-Germans were forced to work at the plant, the number totaled 919, compared with 2,696 Germans. By 1943, the number of non-German forced laborers totaled 11,401.[16]

Especially terrible was VW's (and other German companies) practice of recruiting workers, male and female, from the ranks of Polish and Russian Christians who became refugees during Hitler's campaign of ethnic cleansing. These adults worked under harsh and dehumanizing conditions; the women often had children, some fathered by the German overseers. These babies, sometimes born prematurely (not surprising, considering the stress that the women were under), were taken to a VW-owned children's home that, according to lawsuits filed on behalf of survivors in the late 1990s, were full of insects, cockroaches, fleas, lice, and rodents. Most of the babies died, with their deaths attributed to "unknown causes," or simply "too weak to live."[17]

Many of the workers were pulled from concentration camps. Organizers went to the camps and searched for trained mechanics, plumbers, and electricians. These slave laborers were required in the Fallersleben plant because German mechanics and technicians were needed at the front lines. This was all part of Hitler's plan, the official policy of the Third Reich. Those undesirables who did not die in the ovens and gas chambers would be exterminated by labor.

Volkswagen's acknowledgment of its participation in the slave labor atrocities during the War was slow in coming. As discussed in Chapter 3, it is worth noting that VW's latter-day managers had no ties to the Reich. In fact, the company was not really formed until after the British turned it over to the German federal government in 1949. What existed before that was more a state-owned war materials factory than anything like a private enterprise, such as was Daimler-Benz.

In the 1990s, when lawyers began organizing class-action lawsuits, VW was among the German companies that were trying to shed responsibility for slave-labor atrocities. The company argued that if the atrocities were anyone's responsibility, they lay at the feet of the government. The Nazi government was responsible in the 1930s and 1940s, so remuneration or damages should be paid by the German government.

In 1991, Volkswagen AG provided DM 12 million to a board of curators that dispersed the funds to support projects in the countries from which most of the former forced laborers came—hospitals, nursing homes, and schools.[18] The funds were divided in almost equal amounts among some 30 projects in Belarus, Israel, Poland, and the Ukraine. For the most part, the projects benefited the young, the elderly, the handicapped, and the hospital patients—the very populations who were summarily extinguished by the Nazis because they served no practical purpose in the work camps.

Documents discovered at the sprawling Wolfsburg plant in the 1990s showed that Ferdinand Porsche did contact SS leader Heinrich Himmler directly during the War to obtain labor from the Auschwitz concentration camp.[19] That, in and of itself, however, is not damning, because life at the KdF factory, while still under slave-labor conditions, was a better fate than that meted out to inmates at Auschwitz. Not a card-carrying member of the Nazi party, Porsche was not tried for war crimes by the Americans and the British after the War. He was, as son Ferry Porsche admitted, something of a father figure to Hitler and the Fuhrer's favorite car man. Dr. Porsche wasn't a Nazi, but it's fair to call him a collaborator, opportunist, and a vital cog in the Werhmacht war machine.

After the close of WWII, Ferdinand Porsche was held by the British authorities near the KdF plant. Following his release in 1945, Porsche was invited to France to consult on the building of the people's car, which the French transportation authority told him they were interested in building at Renault. Instead, the French arrested Porsche, charged him as a war criminal, and held him in an unheated Dijon prison. They did actually consult with him about the new, rear-engine Renault 4CV before tossing the 70-year-old into an unheated cell. He was never brought to trial, and his son Ferry paid what amounted to a 1-million-franc bail. Ferdinand Porsche was freed in August 1947 after almost 2 years' imprisonment. He returned to Austria a broken man, his spirit and health shattered, and he died in 1950. Before he died, his son Ferry told an interviewer that he returned to what had been named Wolfsburg where Volkswagens were being built. He saw an autobahn full of KdF-Wagens, a sight that made the old man cry.[20]

Reparations

In 1998, VW funded a sum of DM 20 million to be paid to living veterans of the forced labor at the KdF-Wagen plant.

In 1996, VW published a 1,000-page study: *The Volkswagen Factory and Its Workers in the Third Reich.*[21] Many were surprised that VW, under Ferdinand Piëch, would undertake such a project. By the early 1990s, however, when Piëch took over, his predecessors had embarked on several efforts to confront the company's past. To reverse those efforts would have been public relations suicide. In 1996, as the study was released and more lawsuits were filed seeking reparations, the media in the United States and Europe continued to run stories with graphics of a VW logo intertwined with a Nazi swastika. Both CNN and NBC televised graphics showing the VW logo and swastika intertwined in 1996 and 1999 broadcasts. The company was either going to get in front of the issue once and for all, or endure such hideous images dogging its recovery for the foreseeable future. Publishing the report and being open about the past were the smart things to do.

The Rise

THREE

In the summer of 1945, a few months after Germany's surrender to the Allies in Rheims, France, the Volkswagenwerks factory and fledgling village near Fallersleben could hardly be called "City of Strength through Joy." There was joy that the War was over, and Hitler was dead; however, much of Germany was rubble. There was little food. Fear gripped the slave laborers who were now free, but unsure of what to do or where to go. The Volkswagenwerks was heavily damaged from Allied bombing and looting. Some of the slave laborers directed their wrath on the factory by destroying office equipment, machines, typewriters, and phones, and by burning files. The KdF factory, even in this condition, though, was a prize of war. The Germans were no longer in command. The British took charge of the zone in which the factory lay.

In June 1945, a unit of the Royal Electrical and Mechanical Engineers arrived at the factory and set up a shop to repair British army vehicles. The factory had been tagged for dismantling because most of the British officers who had inspected it believed it was beyond repair.

Major Ivan Hirst was in charge of the installation, and he reported to Colonel Charles Radclyffe who directed all motor vehicle operations in the British zone.

The atmosphere around the factory was a mixture of despair and entrepreneurship. A few German workers who were still there retrieved some of the machinery that had been squirreled away in the final days of the War for safekeeping. Machinery like this was extremely valuable, and the decisions to save it in tunnels in the sub-structure of the plant itself was fortuitous. On their own, despite the factory having a foot or more of water running through it much of the time, workers were keeping busy and had assembled two vehicles from spare parts, having reassembled some of the machinery, includ-ing a heavy press used for stamping body panels.

The British were well acquainted with the wartime Kubelwagens that had been built off the Type 1 chassis, having seen many of them running around North Africa after many of their own British-made and American-made water-cooled vehicles had given out in the desert heat. They were glad to have the vehicles that were beginning to trickle out of the broken factory because there was a shortage of vehi-cles for their use.

One of the first hand-built KdF-Wagens, a Beetle rather than a Kubelwagen, to be made at Wolfsburg was shipped to Great Britain by Major Hirst. There was an idea kicking around that the British might take over the factory and produce the vehicles themselves. The trans-portation ministry in Britain, though, was *officially* unimpressed with the vehicle, and its directors reported their belief that the car was flimsy and unattractive, nothing for the British market and, the report stated, nothing even the German market would embrace. The Min-istry stated: "The vehicle does not meet the fundamental and technical requirements of a motorcar. As regards performance and design it is quite unattractive to the average motorcar buyer. It is too ugly and too noisy." The ministry further suggested that the plant be razed. This, however, would not be the last word from the British.

Workers at the Volkswagenwerks who were fighting for food scraps, blankets, and decent clothes were undeterred. There were enough spare parts lying around to continue hand-building vehicles. To them the cars were a form of currency. Disabled Kubelwagens were cannibalized for parts. Some parts were found in abandoned trains at the end of the War and returned to the factory. Completed cars were then bartered for steel to make more cars, as well as food and clothing. In 1945, according to VW's company records, 1,785 vehicles were produced, all for the British military and other occupying forces. Ten thousand would be produced in 1946 by workers who were still living a hardscrabble life in the village on the other side of the canal with not much decent food or shelter. Under the direction of Major Hirst, makeshift production in 1947 fell below 9,000. Still, given the conditions, even that was remarkable considering none of the other German carmakers had yet resumed production at all.

The future of the factory was very uncertain. Vehicles had been sent to Britain, Australia, and the United States for engineers in those countries to break down to see if the cars might have a future in their markets. Each time, though, it was reported back that nothing important could be learned from Dr. Porsche's design. Meanwhile, Porsche himself was suffering in a French prison for aiding the Third Reich.

The reports, though, were not unanimous. Teams of experts were recruited by Britain's Society of Motor Manufacturers and Traders (SMMT) to travel to Germany and study the factory and vehicle. One account of the factory during a visit by a team reported, ". . . it can be said that the Volkswagen is the most advanced and the most interesting for quantity production. It embodies most of the major requirements considered necessary for speedy and economical production, eliminating hand-work to an unusual degree in the process of cleaning, painting and finishing. Both the car and the factory in which it is produced are wonderful achievements in their respective spheres and should be given a great deal more detailed study. . . ."[1] Other cars of the day in Europe, especially British cars, required extensive hand-work, which was one of the dimensions of manufacturing that made cars cost so much. Porsche had studied Ford's assembly-line production in Detroit, though, and the KdF plant and vehicle had been designed for a minimum of handwork.

That's not all the SMMT study said: ". . . a close examination of the design of this vehicle [should be made] as it would appear to offer, with perhaps a few modifications, a possible solution of the cheap utility vehicle that would be acceptable in the United Kingdom and in the overseas markets."[2] Some Brits clearly understood the possibilities, while others missed it altogether.

While 40 percent of the factory had suffered bomb damage, only 3 percent of the tooling was lost, thanks to the preparations made by the Germans in advance of bombing raids. The stamping machine, for example, that made Type 1 roof panels had been surrounded with protective material. Such machines, had they not been protected, and other tools squirreled away in basement dungeons, would surely have been destroyed in the raids. Had they not survived, there would have been no hope or interest in bringing the plant back to life, as those custom-built machines are what enabled the hand-built production to continue in the aftermath of the War. Indeed, some have theorized that the plant must have been *destined* to survive because one bomb that dropped on the factory next to a huge turbine remained unexploded. Had that turbine been destroyed, it might have been enough to deter interest in the plant altogether, and would have prevented the quick resumption of car building after peace was signed.

Meanwhile, the Americans were contemplating the radical Morganthau Plan, which would have limited Germany to being an agricultural nation only, depriving it of the industrialization that allowed the Germans to mount not one, but two, world wars in 25 years. Anti-German sentiment was running high. The British government, which certainly suffered longer and more dramatically than the Americans at the hands of the Germans, were not interested in supporting such a plan. Winston Churchill was convinced that Germany would have to be built up again, not only to provide jobs for the throngs of refugees, but to become a buffer against Russia.

At the conference at Potsdam in July and August of 1945, during which the four Allied powers made a list of German manufacturing facilities to be destroyed, the KdF plant at Fallersleben was among those designated for destruction. It was a repeat of history, as a similar

Allied commission ordered that most of Germany's industrial assets be destroyed following World War I. Cooler heads prevailed. Because there was overwhelming evidence that the plant had been built for civilian production and only was turned into an armament plant by default and necessity, it was spared—but not completely. Some 1,300 tons of machinery was removed and destroyed as it was deemed to be connected specifically to the production of bombs, aircraft, and other munitions. The machines and tools that were meant for the production of automobiles remained. In 1946, Germans who had removed and boxed parts and tools in the substory of the complex retrieved the remainder of what had been hidden after the British had done their inspections. It is amazing how many places there are to hide such things in a facility that is a mile long, especially in the cellars. Although Britain spared the factory from the Russians, who were after any industrial asset they could get their hands on, the Opel Kadett production plant in Brandenburg did not fare as well, being carried off piecemeal to Russia where it would never be reassembled as the plan had been laid. Years later, in fact, visitors to the Soviet Union reported seeing the machinery rusting away along the sides of railroad tracks.

The primary champion of the factory and the car was Major Hirst. Hirst could see that besides the Type 1 being a capable automobile, saving the factory would be a huge boost to rebuilding the lives of the people who were living in Lower Saxony. Hirst and his fellow British officers became so fond of the vehicles that a great recreation became driving the Schwimmenwagens into the Mittelland Canal at speeds of 40 miles per hour and then running them up and down the canal in races. They did anything and everything possible to keep the factory producing vehicles, diverting coal shipments meant for other places, cajoling their superiors for equipment that would have otherwise gone to British factories. Hirst felt a responsibility to the German people and the refugees who stayed on in the village trying to put their lives back together. He believed it was best to keep the factory and the whole enterprise German.

In 1946, the U.S. forces authorized the Reichsbank in Braunschweig to loan the factory 1,350,000 marks to pay salaries and other mounting bills. In May of that year, the town council renamed KdF-Stadt as Wolfsburg after the name of von der Schulenberg's nearby castle and grounds.

A People's Leader

It was decided in 1948 that a real production manager was needed at the factory to determine what had to be done to make it an ongoing enterprise, instead of the seat-of-the-pants operation it had been for 2 years.

Heinz Nordhoff had been an executive at Adam Opel, the German division of General Motors, when war broke out. He had a promising future with the company. After the War, though, he was told he wouldn't be getting his old job back as a matter of policy. The only job awaiting him in the U.S. zone, where the Opel plants and organization lay, was as a laborer. Nordhoff actually did not think much of the KdF-Wagen, but he needed a job to support his family. In 1945 and 1946, he had even worked as a mechanic and at menial jobs to feed his wife and children.

Nordhoff had held several jobs at Opel. He started out writing service manuals while in his 20s; later, he went into the customer service department. In the early 1930s, Opel sent him to the United States to learn the production and marketing skills that were being developed in Detroit. In 1936, Nordhoff became a member of Opel's board of directors. It was from this position that he, among the executives at Opel, looked with consternation at Hitler's plan for a people's car. He was against the Nazi government going into the car-producing business, and he, along with other Opel loyalists, hadn't appreciated the snubbing that Opel's top management received from Hitler and Porsche. Nordhoff went to Berlin in 1939; in 1941, he took charge of the company's truck factory in Brandenburg. Too old to be drafted and a veteran of World War I, he held that position until the end of the War.

Nordhoff was in the Harz Mountains with his wife and daughters during the last days of World War II. Just as he was about to return to

Berlin to stand with his workers as the Allied forces took over, he was literally cut off from reaching the plant by advancing U.S. forces on the road. It's a good thing. All of the other senior Opel executives in Berlin who did make it back to the plant were taken to Russia, presumably to reassemble the factory that had been dragged off in railcars. Instead, they ended up in the Gulag, never to be heard from again.

Nordhoff was amazed at what he found at the KdF factory. He was shocked that they had been able to build as many cars as they did. The mark was almost worthless in 1947, so they were still bartering for materials. One completed car brought a few weeks' supply of steel. Nordhoff, who was 46, moved into the factory for 6 months. He slept on a cot in a room near his office, kept awake at night by the sound of scurrying rats that were foraging for scraps of food in the dank, wounded, mile-long factory. Most of the windows had been knocked out, and much of the roof was in disrepair. Rainy days brought streams of water onto the work floor. Some 7,000 workers were turning out cars at a rate of 6,000 a year. That could not go on much longer or the plant would be shut down. No one knew how long it took to build one car, but Nordhoff guessed it was something like 400 hours.

Though he knew production methods and was clearly in charge, Nordhoff did not act like a boss, but rather a leader. He addressed workers as *partners*. It was not so much a technique, but a fact. In 1947, the factory was still under the control of the British. Nordhoff was a German. He had only a vague idea that if they could clean the factory up and get real production practices going that something good might come of it. The most likely outcome was that a foreign automaker—British, French, or U.S.—might see that it was worthwhile and invest some capital. Whatever the outcome, he very much felt as if they were all in the same lifeboat.

Nordhoff met several times in 1947 and 1948 with Ford executives, convinced that being taken over by a U.S. carmaker was the only way that the factory could continue. Nordhoff, though, under any plan of Ford's, would have been demoted and not allowed to run the enterprise freely. This was certainly a problem for the fiercely independent Nordhoff. With the factory in the British zone, there was a lack of clarity in the negotiations about who would actually own and operate the Volkswagenwerks, which did not please Ford's negotiators who were not terribly disposed to the factory in the first place. Ford was also not thrilled with the proximity of the factory to the East Berlin border, a mere 5 miles. However, Henry Ford II ultimately refused to take on the plant and the car on the advice of Ford executive Ernest Breech, whose quote that neither the factory nor the car were "worth a damn" lives on as one of the great miscalculations in the history of business.

In 1948, the Soviets, desperate to get a domestic car industry under way, offered to have the boundary between East and West Berlin redrawn by 5 miles so that they could take the plant over. The Soviets had their own experience with Volkswagen, seeing Kubelwagens thrive in the harsh conditions of the Russian battlefront. Too, the Russians had no hope of an established western carmaker investing in communist Russia. They may also have been encouraged by no less than a report published in the British magazine, *Motor*, which in its June 1947 issue said, "The 1947 Volkswagen is a modern looking car, neat in appearance and handy in size . . . Lacking some of the refinement which British cars show, the German people's car that was to have been strikes the driver as a sound job which should give long years of service."[3]

With U.S. and British relations sinking fast, the Soviets were rebuffed by both governments. It was Nordhoff's to make sink or swim.

By mid-1948, Hirst and the British were gone. Nordhoff was still trying to clean up the plant and fix the windows and roofs. He had little money and no distribution system, as yet. He had a workforce that was turning over at a rate of 100 percent because there was no decent place to live near the plant. With the mark of not much value yet, Nordhoff sent a couple of VW Type 1 vehicles (the Beetle) to the United States with a Dutchman named Ben Pon, who had sold some Beetles in Holland. Pon's job was to see if any U.S. distributors were interested in selling the car in the United States. If they did, greenbacks would come back to Nordhoff. Pon was chosen because he had managed to sell the Beetle in Holland at a time when anti-German sentiment was as high or higher than it was in the United States. Pon, with the help of a friend, held a press conference aboard the Holland America ship that had taken him and the car to New York. In one of the great examples of tone-deaf public relations, Pon called the cars *Victory Wagens*. The media, however, knew that this was the car about which Hitler had boasted building in the 1930s, and that it had been used as a platform for many German army vehicles. There was plenty of press about Pon's cars, all of it negative. A headline in the *Jersey Journal* read: "Hitler's Car Looks for American Buyers." A Detroit reporter wrote that it seemed an unheard-of proposition that the fastidious, long-legged Americans should squeeze themselves, with the aid of a shoehorn, into these rattling sardine tins.[4]

Pon was rebuffed by every dealer and distributor he saw. Out of money and owing more than he had in his pocket to the Hotel Roosevelt, he was forced to sell the car and the spare parts he brought with him for $800 to settle his bill. Pon's trip, though, was not for naught. He observed the other European carmakers sending cars into the United States, setting up distribution, but with inadequate service and parts support. He told Nordhoff that it was premature to set up shop in the United States and that he shouldn't try until he could do it right with extensive service support. Deeply disappointed, Nordhoff went to the United States himself with a suitcase of photographs of the car and an allowance of $15 a day. He, too, was rebuffed by dealers and reporters who felt that the car had no future in the United States. Their assessment would prove wrong. The two chief criticisms of the Volkswagen were that (1) it was "Hitler's car," and (2) it was out of date. The latter couldn't have been more wrong. The people who dismissed it knew nothing of the extensive testing that the car had endured before and during the War. More money had been put into perfecting the car's design and engineering than any car before it, and up to 1949. The Volkswagen's problem was not that it was too late; rather, it was too early. Americans back from the War had been without new cars since 1941. What was in demand were large land yachts with as much chrome as paint. Americans had gone without indulgences for so long, they wanted the automotive equivalent of cake, not merely the bread that was the people's car.

———

By 1949, Nordhoff was making progress in Germany and other parts of Western Europe with sales and distribution. In fact, it was the only German carmaker even operating at that time. Fortunes started to turn when there was currency reform in Germany that year. Once that happened, Nordhoff could set a fair market price for the car. That took the British out of the German automobile business. No longer did a German citizen need a permit to buy a Volkswagen. They could buy one as long as they had enough money. Freeing up the market made the whole enterprise more robust overnight and got dealers interested. Things were looking so good that workers demanded higher wages. Rebuffed in the United States, though, Nordhoff knew that he had to reinvest as much money into the factory as possible. He addressed the workers, explaining this. Nordhoff always addressed the workforce as "fellow workers," lest they think they were being ordered around. Worker pride was taking hold at the factory, so Nordhoff appealed to them as genuine stakeholders. He also knew that jobs were scarce and the wages that they were making already were better than just about anything that could be found elsewhere in Germany. That wouldn't last long, though. Soon, Opel, Ford, Daimler-Benz, and the rest would be up and running and looking for trained workers to replace those who were now in Army graveyards and at the bottom of the Atlantic.

As money flowed back into the factory, Nordhoff in 1948 managed to rebuild more than 3 million square feet of plant and office space. The German magazine *Stern* wrote toward the end of 1948:

> On the average, a new Volkswagen leaves the conveyor belt once every three and a half minutes ... During the three months from September to November 1948, only 300 VWs went to the occupation authorities, while 2,154 Volkswagens were produced in October alone. Of these, 1,270 were sold to

Germans and the rest were exported. At the moment, there is a waiting list of 15,000 for Volkswagens in Germany. And about 7,000 export orders are outstanding.[5]

As soon as Nordhoff hit his stride and began making improvements to the factory, and the town started to take shape across the canal, distributors, dealers, and bankers began urging him to abandon the Beetle design for something more modern. Again, there was little recognition that the Beetle was ahead of its time. The exhaustive testing that led to the design was lost on the critics of Nordhoff and the vehicle. Of course, it's worth noting that Nordhoff himself was still no big fan of the car. What he did understand, though, was that the vehicle's heart was in its engine. In 1949, the engine was not the engine that had endured tests in North Africa and the Russian front. The quality of the materials that Nordhoff was using was not as good as what the plant had used in 1940 to build Kubelwagens. The engines did not last long without substantial part replacement and maintenance. They were noisy. Interior textiles were not durable. Critics were urging Nordhoff to change the outer skin of the car; however, he believed that doing that before refining the engine and drivetrain and fixing the rattles and substandard material would have been a mistake.

A problem cropped up in 1948 when the 336,000 faithful Germans who had money taken from their paychecks in exchange for coupon stamps for a KdF-Wagen came demanding their car, now that they were coming off the factory line. Nordhoff told organizers and lawyers representing the savers that the current factory and its product had no connection to the scheme and that, because the Reich was no more, their coupon books were worthless. In October 1948, a group of savers banded together and began the equivalent of a U.S. class-action suit against the government-owned VW enterprise. The regional court in Hildesheim rejected the claims of two plaintiffs in January 1950, though the decision was appealed. The disputes of the savers would drag through German courts until 1961, when a settlement was reached that granted savers a coupon of varying worth toward the purchase of a vehicle.

Constant Improvement

Improvements to the VW's engine and drivetrain were desperately needed to improve reliability and durability. Nordhoff hired Dr. Alfred Haesner, with whom he had worked at Opel, to be chief engineer in 1951. Between that year and 1954, Haesner and his staff made constant changes and improvements, upgrading every part and pinion to work more smoothly and to last longer. It is during this time that the Beetle was transformed from an advanced design to an advanced machine. Hydraulic brakes replaced cable ones. A new gearbox was introduced with synchromesh shifting, which required no manual clutching on second, third, and fourth gears. Wheel diameter was reduced from 16 to 15 inches, and rim width was increased from 3 to 4 inches. Better tires were fitted for the car. The dashboard was redesigned, with the speedometer relocated to where the driver could clearly see it. The split window in the rear was replaced by one large window that increased visibility by almost 25 percent. The engine was enlarged from 1,131 to 1,192 cubic centimeters. Larger valves, redesigned cylinder heads, and a higher compression ratio were all key changes to improve performance and drivability. Peak power was increased by 20 percent, from 30 to 36 horsepower. Fender-mounted lamps replaced the semaphore turn signal arms, and the fuel tank was reshaped to enlarge trunk space. There was constant tinkering with very little change to the exterior and no changes to the sheet metal. The Porsche shape and curves needed to be maintained to retain aerodynamic performance. To change it haphazardly would have resulted in the car being out of balance and possibly requiring changes to the engine just to boost power to make up for lost speed due to wind drag.

In 1952, *Road & Track* tested a Beetle.

How could you improve on a car which will cruise effortlessly all day long at top speed? What changes would you suggest in a vehicle which will seat a driver and three passengers in adequate comfort and which will handle light as a feather? Could you ask a 94-inch wheelbase automobile to give any more than 30 to 35 miles per gallon . . . on regular gasoline? These are the questions for which *Road & Track* is hard pressed to find answers.[6]

Production at Wolfsburg climbed from 81,979 in 1951 to 279,986 in 1955 to 725,927 in 1960. By the end of the 1950s, Beetles were being shipped in completely knocked-down (CKD) form to several other countries for assembly at factory-authorized plants. The 1953 annual report of VW states that it was exporting vehicles to 88 countries and had established subsidiaries in Canada (1952) and Brazil (1953), both of which were operating profitably. The city of Wolfsburg was not the ramshackle affair it was in 1948. Wages were 5 percent above the other automakers in Germany. Pensions were being funded. Employees were being given financial help to buy houses. Over 2,000 workers lived in apartments built by VW. The company had even built two churches in town, one Catholic and one Protestant. Nordhoff lived in a small detached home in the midst of others that were occupied by workers, and other white-collar executives followed his lead.

In 1958, VW had about 2 percent of the U.S. market, with all other imports holding another 2 percent. It was being noticed and taken seriously by most of Detroit. *Time* magazine ran a piece that year on the VW popularity, noting that a middle-class housewife was typical of the U.S. buyers who had discovered the Beetle.

At a time of crowded streets and filled-up parking places, we are taken aback every year by a longer and wider model from Detroit. While the price of gasoline and oil shot up, we were invited to buy a car with 300-horsepower which soaks up the gas. We were told that every family should have a second car, and for twelve years prices went up yearly. Well, we shall follow Detroit's advice and buy a second car, but it's going to be a Volkswagen.

This was remarkably consistent with what some dealer promotional material from the late 1950s taught salespeople on how to think of the VW when selling it. "Volkswagen, the ideal second car for town traffic. What the helicopter is among aeroplanes, the VW is among cars."[8]

Many U.S. journalists, seeing the success of the VWs, became highly critical of the Detroit companies and the path down which their product developers had taken U.S. drivers. Journalist Eric Larrabee wrote:[9]

> Once upon a time Detroit became great and rich by means of a cheap, compact family car . . . But that did not satisfy the public, and certainly not the people of Detroit. In the belief, which up to a point is justified, that the American wants to buy "something better still," i.e. bigger and more showy, the industry turned the once cheap, maneuverable mass-produced cars into dinosaurs of the high road, fashion salons on wheels. Out of its desire for that last word in external line, for the latest technical gadget, and for an absurd horsepower figure, Detroit has forgotten the actual meaning of a car, namely a sensible and economic means of transport, adapted to traffic conditions . . . This development was bound to defeat its own purpose one day.

The opening paragraph of a *New York Times* article in 1955, written by Grace Glueck, is worth reading, too, as a milepost of mounting attitudes about cars in the United States.[10]

> The complaint voiced recently by New York City Traffic Commissioner T. T. Wiley that the new American automobiles are too long, too wide and too powerful recalls a drive to and from Florida taken recently in a European pygmy automobile that is none of these things. Two of us shoehorned two suitcases, two overnight bags, a box of footgear, a couple of cameras and ourselves into the pocket-size interior of a two-door four-passenger Volkswagen sedan. It got us down and back, not so fast nor as comfortably as a big American car, but for very little money.

And it provided jokes and wisecracks, horn-tooting and whistling, curious questioning and pursuit by truck drivers wherever we went.

Beetles and Other Insects

As VW was picking up steam in the early 1950s, so was a German coachbuilder, Karmann. It was Karmann that was taking Beetles and turning them into cabriolets. The story of the Karmann Ghia, though, begins with Mario Boano and Luigi Segre of Carrozzeria Ghia in Turin, Italy, also a coachbuilder. Ghia had done some work for VW, suggesting changes and refinements to the Beetle that went largely ignored. Karmann, too, had suggested changes, but Nordhoff wasn't having any of those, either. Dr. Wilhelm Karmann turned to Ghia to see if they could think of something together that might tickle the hard-to-please Nordhoff. Mario Boano and his son, Gian Paolo, took a Beetle into the Ghia studios, removed the standard body shell, and within 5 months had created a new coupe body for the Beetle. Though Ghia and Karmann have never admitted to it, auto historians point to an American, Virgil Exner, as the inspiration for the Karmann Ghia. Exner was a stylist with Pontiac and the Raymond Loewy Studio, where he worked on Studebaker. In 1950, Exner had gone to Chrysler, becoming styling director in 1953. Ghia worked with Exner on show cars meant to spice up the Chrysler lineup. One of the results was the Chrysler K-310, which was first shown in 1952. That car led to the Chrysler/Ghia D'Elegance of 1953. The Ghia De Soto Adventurer, a limited production, followed. Chrysler had commissioned a run of 40 D'Elegance coupes, but that was pared back during the Korean War. The VW–Karmann Ghia design is very clearly influenced by that car. Nordhoff fell for it, seeing it as a way to expand the lineup into a segment where there was obvious demand. He gave the project to Karmann to build the coupes. Complete Beetle platforms were shipped to Karmann, where the graceful bodies were applied and then the completed cars were put into the VW distribution stream. The price of the coupe was $2,455, about $1,000 more than a Beetle. Karmann Ghias were things of beauty to their owners and enthusiasts, but they were sports cars in look only. The original Karmann Ghia did but 72 miles per hour, a little faster than a Beetle, owing to its more aerodynamic shape.

Before the Karmann Ghia, though, was the Transporter, or Type 2. The inspiration for a van came from the Dutchman, Ben Pon. While in the United States, he saw a great demand for vans and trucks used by plumbers, electricians, carpenters, and small businesses of all kinds. In his notebook, he made a crude sketch of a rectangular box atop a Beetle chassis. The idea appealed to Nordhoff, as he was well aware of people adapting the Beetle into wagon-like and open-bed vehicles. Other manufacturers were producing tall-panel trucks, such as for bakeries; however, no one had yet produced such a vehicle for passengers. It was the first minivan.

The Transporter made its debut just a year after Pon made his sketch, and without any input from the Porsche studio. At almost 169 inches long, it was more than 8 inches longer than a Beetle, but it had vastly more interior room than either the Beetle or the station wagons of the day. Passenger versions could carry nine passengers on three rows of bench seats. Enclosed versions that had no windows were adapted for use as ambulances and delivery trucks. The Transporter had a slow start in the United States, and it didn't really catch attention until 1954. There were three models: (1) the base-model Kombi, priced at $2,200; the Microbus, priced at $2,365; and the deluxe Microbus, priced at $2,500. From the start, VW offered a camper version with a foldout bed, a built-in table and cupboard, window curtains, and an opening for a roof transom. The early versions of the vans had swing-open doors and a lift-down gate. *Mechanix Illustrated* in 1955 wrote:

It is as versatile as a steamship con man and twice as useful. . . . It will climb anything, but not fast. . . . When the grade gets real grim, the Kombi speed is not much better than a fast walk, but it will get you there.

Motor Trend in 1956 would write:[11]

> More a way of life than just another car, the VW bus, when completely equipped with the ingenious German made "kamper kit," can open new vistas of freedom (or escape) from humdrum life.

The Salesmen

There were some Americans who had affection for the VW. Handfuls of servicemen who had encountered them in Europe during the War had arranged to have them sent home. Two were officially exported in 1949, though, to New York dealer Max Hoffman. Hoffman, on a lark, had agreed to be the exclusive distributor of VWs east of the Mississippi. In 1950, he imported 330 of them. Hoffman also distributed Porsche cars being turned out by Ferry Porsche. When dealers went to Hoffman trying to get Porsches, they found that their orders were handled more promptly if they also asked for a few VWs. And so VW's beginning was under way in the United States, again on the back of the Porsche family.

Volkswagens were sold by the seat of the pants in those first years. Foreign car dealers who were selling MGs, Jaguars, and Porsches were also selling VWs to curiosity seekers who appreciated the low price. In fact, these dealers were selling more Beetles than the higher-priced cars. Auto enthusiasts would buy them, resell them, and then go back to Hoffman for more.

By 1953, VW was exporting 70,000 cars a year. Total production in Wolfsburg was 180,000. The United States, Morocco, and Western Europe were finding the car a great value and a durable performer. Nordhoff, however, was concerned about the patchy sales network in the United States, which didn't offer reliable service and parts support for people—Ben Pon's warning. In other developing markets, new territories were opening based on a policy of service first and sales second. Dealers would have to set up parts and service facilities before they could sell any cars. This is what the United States demanded as well. Hoffman's agreement expired and was not renewed. Nordhoff sent an old Opel hand, Gottfried "Geoffrey" Lange, to the United States to find qualified distributors. And he did: Don Marsh in Columbus, Ohio; Carl and Oliver Schmidt (not related) in Chicago; John von Neumann in Los Angeles; Reynold and Luther Johnson (brothers) in Oakland, California; William Boeing, Jr. (aircraft scion) in Washington State and the Pacific Northwest; Kjell and Knute Qvale in Oregon, Montana, and Idaho; Donald McKay in Hawaii; and Arthur Stanton in New York.[12] These were the first distributors of VW. Sales in the West got off to a booming start as California became a hotbed of interest for import cars, as it still is today. Volkswagen sales in 1954 were 11,265, with more than half being sold in just four Western cities. Even in 1957, the percentage would be 33 percent. East of the Mississippi, Lange's counterpart was Will van de Kamp. He arrived in New York in 1954. Van de Kamp was a zealot about VW. A polished sophisticate, van de Kamp wore Saville Row suits and set about to comb through the Hoffman dealers, eliminate some, and make all who remained understand that selling VWs was not like selling anything else. From the start, he was hard on dealers who wanted to sell more than one import marque out of the same showroom, believing that VW should have its own selling space and repair bays. Though inspired by Nordhoff, van de Kamp was the one who first established that there was a "Volkswagen way" of doing business and that there are "Volkswagen people." Van de Kamp found *his* people: Hubert Brundage in Miami, Florida; John MacPhee and Tage Hansen in Massachusetts, Maine, New Hampshire, and Rhode Island; the Schmidts in Chicago, covering Illinois, Minnesota, Iowa, Wisconsin, and the Dakotas; Cook, Heckman, and Sluyter in Grand Rapids, Michigan, covering Michigan and Indiana; Charles Urschel, Jr., in San Antonio, Texas; Willard Robertson in New Orleans, Louisiana, covering the Delta states and Tennessee; and Jack Pry in Washington, D.C.[13]

Van de Kamp was very much a one-man band, impressing on his fledgling network of distributors that the dealers they selected must be of equal caliber and enthusiasm as themselves. By 1955, it was becoming too much for one man, and so van de Kamp hired 25-year-old Britisher J. Stuart Perkins. The two men and a secretary worked out of a room at the St. Moritz Hotel in Manhattan. No sooner did they get to know one another that they started looking around on behalf of Nordhoff for a manufacturing plant at which they might build VWs in the United States. They were given permission and capital to buy a Packard-Studebaker assembly plant in East Brunswick, New Jersey, on the Raritan River, which was a tributary to Elizabeth Port, the largest saltwater commercial port in the country. However, financial estimates on what it would cost to outfit the factory, how quickly it could ramp up, how many cars VW could produce, and how many had to be produced to be profitable had been flubbed. Nordhoff made the decision just 6 months after buying it to sell it.

Waves of Germans from Wolfsburg began arriving in 1956 and toured the country in some three dozen panel trucks, stopping at dealerships to help set up service bays and train mechanics. The first corporate office was established in New York as Volkswagen United States. That first try at incorporation did not go well, though, and was dissolved in 1958. After that experience, Volkswagen of America was formed as the sole importer of VWs. This was a big step. Each distributor had been importing their own vehicles from Wolfsburg. Now, all cars would flow through this small operation in New York. Perkins, who knew nothing about importing, simply began cold-calling ports of entry and asking the brokers at each port to advise him. Meanwhile, the German mechanics crisscrossed the country. These VW rovers worked with dealers, sometimes willing and sometimes not, instructing them that service departments should be as clean and well kept as the selling area. In fact, they were striving for total uniformity in the workshops, dealership to dealership, a first for the U.S. car business. Through repetition comes quality. It was a mantra of Nordhoff's about the cars, and so it would be about the stores as well.

The car was catching on in the United States. *Road & Track* in 1956 wrote about the Beetle:[14]

... enough figures are in to confirm that Dr. Ferdinand Porsche's little people's car has done what no other vehicle manufactured outside the U.S.A. has ever been able to do: it has gained an unmistakable wheel-hold in the garages and hearts of the American car buying public . . . The only mystery is: how did it happen? Especially with practically no national advertising? Of the various explanations, probably the simplest is that the Volkswagen fulfills a need which Detroit had forgotten existed—a need for a car that is cheap to buy and run, small and maneuverable yet solidly constructed, and perhaps above all, utterly dependable and trouble-free.

That Beetle cost a U.S. buyer $1,495.

Van de Kamp was nutty about his "Volkswagen way." He would tour dealerships and perform the equivalent of snap inspections, yelling at a dealer who allowed his salesman to smoke in the showroom or to lounge about reading a newspaper in between customers. He became a legendary character for his antics, such as calling the head of an airline or hotel company demanding a flight or hotel that his secretary had discovered was full. His overbearing ways, though, got the better of him. Nordhoff realized in 1958 that the U.S. operation, although off to a good start, was not going to flourish under such a man. He couldn't operate in a system. He was obstinate and no good at taking direction from Wolfsburg. He could lead, but not run staff. This is a pattern that would repeat itself well into the 1990s, visionary and creative men who had difficulty taking orders from Wolfsburg, which was a far distance from the United States and out of the know about what was happening in the United States. Van de Kamp was sacked. After he left VW, he wouldn't go far. Van de Kamp bought into the Schmidt's distributorship in Chicago. Although he had intimidated and harangued most of his distributors, the Schmidts welcomed him. To his credit, van de Kamp attended the very next distributors' meeting and took his place in the group just like any other distributor. He was a class act.

In 1959, while on personal business in Germany, van de Kamp was killed in a car accident. It was not a VW, though, but a Porsche that he was driving on the Autobahn.

———

Detroit started trying to catch up in the demand for small cars beginning with the 1958 model year. American Motors (AMC) dropped its Hudson and Nash lines to concentrate on Ramblers. American Motors Corporation revived a 100-inch-wheelbase Rambler that year. It sold for $1,850, $200 less than the larger Ramblers. Renault had been marketing the semiautomatic Dauphine with some success, though Renault did not have the service success of VW. Studebaker-Packard, too, began making noise about importing the Goggomobile, an Australian minicar built by Buckles Motors, which was selling in Germany for the equivalent of $735. General Motors, not convinced yet that they should build small cars in large quantities, began importing Vauxhaul cars from Great Britain and Opels from Germany, and they distributed them through their Pontiac and Buick networks, respectively.

———

Carl Hahn worked his way to Wolfsburg by way of a letter that, at the suggestion of his father (a board member of the German Auto Union), he had written to Nordhoff. The letter was about Hahn's ideas on the Europeanization of the auto industry, which he formed while he was an economist at the Office of European Economic Cooperation in Paris. Nordhoff didn't think much of the idea, but he invited Hahn to come to Wolfsburg anyway. The 27-year-old did and was quickly taken in by Nordhoff to be his personal assistant. This didn't prove to be much of a job, as Nordhoff was notoriously independent; therefore, Nordhoff made the restless Hahn head of sales promotion in the export department. Hahn was clearly a comer and a Nordhoff favorite. Shortly after van de Kamp's ouster, Nordhoff went to the United States to be treated for ulcers at the Mayo Clinic. After being released, he stopped in New York City. From there, he sent for Hahn and export chief Manuel Hinke. Seeing that the United States needed a man to replace van de Kamp, and Perkins was deemed not ready for the task, Nordhoff made Hahn the head of Volkswagen of America.

Despite van de Kamp's efforts to make dealers carry VW exclusively, Nordhoff was distressed that so many of VW's dealers in the United States were selling multiple brands of cars in the same showrooms. This is called a *dueled franchise* in the trade. Volkswagens were alongside Jaguars, MGs, and Renaults. Nordhoff wanted Hahn to comb through the dealers, shake out the substandard operations, and insist they dedicate real estate and facilities to VWs. There was enough product to justify the investment, as VW was offering not just the Beetle, but the Cabrio, the Karmann Ghia, and the Transporter.

Carl Hahn believed in systems. Dealerships and distribution were modeled after Howard Johnson restaurants. Each dealership was formatted with strict standards so that each would have a distinct VW look from market to market. Cleanliness and neatness of design was mandated not just for the selling floor, but the service bays and employee lunchrooms. Lockers and showers were to be provided for dealership staff so that customer areas were not cluttered. Dealers received designs and plans for different-sized dealerships that specified furnishings down to chairs and desk lamps. Every dealer was required to have at least four work stalls, each 200 square feet. In addition, every dealer had to carry a 5-month supply of parts. Dealers were required to attend standard training programs, and salespeople had to go through product and sales training sessions.

Volkswagen's attention to service over sales was pioneered by Detroit. By 1960, however, U.S. carmakers had become more motivated by sales than driven by service. The British had met ruinous results by not putting service ahead of sales when they started in the United States after the War. Renault was suffering for it as well.

In 1960, VW sales in the United States topped 100,000 for the first time. The Beetle got an antisway bar that year to better stabilize the ride and handling. An automatic choke was added, along with new colors and a steering damper. The Beetle was growing up a little, becoming more refined just in time to meet the new U.S. competition.

In 1961, VW had produced its five-millionth vehicle. Nordhoff marked the occasion with a speech in which he articulated what com-

panies in 2001 might call a mission statement. While longer than many
mission statements of the twenty-first century, it bears repeating.

> To develop one model of car to its highest technical excel-
> lence . . . to dedicate ourselves to the attainment of the highest
> quality . . . to destroy the notion that such high quality can only
> be attained at high prices . . . to subordinate technological con-
> siderations to human ones . . . to give the car the highest value
> and to build it so that it retains that value and . . . to build up an
> enterprise which belongs to its workers more than any other
> industrial concern in the world.

In 1960, Detroit discovered the compact car: the Ford Falcon,
Dodge Dart, Mercury Comet, Chevy Corvair, and Plymouth Valiant.
This hit the European imports hard. Import sales were cut in half from
1960 to 1961 to 378,000. Opel, Volvo, MG, Datsun, Toyota, and Saab
were all decimated. Not VW, though. Sales continued to rumble
along. Ed Cole, then chief executive at Chevrolet, who had a lot of
faith and confidence in the Corvair, predicted publicly, "In two years,
Volkswagen will be broke in the U.S.A."

Volkswagen's emphasis on service was not just good planning, it
was practical. The quality of service made up for what was mechanically a thoroughly sensible but unexciting car. By 1960, the Beetle's
lack of power was almost laughable. It's puny 36 horsepower meant
that each horse had to pull 45 pounds of weight, as the Beetle weighed
1,610 pounds. In Detroit, the norm was 15 pounds per horse. At 55
miles per hour, everything was hanging out, and there was no reserve
power for accelerating. The Beetle defeated the best attempts at soup-
ing the engine. The intake ports were built so skimpily that they
passed a minimum of fuel-air mixture. This meant that supercharging
the engine was impossible. As every VW owner knows, too, the cars
could be devils on the highway when the wind was up. Because of the
weight distribution, with more on the rear wheels, the car's natural
center is not in the actual center of the car. Also, it took but 2.4 turns

of the wheel to lock. This combination made such drives harrowing to say the least. *Speed Age* magazine in 1957 made an interesting observation about VW in its April issue.

> . . . there is no denying that the modern VW, particularly in export trim, is a cheap and completely dependable car. And it is definitely the best serviced foreign car in the U.S. But overrated it certainly is—in originality, appearance, in performance and in workmanship. In short, the most overrated car in the world.

Maybe so. But Americans were still buying the heck out of them.

The Magic

FOUR

———

It was with reluctance that Will van de Kamp gave in to paying for a booth at the 1957 New York Auto Show. However, he wouldn't give in to what he considered an absurd request. It was the custom of the day to have buxom, scantily clad girls showing off new cars, but he would have none of it. Instead, he wanted engineering types in white lab coats to explain the cars to the press and public. For Pete's sake, he didn't want *women* at all talking about the cars. He was dogged by his U.S. associates to follow the popular auto show tradition and finally relented, but no evening gowns. Volkswagen secured a few airline stewardess uniforms for the women and made them go through 2 weeks of product indoctrination so they understood what they were talking about, not just parroting scripts. Honesty. Volkswagen was, and would continue to be, an honest product. If the cars and the brand had to be pitched at all, they would be pitched honestly.

Though Carl Hahn was in charge in 1959, succeeding van de Kamp, he felt the same way. He hated the nonsense with which U.S. car companies sold cars. Germans took automobiles seriously—and the Volkswagen, though full of emotion as far as it concerned its U.S. buyers, was a serious machine to Hahn and the other Germans charged with getting the U.S. operation on track.

At 32, Carl Hahn took over Volkswagen of America in 1958. Now a Nordhoff protégé, Hahn came from an established family in Germany, was well educated, and spoke excellent English. Along with Hahn came Helmut Schmitz, a puzzlement to his U.S. coworkers because he couldn't drive and had little interest in cars. As a research director and eventual ad manager, though, Schmitz worked with Hahn to analyze what was happening in the United States between the car, the brand, and the people who were defying convention by buying VWs. The two men hired research firms to interview people buying VWs, as well as people who chose not to buy after looking over the brand. Despite the speed bumps that were encountered in setting up a dealer and parts distribution network, training mechanics, and the rest, Hahn was smart enough to realize that it took no act of genius to sell the small volume of vehicles that VW was exporting to the United States. Over 600,000 cars sold in 1959 were imports; about 150,000 of those were VWs. The goal was so modest, early dealers could stay afloat selling just to curiosity seekers. There was little else to compete with the Beetle—a temporary advantage, Hahn knew. There were 6-month waiting lists for Beetles in the United States, but Heinz Nordhoff was in the midst of a major expansion of the Wolfsburg plant. More cars and vans would soon be flowing to the United States, and those waiting lists could evaporate. However, it was only a matter of time, probably just a few years, before Detroit awoke to the demand for compact cars. The U.S. automakers couldn't help but see the trend.

Heinz Nordhoff was no fan of advertising, and neither had been van de Kamp. Sensing, however, that the limits of word-of-mouth marketing were being reached, Hahn decided to begin a national advertising effort in 1959. Some of the U.S. dealers and distributors had, in fact, done some newspaper advertising on their own. This worried Hahn because each distributor and dealer was out there alone with no central control. They could be doing anything to move cars. And dealers left to their own devices could produce unpolished, amateur, decidedly un-Volkswagen, advertisements.

Hahn and Schmitz began making the rounds in New York, visiting ad agencies that were anxious for VW's business. In those days, like today, a car account is a highly desirable piece of business for an ad agency. A car company's heavy spending and the romance of the automobile anoints a small agency as having arrived; everyone sees their work. Likewise, big agencies with no car account were seen as lacking. For agencies with enough space, a car in the lobby was a great first impression to make on prospective clients.

What amazed the two Germans as they went from agency to agency was the absence of understanding and appreciation the advertising men (not too many ad women at this point) had for VW. None of them seemed to care about the car's uniqueness, its very reason for catching on in the United States. For the meetings with Hahn and Schmitz, the ad agencies pasted sample VW ads on their conference room walls. For the most part, they'd just substituted the car for a tube of toothpaste, a bottle of aspirin, or a washing machine, slapping a picture of a VW on an old piece of work.

Car ads of the day were campy, unrealistic-looking things, with illustrations rather than photographs. This allowed artists to exaggerate features. People depicted in the ads were drawn out of scale, shown smaller than in life compared with the car. Sunbursts, little jewel-like explosions of light, were drawn in to illuminate the precious value of the car. It was all dishonest and false. Bill Bernbach, an ad man who'd been gaining notice for a new philosophy of advertising, despised these tactics. The new philosophy was—honesty.

The Magicians

Bill Bernbach and Ned Doyle formed the ad agency of Doyle Dane Bernbach (DDB) in 1949. Both had previously worked at Grey Advertising, one of the big old-line agencies. They teamed up with Mac Dane, who had a small agency of his own, and formed DDB. The agency did smart stuff for New York retailer Ohrbach's, El Al (the Israeli airline), and Levy's (a breadmaker). An ad for El Al, for example, showed a photograph of open ocean. The headline, touting a new jet that would make the trip across the Atlantic faster, read, "On Dec. 23, the Atlantic Ocean became 20% smaller." It was totally unique to show a picture of open ocean, as the prevailing school of advertising said that such a picture would make people think of plane crashes. It also produced ads for Dreyfus & Co., a financial services firm, and Barton's Candy. Doyle Dane Bernbach was being talked about, if not by the older, staid agency owners of the day, then by the young copywriters and art directors who were toiling away for insurance companies and soap makers. Filtered through business school models of persuasion and frequency, most of the ads being produced by Madison Avenue were static and saccharine. There was no soul in advertising. It would take Bernbach's agency to craft one.

Based on the total advertising billings of its clients, DDB was nearly 80th in ranking among U.S. ad agencies in 1959, according to the American Association of Advertising Agencies (AAAA). It was an agency, however, that all the young lions wanted to work for because of Bernbach's willingness to flout conventions; indeed, he believed conventions had to be broken in order for anything good to result.

Doyle Dane Bernbach came by the business in the usual way: His people knew people who knew people. Richard Avedon, one of the top photographers of the twentieth century, was shooting Ohrbach's ads for DDB. Avedon knew VW distributor Arthur Stanton, who just happened to be a fan of the Ohrbach's ads and among those who were pressuring VW's Hahn to do national advertising. Stanton hired DDB to do an ad for the opening of one of his dealerships, Queensboro Motors. Hahn and Schmitz were present for the meeting when DDB presented the Queensboro Motors ads to Stanton. Hahn liked what he saw in Bill Bernbach. Doyle Dane Bernbach Account Director Edward Russell showed an ad for the dealership to Hahn and Schmitz, and they argued over a relatively small copy point in the ad for more than 45 minutes. Russell refused to make the change that Hahn thought was needed. Hahn responded by only giving DDB the VW car business; he gave the van business to another agency. Punishment for the argument was short-lived, however, as Hahn consolidated all of VW's advertising with DDB the following year, 1960. Hahn would later tell the DDB team he chose them because at that meeting, he knew he had come across men of principles.[1]

After winning the business, Bernbach and his team went to Wolfsburg to visit the VW factory. They walked the floors, talked with factory workers, and saw raw materials—steel, textiles, and rubber—turned into cars. Of particular interest to Bernbach was the care that VW took in making the cars *right*. The sheer number of people making sure that duds didn't get put on the train out of Wolfsburg astonished him. There was an incredible honesty, Bernbach saw, in the way the cars were made. Through repetition and constant improvement of the basic designs year after year, the vehicles became superior. There was a lack of guile in the factory, in the workers, and in the cars. Volkswagens were to cars what DDB's advertising was to marketing—the two were a match.

Julian Koenig, a DDB copywriter, and Helmut Krone, the agency's soon famous art director, were on that first trip to Wolfsburg. Both men worked on the VW account from the start. "There was an attitude at Volkswagen, everywhere we went, whoever we saw and met, that was different than any company we had ever heard of or worked for," said Krone in a 1999 interview. "Today, people talk a lot about the way advertising needs to be tied into the 'essence' of the brand. But up to that point, clients pretty much came up with the way they wanted to sell a product, and then the agency tried to figure out a clever way to make the top man happy, and that's the way campaigns got created. What we were doing was discovering the advertising from within the company. We had done good work before that for some good clients. But with Volkswagen, it was a matter of finding out and soaking up what this company was about, what motivated the people who worked there, how they felt about the product they were turning out. It was a mining expedition."

In 1959, print ads for the VW Beetle took on a decidedly different tone and tenor than any other automotive ads to be found in *Life, Time* magazine, the *Saturday Evening Post,* or *Colliers.* Rather than a headline bellowing some tactless sales message, there was a bold photograph of the car, which looked like no other car, and a headline that was more caption than sales pitch. Those caption-like headlines were coy and inviting. Prose more than copywriting, the ads were different from anything else the U.S. magazine reader had seen. And why not? The car was like nothing else on the U.S. roads. One ad showed a Beetle with an overheating radiator, with the caption below, "Impossible." Then, a factual explanation of how the Beetle was air-cooled and why it would never overheat like a traditional water-cooled engine. Another ad showed a Beetle chassis without the engine or guts, freshly painted, as it might appear on the assembly line just coming out of the paint shop. The underlying caption: "After we paint the car, we paint the paint." Under that, text explained the rust- and pit-inhibiting paint process. This contrasted sharply with the approach that other carmakers were taking in their advertisements. One ad headline for the 1957 Chevy Bel Air, for example, read, "Filled with grace, and great new things." A Mercury headline from the same year read, "You ride in a wonderful dream car world of space and light and color." Even the up-and-coming Toyota bored potential customers with "The world's greatest automotive value," advertising its Toyopet. It wasn't writing—it was laying pipe.

Doyle Dane Bernbach's ads for VW were recognized not only by consumers but by their peers as well. "The average American may be somewhat confused by Comets, Corvairs, Darts, Falcons, Hawks, Larks, Ramblers, Tempests, Valiants—not to mention such imports as Austin-Healeys, Fiats, Jaguars, MGs, Mercedes-Benzes, Peugeots, Renaults, Saabs, Triumphs and Volvos," said *Sales Management* in 1959. "But chances are he'll know one little bug by its changeless shape, and even know that its engine is rearward and air-cooled."[2]

———

Volkswagen and DDB were the first to use undoctored photographs in auto ads and brochures. That was honest. There also was no sales hyperbole. The car was so unlike anything else being sold that much of the public thought the car was downright ugly. Certainly, the Detroit old guard did. As a result, Bernbach felt strongly that VW should not take itself too seriously. It should be neither the backslapping salesperson nor the lecturer. Volkswagen advertising would be the man or woman at the cocktail party around whom people naturally gathered because of his or her witty, entertaining, and smart conversation.

Volkswagen's products had people talking, so the advertising should as well.

Another tenet of Bernbach's strategy for VW was that no ad should knock Detroit. Although VW was becoming as much a part of the United States as Chevrolet, it was still a guest in the United States. Many buyers and potential buyers would have to justify purchasing a German car so soon after World War II, not just to themselves, but to their families and their neighbors as well. For example, one ad that *didn't* run merely showed a Ford, a Chevy, and a VW converging on a road from three different directions. The caption read, "There's room for all of us." Bernbach rejected it, thinking it presumptuous for VW to say such a thing. Besides, the ad broke a key Bernbach rule: It didn't inform the reader of anything about the car. It merely put forth a sentiment that VW hoped people would come to feel. Telling people what you hope they feel is no way to market anything, yet into the twenty-first century, companies, especially car companies, fail to grasp this.

Bernbach also believed that ads, whether print or TV, should deal with only *one* point. Too many ads of the day were so cluttered with information that no selling point could be discerned. A typical headline in a VW ad was, "It won't drive you to the poor house." Roy Grace wrote hundreds of VW ads during the 20 years he worked for DDB. In 2001, he reminisced, "One message ads are a lost craft. But it's what that campaign was built on. One idea per ad. Period."

Bernbach told a 1961 gathering of the AAAA: "Properly practiced, creativity can make one ad do the work of ten. [It] can lift your claims out of the swamp of sameness and make them accepted, believed, persuasive, urgent. Is creativity some obscure, esoteric art form? Not on your life. It's the most practical thing a businessman can employ . . . [But] you've got to have something to be creative about."[3]

Bernbach didn't think advertising's role in the car business was to sell cars. That was the job of the salespeople in the dealerships. Advertising's role, he thought, was to get the ad read or seen, and it must be done in a believable way. So revolutionary was DDB's brand of advertising that VW began using U.S. ads around the world. They prodded

DDB to open offices in VW's main markets: Germany, France, South Africa, Australia, Italy, Spain, the Netherlands, the United Kingdom, and South America.

———

Did Bernbach know what he was talking about? Starch readership studies, which measure how well consumers recall the print ads to which they've been exposed, reported in 1966 that VW ads had twice the readership of other car ads. Essentially, VW doubled its ad budget just through creativity. This is a principle long adhered to at clever agencies with small-budget clients. It seems, however, that the larger the ad budget, the further from this ideal advertisers and their agencies stray. The bigger the ad budget and sales volume projections become, the less interesting the campaigns become. At least, that's what advertising history shows. Countless times have bland marketing directors and cowardly agency heads defended milquetoast advertising by saying something like, "We have a lot of different people to whom we have to appeal, so we can't be a Volkswagen."

In 1959 and 1960, the most popular movies were *Spartacus*, *Psycho*, and *The Apartment*. Hit songs included Chubby Checker's "The Twist" and the Everly Brothers' "Cathy's Clown." *Advise and Consent* won the Pulitzer Prize for literature. The hit TV shows were *Gunsmoke*, *The Andy Griffith Show*, and *Wagon Train*. The country sat on the brink of a serious cultural shift. Films were becoming racier and themes more sophisticated, whereas TV shows were still innocence and cotton candy. Popular music was still about boys and girls in love, but a more political and cerebral form of music was starting to get a toehold in New York's Greenwich Village and San Francisco. In some ways, the shift had already begun. The United States was transitioning from the Eisenhower years with an election that would find half the country looking forward with votes for the charismatic John F. Kennedy, and half the country looking backward to Richard Nixon. The front end of the baby boom was just 14, not yet old enough to buy cars. The ones doing the buying were the veterans of World War II who were in their 30s and early 40s. In just a few years, their children would be giving them hell, either fighting in or protesting another war, and welcoming a British musical invasion.

Consider the car names of the day: Monte Carlo, Bel Air, LeMans, Corvair, Catalina. Cars designed and marketed with escapist fantasy themes and imagery. Volkswagen's best-seller was not being advertised as a Beetle, but that's what it was being called on the street and in the VW offices. After all, it's what the car so clearly looked like. It was hardly an escapist image, though. After all, where do you have to go to find a Beetle, but under a rock?

There were a couple of other four-wheeled insects being marketed: the Hornet, the Wasp, and the Super Bee, bugs with menacing, aggressive qualities. Order your Hornet in green and you'd be driving a comic book superhero, even if the cruddy car under the paint was hardly worthy of the analogy.

Necessity being the mother of invention, paltry ad budgets have been mother to some great advertising. Most of the bland advertising (and the sheet metal) coming out of Detroit has been cursed by one thing: volume. When so many cars are produced for so many people living in so many zip codes, it's pretty imperative to hit the lowest common denominator. And so it has been for most of Detroit's advertising, certainly as it was in 1960—and pretty much is in 2001. With ad budgets topping $100 million for a single model launch in 2000, "creatives" at Campbell-Ewald (Chevrolet's agency) and BBDO (Dodge's agency) often produced the creative equivalent of oatmeal or white noise because they know they have weight on their side. They produce graphs, charts, focus groups, and tracking studies showing how the cumulative effects of any ads work to drive sales. Volkswagen of America and DDB didn't have that luxury in the early 1960s, however. The company sold 150,000 cars in the United States in 1959. In 1960, the ad budget was a little over $1 million. By necessity, each ad created was a kind of campaign all its own. Each VW ad was so complete that it could stand alone for the whole brand, despite the fact it might only address one aspect of the car.

The exterior of the VW Beetle by 1960 hadn't changed substantially in 20 years (although the guts of the car certainly were improved). It looked very much like Dr. Porsche's mid-1930s design. That was remarkable for an industry, indeed an economy, built on planned obsolescence. The way to assure production, after all, was to keep churning out new product, a practice that car manufacturers and college textbook publishers elevated to an art form. According to General Motors' famed research chief Charles Kettering, one of the primary purposes of market research was to foster a healthy dissatisfaction on the part of the consumer. The Beetle made sense precisely because it made no sense for its time. Its exterior was hardly changed from 1940 to 1960. One print ad attested that a person could assemble a full Beetle quite easily from parts of a 1947-, 1955-, 1956-, 1958-, and a 1960-model Volkswagen. The Beetle was for the person who didn't want to go to the restaurant that was so popular that you couldn't get a table, or to the movie with the longest lines. It was for people of the cultural intelligentsia. The idea of individuality in a wildly conforming society appealed to a few—but to a growing few.

All this suited VW just fine. There was a limit to how many cars it could bring into the United States. In addition, the company didn't want to grow too fast. Volkswagen sat back and waited to see who showed up to buy the car. It's the same strategy that Arnold Advertising, VW's ad agency in the late 1990s, employed to the mutual success of the agency and the VW brand. (Between winning the Volkswagen account in 1995 and the writing of the book in 2000, the agency underwent a few name changes. In 2000, it was called Arnold Advertising.) (See Chapter 9.)

Consider what *Time* magazine wrote of the VW in 1964:

It is as though Bing Crosby came to a party in a polo-neck sweater: he can afford to do so, for everyone knows that he has a dozen dinner jackets in his wardrobe at home . . . A young mechanic only needs to scramble into a VW, and put on a golf cap, and he immediately passes as a Harvard student . . . The acquisition of a VW automatically makes the buyer into a member of the intelligentsia.[4]

Not everyone embraced this ad strategy. There always were a few dealers who objected to the sophisticated approach. Many believed that the advertising wasn't forceful enough to convert people who were not considering VWs.

A letter from one of these VW dealers remained in the company files as late as 1983, preserved like an artifact in a museum. The dealer's name was blacked out like in an FBI file.

Dear Mr. Hahn

I am not an advertising expert, but nevertheless I write this letter to you in a desperate attempt that I may be able to convince you to do something about changing our advertising approach.

For many years when we owned the market we could afford the luxury of writing cartoons and not ads. We could do and say what we wanted to and not hurt ourselves, because we had no real competition. That certainly is not the case today. Buyers have alternatives, and they are going to have more of them.

Our prices keep going up so we must give strong reasons why Volkswagen is a good deal. And you don't get that message across with cute stuff. You do it with hard sell.

We have, at best, one more year if we don't begin now, to get into the business of advertising cars and stop selling flowers. The truth of the matter is, Mr. Hahn, that Volkswagen advertising doesn't work any more.

May 15, 1964

Au contraire! The genius of the DDB work was that Bernbach and his mates understood that advertising didn't sell product, especially to people who weren't really considering the product in the first place. Why spend money trying to sell a cruise vacation to a man that hates the open sea? Bernbach's idea about advertising was to find people who liked cruises and get them to buy *the right* cruise, his cruise. Even more important, said former Volkswagen of America President J. Stuart Perkins, was keeping the customers you already had. "Each ad provided owners with additional information about their car. So they have more arguments to use in talking their cars up." The DDB VW ads tapped into something that only came into vogue in the 1990s: creating and nurturing "brand ambassadors."

As Will van de Kamp knew, VW owners became the best salespeople of all. The advertising was so likable and memorable that it served to reinforce and reward people who'd already bought their VWs. Customers regularly wrote to company headquarters and to DDB praising the ads, describing how they framed their favorites and hung them in their homes. It was a fairly radical idea to aim ads at customers who had already bought the product and probably wouldn't buy again for several years. Keeping VW people plugged into the brand through advertising, however, was a principal tenet of the strategy. Even in 2001, vintage VW ads are carefully cut from magazines and are bought, sold, and collected on eBay.com every day.

One of the most likable qualities of the DDB ads was that consumers were not treated like idiots. The ads were conversational and witty. They were enjoyable to read rather than intrusive. It was a quality that Hahn brought to the dealer showrooms as well. For example, nothing in the dealerships was allowed on a wall with cellophane tape. Everything, including salespeople's favorite ads, had to be framed if it was on the wall.

"The difference between working at DDB in those days and other agencies was the difference between sticking your hand on a hot range and on an ice cream cone," said DDB Art Director Roy Grace. Run by account men, most other agencies were confining for creative people. Especially in the early 1960s, DDB's lack of a stifling organization provided a fertile environment for writers and art directors. "Bernbach got really excited about great advertising. He set the standard and we followed droolingly," says Grace.

Consumer research was big at VW in the late 1950s and 1960s, but it was a dirty word to the agency creatives. Hahn, Perkins, and other key VW executives used it extensively, but as a tool to guide rather than as a straightjacket in their ad agency. The creatives who were working on the ads, such as Roy Grace, Helmut Krone, and Bob Levenson, distrusted research and preferred to be the strategists. The essence of great advertising, said Grace, is taking out the garbage every day. "You just have to make sure you know what the garbage *is*."

The art direction that Helmut Krone established for VW advertising made each print ad unique. Not only was VW using photographs instead of embellished illustrations, but the consistency and simplicity of each ad set it apart from the ad clutter in the rest of a magazine. A reader could easily thumb past a Chevy, Pontiac, or Mercury ad, as one tended to resemble the other. A Volkswagen ad, however, regularly stopped readers in their tracks. Research by the Starch Company, in fact, found that VW ads had higher reader scores than editorial content in many magazines, including cover stories. Sobering stuff for a magazine editor.

One of the worries of many would-be Beetle buyers was its low price. How could a car costing under $2,000 be any good? A representative ad positioned a Beetle, small in a white background, taking up only about one-fifth of the page. The headline read, "Don't let the low price scare you off." Again, this ad, like many others, attacked a consumer worry head-on with tongue planted firmly in cheek. Another ad attacking the same issue showed a Beetle, this time filling up the page. The headline read, "Live below your means." These headlines showed something else about the honesty of the language that Bernbach wanted. Each headline was written as a sentence that started off with a capital letter for the first word. There was a subject, a verb, an object, and a period. Not only were most other headlines of the day *not* complete sentences, but all of the words were capitalized or made all lowercase for graphic effect. The typeface in VW ads, Franklin Gothic, was as plain as the cars and the truth in the ads.

Consider a print ad for the Microbus, which VW referred to as its "stationwagon" in ads. Below a beauty shot of the vehicle read the line, "Somebody actually stole one." The copy then went on to describe how the owner of a "bus" reported his vehicle stolen. Copywriters used the occasion to not only poke fun at the vehicle, a mainstay of VW advertising, but to talk about how the air-cooled engine would see the robber through, no matter how far south of the border he took his prize. "You can go farther in a VW than in any police car (24 mpg is our average). You have 21 windows to spot anyone who's tailing you."

A Study in Devotion and Revolution

The success of the VW Beetle became the subject of study by psychologists and sociologists. Viewed by the masses as hopelessly out of date and fashion, academics viewed its popularity as a profound shift in the attitude of the U.S. consumer. "The Detroit monster has ceased to be a sign of social success," said sociologist Reuel Denney. "Too many people are in possession of this symbol and it has lost its meaning. . . . The popularity of the small foreign car is a protest against it. . . . In a society like ours, where upstart extravagance has become an everyday occurrence . . . the only way left open to the elite is simple elegance . . . functional common sense."[5] The diagnosis of German market researcher Ernst Dichter is less theoretical. "The Americans are simply fed up with spending enormous sums on cars. They soon find new, and more interesting, symbols of success, vitality and individuality. They are returning to a means of transport which serves the purpose and which retains its value, for they need their dollars for motor boats, swimming pools, fishing tackle, ski equipment and extra holiday travel. . . . I believe they have begun to outgrow that stage of development at which the sum total of bliss is represented by a Detroit monster glittering with chromium plating."[6]

Paul Davidson had just graduated from New York University in 1960. His friend, Carl Schmidt, had just bought a Beetle, a used 1953 model, for $250. "What impressed me was that Carl knew nothing about cars really, but he could tinker on the car and fix it pretty easily, when it did need fixing, which wasn't very often. We were roommates in the East Village of Manhattan, making almost no money. But we each had girlfriends who lived outside the city, and our folks lived off the track up in rural New York State, a pain in the neck to reach by train. We kept it parked in a cheap lot on the West Side. When I think back, one of the great things about that car was that we felt smart about owning it. It gave us no trouble. And when it acted up a little, there didn't seem to be anything we couldn't do ourselves. Sometimes it would just die on the highway. I would pull it over on the shoulder, unplug cables and plug them in again, or replace the fuel filter (we kept a few in the glove-box). Then, it would just start up again. It carried us all over the tri-state area on the weekends, sometimes together, sometimes taking turns. We got the best gas mileage of anyone we knew. Forty miles per gallon many times. It was a dream in the snow. The only scary thing I remember was how the car would get whipped around on a windy day, especially when we were crossing the George Washington Bridge, or if we were stuck in traffic on Sunday afternoon coming back to the city. The bridge would move and so that little, light car would feel every movement. But we felt like we were in on something, I think, with the Beetle. Our parents thought it was a crazy car, and my Dad, who had been in the war, really hated seeing it, because he knew it was German and associated it with the Nazis. Carl's father was second generation German and was real sensitive about being German. His father even changed his name to Smith, but Carl didn't follow. When Carl and I went our separate ways in 1963, I offered to buy it from him, but it was his, like a kid that had been born to him or something. There was no way he was going to sell it to me. I think he still had it in the 70s when I saw him last, using it as a second car."

———

Deborah Fein is a middle-school English teacher in the state of Washington. Single and 33 years old in 2001, she drives to and from work in a 1968 VW Squareback that she inherited from her father. "I live a mile from my school, and use it extensively. I also take great care of it. It's like my baby. I never drive more than a fifty-mile round trip in it, because I am trying to make it last as long as possible. I can't imagine feeling the way I do about any other car. I take my dog, a German Shepherd named Helmut, to the park in it. I feel like I am driving a better car than anyone else on the road even though it doesn't really go over 65 miles an hour any more. I can't explain how I feel about this car. I could afford a new one. But I only have a one-car garage, and I can't bear to give it up. I imagine one day I will have to put it to sleep. But for now, it's my family, along with Helmut. Who would have thought a nice Jewish girl like me would have fallen for two Germans?"

Friendly Persuasion

Doyle Dane Bernbach practically invented wit in advertising. Ads made extensive use of self-deprecating humor married to wit. The cars were ugly to just about anyone who didn't love them. They were like English bulldogs: so ugly that they were actually beautiful and lovable.

Doyle Dane Bernbach's ads didn't hard-sell the car's features; rather, they favored indirect marketing. The difference between direct and indirect marketing is easy to explain. If a company wants to tout the car's traction, it might show the car driving up or down a steep icy road. A direct-marketing ad isn't necessarily bad, but it often is. An exception to this rule is a GMC ad in the early 1990s that showed a Safari van driving down a steep ski jump, seeming to defy the laws of good sense and gravity. If that wasn't impressive enough, when the van reached the bottom of the ski jump, it went into reverse and backed up the ramp. Tactless, maybe, but a pretty good demonstration—and very direct.

Such an ad would be too direct and obvious for DDB. To show off VW's traction, excellent because of its rear-mounted engine that put weight over the wheels that drove the car, DDB created an ad considered the best advertisement for traction control ever. It was called "Snowplow." In this TV ad, a door opens and a man's shoe steps outside into an arc of light, breaking the snow crust. Headlights go on, an engine comes to life, and a VW Beetle surges through the snowy mist of this black-and-white-filmed landscape. A male voice asks, "Have you ever wondered how the man who drives the snowplow drives to the snowplow? This one drives a Volkswagen." He adds, "So you can stop wondering." The shoe print reappears and now the snowplow roars to life, out of its garage on its appointed rounds, leaving the VW poised in the picture-perfect three-quarter shot that would become the norm for car advertising for the next 2 decades. A commercial featuring snow would not normally run in hot-weather climates such as Florida and Arizona, but VW discovered that people in those regions like to see snow. Not only did the ad run in those markets, TV stations reported that people were calling the station asking that it be run again. That's when you know an ad is pulling.

So many of VW's TV ads in the 1960s played like short 30- or 60-second films. Each one had an idea that sold *one* leading element of the car, not three or four. They were so pleasurable to watch that they could be rated higher in viewership than some of the programs running at the time.

One memorable TV ad spoke to VW's commitment to quality. Instead of the approach taken in the 1980s and 1990s of citing third-party endorsements from automotive research firm J. D. Power and Associates or *Car & Driver* magazine, DDB created a 60-second film out of the legion of quality inspectors it had encountered on its trip to Wolfsburg. In a set that resembled the Colosseum in Rome, a Beetle is driven into the center. The arena is filled with inspectors in white lab coats ready to put thumbs up or down. "Welcome to the Volkswagen factory, where every day a bloodthirsty mob of 8,397 inspectors decrees whether or not a Volkswagen will live or die. Should it lose favor with any of them, even for the slightest whim, it will die." Doyle Dane Bernbach creatives went on for years mining tidbits of information, like the number of inspectors at the factory, so that every ad was grounded in truth. "It was important to start with a truth about the product and the company, and create an ad from there, not start with something we had to sell and then figure out what we could come up with," said Helmut Krone. The ideas were used in print *and* TV as much as possible to reinforce the powerful images. A print ad, which had to run as a two-page magazine spread, was filled with over 1,000 white-coated inspectors standing in front of one Beetle. The headline: "It takes this many men to inspect this many Volkswagens."

The standard car ad at that time, notes advertising reporter and historian Bernice Kanner, "showed artfully elongated cars in lush settings with models in diaphanous gowns draped over their hoods. Two-toned

De Sotos were in. Carmakers were following a formula of success that said to change the car every year so people would feel they were driving an out of fashion suit, and would aspire to buy a new car before they had to for mechanical reasons." Kanner says, "Narrators boasted of superior performance or suggested visions of virility or romance."[7]

Ideas like "Snowplow," which is big enough to serve as a whole campaign on its own, are in short supply at the start of the twenty-first century. The ad ran for only 6 months when it first aired, but has lived on in the heads of most people who saw it. Worth noting is that subsequent creative teams at DDB tried to reprise "Snowplow" scene for scene for the Rabbit in the late 1970s. (See Chapter 5.) It was a terrible idea, because the Rabbit, not nearly as loved or respected as the Beetle, couldn't make the claim. Knowledgeable VW devotees were put off that the company would steal from itself in an attempt to foster credibility for the struggling car.

There was no written law in the 1960s saying: No funeral in ads. There might as well have been, though. It seemed an unlikely setting or premise in which to sell a car, but that didn't stop Roy Grace from writing it into one of the most highly regarded ads in history. A funeral procession passes by on the TV screen. As the voice of the deceased announces the will, we see the various mourners in their large luxury cars anticipating how they will benefit from the deceased. From beyond the grave, though, we learn that the departed, a very wealthy man, respected the value of a VW. His crotchety voice intones, "I, Maxwell Snaberly, being of sound mind and body, do hereby bequeath the following: To my wife, Rose, who spent money like there was no tomorrow, I leave $100 and a calendar. To my sons, Rodney and Victor, who spent every dime I ever gave them on fancy cars and fast women, I leave $50 in dimes. To my business partner, Jules, whose only motto was 'spend, spend, spend,' I leave nothing, nothing, nothing. And to all my other friends and relatives who also never learned the value of a dollar, I leave a dollar. Finally, to my nephew Harold, who oftentimes said, 'A penny saved is a penny earned,' and who also oftentimes said, 'Gee, Uncle Max, it sure pays to own a Volkswagen,' I leave my entire fortune of $100 billion." Harold then drives a lone black Beetle at the end of the procession and wipes away a tear.

Roy Grace came up with the idea for the ad while driving around New Jersey. He owed VW a commercial and was late in delivering. "I stopped at a light and saw a funeral cortège. At once, I thought that a funeral would be the last thing on which you would base an ad. But then I thought, why not? It was relevant. It was full of cars. It was also wrong and irreverent, which was, of course, the point." It so happened that the day Grace presented the ad, the VW executive who approved it had just come from his own brother's funeral. Why he was at the office that day, none of the players can recall. Irreverence was key to the VW advertising playbook, recalls Grace. "But it had to be intelligent irreverence, and completely tie in to the values we had established for the brand. Too often in recent years, as agencies have sought to create 'likeable irreverence,' they forget to tie it to the brand, or to a strong idea that connects to the brand."

Legendary ad man David Ogilvy said that "Funeral" blew up his theory that people don't buy on laughs. The key to this ad, though, is that it used a funny and arresting image to convey something unique and integral to VW's brand equity—the economy of owning it. Perhaps most important, the ad was clever, and did not, as so many ads did, insult the intelligence of the viewer/consumer.[8]

Not to be given short time in any discussion of DDB's VW ads is the element of surprise. Surprise and delight are two critical ingredients to effective ads. One ad in 1961 showed a blank page. No picture of a car at all. The headline read, "We don't have anything to show you in our new models." It is the only ad that Stuart Perkins could recall raising eyebrows in Wolfsburg. The German executives had seen plenty of creativity from DDB. An ad with no picture, though, was hard to fathom, considering an ad page in one of VW's regular magazines cost $30,000. The point of the ad, of course, was to push what had become one of Volkswagen's principal *unique selling propositions*, the fact that the cars only changed year to year under the skin, allowing for easy fixes, ready availability of parts, and thrifty value. It was an ad that stopped readers. It was unexpected. When VW devotees realized what the point of the ad was, there was *delight*.

Doyle Dane Bernbach also used a tactic known as *misdirection*, which is also a lost art in advertising. To highlight the roominess of a

VW, the agency hired Philadelphia 76er Wilt Chamberlain, who was 7 feet 1 inch tall. In the ad, the basketball star is standing next to the Beetle looking like he is either just getting out, or just getting in. The headline reads, "They said it couldn't be done. It couldn't." The copy goes on to explain that the company tried to make Chamberlain fit behind the wheel of a Beetle, but couldn't. "At 7'1", he was just too tall." The copy then goes on to explain how much room there really is and that a man, for instance, 6 feet 7 inches tall, would fit just fine.

In the 1960s, companies of all kinds, especially car companies, were fond of slogans. Volkswagen didn't have one, and wouldn't until the 1970s. Throughout the company's best decade for sales and advertising, each ad was punctuated with just the VW lollipop logo. It is a strategy that no less a brand than Mercedes-Benz would discover and cling to in the 1990s. The reason was that in the mid-1990s Mercedes-Benz had the one thing that every other car company desired to have—the tri-star logo. In the 1960s, the same could be said of VW and its lollipop.

One of the biggest challenges of the 1960s was selling the VW Type 2 Transporter. Ben Pon, the legendary early VW seller in the United States, had come up with the idea for the vehicle by sketching a box on top of the Beetle platform. In a questionable act of honesty, DDB began advertising the Transporter as a station wagon instead of a bus. No one wanted to buy a bus, though the people who bought the Transporter called it that when they got it home. To start, no one wanted to buy the Type 2 except camping enthusiasts and small businesses, such as landscapers and plumbers, who used it as a van.

Women especially did not like the Type 2—at first. For one thing, they did not like having to climb up into it in their skirts and high heels. One of the first ads that DDB created read, "Why won't your wife let you buy this wagon?" The idea attacked the biggest knock against the vehicle, and used the opportunity to address all of the great features of the wagon. To appeal to women in greater numbers, a two-tone version was brought to the United States, and it had a sunroof as well. Also, the engineers in Germany modified the entry so that it wasn't such an awkward climb.

One of the characteristics of owning a VW, the agency discovered, was that VW owners often had to justify their purchase to others. They delighted in doing so, however. That was part of the magic formula. For the bus, an ad was created that read, "How does it feel to show up in one of these?" The ad depicted a leggy woman in an evening dress in the front seat of the Microbus parked in front of the Plaza Hotel. Another ad, though very questionable by 1990s standards, read, "Do you have the right kind of wife for it?" The ad went on to ask, ". . . the kind of wife who can invite 13 people to dinner even though she only has service for 12? Name a cat 'Rover'?"

With few missteps along the way, VW and DDB were ahead of their time in advertising to women. It was the norm in the 1960s and before then that advertisers created ads for women's magazines that were different than those running in men's or general interest magazines. Also, women were patronized. The honesty and straightforward style of VW's ads, though, could run anywhere. This was in evidence when feminist Gloria Steinem launched *Ms.* magazine in the 1970s. Volkswagen was the first automotive advertiser to buy space in the controversial magazine. Volkswagen had always been a hit with independent-minded women, as it had been a success with independent-minded people. When it came to run in the magazine, no special ads had to be created. In fact, the ad that did run stated, "We never ran an ad in another magazine that we wouldn't run in *Ms.*," and included four VW print ads in cut-down size. "We had already discovered that the purchase of a car for a woman was a really important one," says Steinem. "It meant symbolic freedom and independence and mobility, and gradually as the rest of the auto industry caught on to the fact that women were buying cars, they also started to address women in ads, but they were still condescending, as if they were talking to a child," said Steinem. Later, when an ad was created especially to run in *Ms.*, the ad showed that while even though VW was losing its way in the United States, DDB could still be counted on to pull out a winner. The ad was for the Dasher wagon, and the headline read, "I bought a wagon out of wedlock." It was to position the VW wagon as not just a grocery and kid hauler, but a utility car for an independent woman.[9]

———

Volkswagen and DDB waded into television gradually for reasons of cost, as well as strategy. When they did, though, they had much the same success as they had in the print medium. Irony, honesty, and self-deprecation, all the same qualities of the print campaign, were translated into TV. Volkswagen was the first to make fun of what other companies and agencies were doing with TV. A well-worn image in the early 1960s was the sight of a car bursting through a paper wall. To make the point that the VW Karmann Ghia was a graceful and snazzy-looking car, but not the fastest sports car on the street, a Ghia was seen heading for a paper barrier, only to nudge it. The wall sort of gave a bit, but then the car fell back, the paper barrier still in tact. The narrator on the ad said, "The Volkswagen Karmann Ghia . . . is the most economical sports car you can buy . . . It's just not the most powerful."

Were DDB and VW perfect? Hardly. The 1960s was a special time for the two, like it was for the country. Certainly, by the early 1970s, both began wondering what was coming next in terms of product and marketing strategy.

The preceding Ghia ad, although clever and funny, was actually based on a bad strategy. Research done by VW on the Ghia buyers showed that the customer believed, or wanted to believe, that he or she was purchasing a real sports car with performance, handling, and power. The research said one thing, but the ads were saying something else—that this was VW's version of a sports car and, therefore, is no sports car at all. It's a cute alternative. Volkswagen was saying to the buyer, "Look, Walter Mitty, even the manufacturer knows it's a joke." The Ghia, of course, was a Beetle with a different hat on. It was of beautiful Italian styling, but its horsepower and top speed were equal to a Beetle's. This ad showed that the abhorrence of traditional research by DDB's creative team was not always the wisest course. Still, the team had a fabulous batting average throughout the 1960s.

"It would have been kinder to call the buyer at home and say Volkswagen just wanted you to know you did not buy a sports car. You bought a Beetle with a different body, or even, inform the buyer with a direct mail piece," said then Director of Advertising John Slaven. "To go on national television and inform the poor customer's neighbors of his image problems just was not smart." The ad was quickly pulled off the air. Slaven noted, "The ad would have worked fine for the Beetle, but not the Ghia." The lesson in that experience was not to let the successful positioning for one product dominate the brand to the point where models that need different messages get swamped. It is also worth noting that the ad won numerous ad industry awards, showing the real connection between those awards and truly successful advertising.

———

As 1970 approached, VW was a different company than it had been in 1960 when DDB was just getting started. Kurt Lotz had replaced Heinz Nordhoff when the latter died in 1968. The Beetle had been improved in the late 1960s with two engine and suspension upgrades. Its top speed in 1968 was 78 miles per hour, and a driver could actually get well into the 50-mile-per-hour range in third gear. Zero to 60 miles per hour could be achieved in about 22 seconds. An automatic stick shift was introduced in 1968, which meant the driver didn't have to depress a clutch pedal when shifting gears. Beetle sales that year reached 390,000, accounting for 5 percent of all cars sold in the United States.

Volkswagen of America executives, though, were not stupid or blind. In 1969, they had seen waiting lists start to dwindle in California, a bellwether market for VW. *Road Test* magazine in 1968 did a comparison between the Beetle and the Toyota Corolla. It was embarrassing for the poor Beetle, like Babe Ruth having to compete against Muhammad Ali in the boxing ring. The Corolla beat the Beetle in every category, with the possible exception of personality. However, the auto press was drooling over the engineering feat of the Corolla and the new fit-and-finish standards of the Japanese. The Corolla, too, was cheaper than the Beetle.[10]

Lotz was gearing up for a new era of front-wheel-drive cars to replace the rear-wheel-drive cars on which the company was built.

Volkswagen had purchased majority control of Auto Union in 1964 and, in 1966, introduced the first modern Audi, the Audi 60. The Audi marque came to the United States in 1970 with two front-wheel-drive cars, the Audi 100 and the Audi Super 90. Lotz engineered the takeover of German premium carmaker NSU, which had a front-wheel-drive car it developed, called the Ro80, a rotary-engine car with durability problems, and the front-wheel-drive K70. Lotz took the K70 and gave it to VW's engineers to learn about front-wheel-drive, water-cooled cars and to see if they could fix some of the durability issues. The K70 was further developed and refined as the first conventional VW. Though it only lasted 5 years due to poor sales and harsh reviews, it turned the tide at VW and ushered in a new era of design and engineering for the brand.

Rudolph Leiding took over as only the third of VW's chief executives in 1971, succeeding Lotz. Leiding was known for his crisis management skills, having gone to Auto Union in 1965 where he created what became known as *the Audi miracle,* straightening out product development and finances in just a few years. He then went on to Brazil where he achieved record profits and production. Lotz had overburdened VW through acquisitions, and the supervisory board felt someone with Leiding's organizational prowess was needed to streamline and prioritize projects.

Leiding ushered in the Golf, Scirocco, Passat, Polo, Derby, Audi 50, and Audi 100 in 1974 and 1975. The company was definitely not the one-car company that it had been criticized for being under Nordhoff. Now, with a stable of new so-called state-of-the-art cars, all they had to do was sell them.

The Wall

FIVE

Volkswagen sales in 1971 were sinking, torpedoed by a falling dollar, new Japanese competition, and a lack of credible new products in its own showrooms. Despite continuing improvements in the venerable Beetle, it was losing more ground. In 1972, *Road & Track* magazine noted that it was "the Best Beetle yet, but still not as good as its competition." The four-speed Beetle was priced at $2,349. Gas mileage was better than 27 miles per gallon. The old shortcomings, however, were losing their charm in the face of the quickly improving Japanese models—the wind and engine noise, jouncy ride, and spare interior. The people to whom the noise was music and the ride "German" were coming to the dealerships in fewer numbers. The enthusiast magazine further noted:

> The Beetle, whether in standard or Super form, has three main points to recommend it: fuel economy, workmanship and its reputation for long life and good service . . . If you value those three virtues above all others, then the Beetle is for you. Other-

wise, it is hopelessly outdated and undone by both Japanese and American economy cars.

In 1972, VW began offering spiffed-up Beetles to jump-start sales and interest. The Baja Bug played off the Beetle's success in the demanding off-road races in Baja, California. The dealer-installed option consisted of striping, superior speed shifter, Bosch fog lamps, leatherette steering wheel cover, mag-type wheel covers, a walnut dashboard applique, and tapered exhaust tips. Curved windshields were added to the Super Beetle in 1973, and the Sport Bug was introduced. The Sport Bug featured special contoured bucket seats, a padded steering wheel, and short-throw shifter. Brighter paint colors were added, too. All of this stuff was to make up for the fact that the Beetle was getting pricier. Between 1960 and 1969, the Beetle's price had gone from $1,595 to just $1,799, an amazing value. However, the falling greenback was making that price stagnation a thing of the past.

It was the beginning of the end of VW's rear-wheel-drive era in 1974. The Dasher, Rabbit, and Scirocco, all front drivers, were on sale; Beetle sales plummeted from 226,000 in 1974 to just 82,000 in 1975.

Multiplying Rabbits

The replacement for the Beetle, the Golf, was a crapshoot for VW because, if it failed, there may not have been much of a company left to go forward. The Beetle had become an antique both in Europe and the United States, leaving only developing markets open for growth. Furthermore, the Japanese were knocking on those doors as well with newer cheap-to-build products of good quality, not the inferior cars they brought to the United States in the 1960s.

The Golf was the big bet for the future. The transition from the Beetle to the Golf in Europe wouldn't be as traumatic as in the United States, because Europe had already seen a ready acceptance of VW's other products. In the United States, the Dasher, which was the forerunner of the Quantum and the Passat, preceded the Golf/Rabbit in 1974 and didn't catch on in significant volumes. A particularly desperate product introduction in the early 1970s, which was meant to broaden the customer base but is recalled with a chuckle by most dealers, was the Thing. It was actually an updated version of the Kubelwagen jeep that German soldiers had driven across Europe and North Africa during World War II. The Karmann Ghia, while having a following, was, like the Beetle, old and feeling price pressures. While all this mishmash of product was trotted out, Volkswagen of America and DDB were in a quandary about what marketing direction to take.

The 1975 introduction of the Rabbit in America looked like a raging success at the start. Sales that first year were 98,000. The ad campaign from DDB seemed to transition successfully from the Beetle, Karmann Ghia, and Microbus ads to the more sophisticated Rabbit. Despite the fact that the price was $3,500, $500 or more than the competition, car buyers seemed ready to pay it, especially given its front-wheel-drive advantage over the domestic cars in the class. Up to that point, the only front-wheel-drive vehicle had been the Oldsmobile Toronado. However, it was the Rabbit that got the industry and consumers interested in front-wheel-drive cars, which is what most of the industry is today. The fuel crisis, along with higher prices and outright shortages, was good news for a new small car. The Rabbit came with a 70-horsepower 1.5-liter engine in both a two-door and a four-door hatchback package. Prices ranged from $3,000 to $3,500. It got 30 miles per gallon and, at first, impressed the automotive press more than Honda Civic, Ford Pinto, AMC Gremlin, and Chevy Vega. In Englewood Cliffs, New Jersey, though, staffers were worried. The cars were noisy and had cold-start problems, the latter being a far cry from the Beetle's reliability that VW customers had come to expect. That wasn't all, however.

"The Rabbit was a transforming car for the company," says Dave Huyett, then a marketing staffer at Volkswagen of America. "We suddenly had to sell a car that was meant to become *the* volume car for the company, and it flew in the face of most of what we had been marketing for twenty years: great in the snow, air cooled, cold starts, thrifty, unique one-of-a-kind design. The Rabbit was none of those things, and it was a shock to the system. There was the added complication of not really knowing who we were going after. Were we going after Volkswagen owners with a new car? Or people who had not bought VWs in the past because they didn't like the product? The Rabbit was a totally different car, which might be a positive to people who had passed us over before. But how Volkswagen devotees were going to react was vitally important. And we were all very conflicted about how to deal with both audiences."

The Rabbit was extremely well timed as gas prices were up in the United States, and Detroit had not yet come out with its own gas sippers. This bought some time for the crew in Englewood Cliffs. Sales of the Rabbit in 1975 topped the Beetle's.

Things were looking so good for the Rabbit, in fact, that Volkswagen AG had begun thinking about the future in the United States, and how it might guarantee big volume growth. A study to build a plant in the United States had begun in 1973 in advance of the Golf's introduction, but was scuttled, in part, because of management instability in Wolfsburg. Rudolph Leiding began the study, but his position became tenuous. When Toni Schmücker took over as chairman in 1975, he immediately picked up the plan. Schmücker hated being left so vulnerable to the vicissitudes of the currency markets. The company had been knocked off its feet in 1972 and 1973 when the rise of the German mark against the U.S. dollar had sent the thrifty Beetle's price up 40 percent in 1 year, and 20 percent the next. In 1974, the U.S. dollar was down to around 2.5 marks, where it had rested since about 1970; this compared unfavorably with 4 marks to the buck between 1961 and 1969.

Schmücker decided that VW should build cars in the United States as a hedge against currency swings. What's more, say colleagues, Schmücker had been poorly treated at Ford Motor Company and was anxious to take on his old employer in its backyard. The rest of VW's board in Germany wasn't so sure. Heinz Nordhoff flirted with building VWs in the United States as early as the 1950s. When it was determined, however, that the numbers had not been run properly to assure a profit in a reasonable time, he backed off. The company had gone so far as to buy a plant close to the Elizabeth, New Jersey, port where cars arrived from Germany, all the easier to blend the domestically built Beetles with imports before shipping them out to dealers. However, despite Schmücker's plan, the Vorstand (Volkswagen AG's operating board), in 1975 and 1976, opposed getting into bed with the United Auto Workers. Another hurdle for a U.S. plant was that the Americans were notoriously independent and difficult to dominate once they sourced their own product. Americans were not as malleable as managers in Brazil or South Africa.

As chairman of the board, though, Schmücker had considerable influence. He was committed to the idea, and ultimately the board wouldn't stand in his way. Well respected and newly appointed, Schmücker could have a chance to make it work. Born and raised in Germany, Schmücker served in World War II and became a prisoner of war. He left Ford in 1968 to go to the Rheinstahl Group, a diversified steel and iron company, where he quickly became chairman. Volkswagen turned to Schmücker to replace Rudolph Leiding who ran the company for just 4 years.

To present it to the board, a paper was commissioned to see if a plant could be operated profitably. Could VW sell enough Rabbits in the United States to justify the investment in a new plant? Dave Huyett worked on the analysis and said the arithmetic supported a plant. The market share requirement for supporting a plant was 5 percent, a lofty target buttressed by a fuel crisis of uncertain duration.

Says Huyett, "There is no question that, as an organization, we had become enraptured with ourselves and our own success. The idea of our own plant was kind of intoxicating to a lot of us. It gave us a sense of importance."

Up until the early 1970s, the VW brand had been built in the United States on sales, marketing, and distribution savvy. No one at Volkswagen of America had enough experience to undertake running a manufacturing plant. A search of candidates turned up a handful of experienced manufacturing men from General Motors, Ford, and American Motors. Schmücker, being from Ford himself, knew of a few people worth approaching. However, the man whom the search firm seized on was James McLernon from Chevrolet. McLernon was 50 and had recently brought the Chevrolet Chevette to market under cost and ahead of schedule by GM's standards. He was affable, personable, and patrician, and VW hands remember him having a dazzling memory for faces. "Jim could go more than a year between meetings of a dealer, a dealer's wife or a staffer's wife, and remember their names without any problem. I'd see him do this in the course of a night with 100 people. The guy was a pro," says Charlie Hughes who was a marketing director, first at Porsche-Audi, then at VW in 1982.

Schmücker offered right away to make McLernon the boss of both the new manufacturing company and the sales and marketing company, says McLernon. He declined, though, wanting to concentrate on building the plant in Pennsylvania. After Rabbits started production, he agreed he would take over the whole operation, not believing that the two entities could remain split over the long haul. That deal, though, was contingent on McLernon staying on schedule—2 years to get Rabbits hopping out of a U.S. plant. After that, Stuart Perkins, who was running Volkswagen of America, would be working for McLernon, not reporting directly to Wolfsburg.

McLernon decided to base the manufacturing company in Warren, Michigan, Chevrolet's home, to be close to suppliers and the rest of the industry. Meanwhile, Perkins wanted no part of a plant and no part of a VW led by a Detroiter.

McLernon was typical of Detroit. Born in New York State and schooled in Buffalo, he had worked his way up the GM manufacturing ladder, serving as head of manufacturing at Chevrolet for the 7 years before joining VW, working for legendary GM executive John DeLorean.

McLernon surrounded himself at VW with other Detroiters, especially people who had come up with him at GM. The problem from the start was culture clash. Volkswagen enjoyed a storied history of technological excellence and innovation. The company had long been successful by eschewing the Americans' postwar reliance on planned obsolescence, with models shedding skin every other year while remaining marginally improved at best under the hood. Volkswagen, of course, stayed famously the same on the outside for 30 years, with thousands of improvements being made over the years to make the cars better performers. The strategy had succeeded throughout the 1960s and helped earn VW the badge of the honest, antiestablishment car. The men in Englewood Cliffs, New Jersey, almost all of them urbane and sophisticated, understood all of this. They had a healthy disdain for the brand of business that was practiced in Detroit. They were New Yorkers, by birth or choice, and the Englewood Cliffs, New Jersey, vicinity was packed with import car companies: BMW, Volvo, Jaguar, Ferrari, and Renault. Many of the office buildings along Route 9W, which ribboned the Hudson River near the George Washington Bridge, had numerous Europeans sprinkled among the Americans. It was a culture very different from Detroit. There was, after all, a wine cellar at the VW office. And now, VW was entering into a pact that might well turn the whole company over to Detroit Incorporated.

In 1975, Stuart Perkins was running Volkswagen of America. He had been the first employee hired in North America in 1957 when Carl Hahn was sent by Heinz Nordhoff to revamp the fledgling U.S. operation. He had VW in his veins and VW stamped on his nose. And here was Schmücker, a comparative newcomer himself, handing over the keys to a Chevy man.

"It was a terrible period," recalled Advertising Director John Slaven. "It became a real us-versus-them thing from the beginning. Most of us loved Perkins, and really distrusted what Schmücker was up to."

Meanwhile, the Volkswagen AG board under Schmücker had been grappling with what course to take in the United States. Despite the success that VW was having in the the United States and Canada, several on the board had misgivings about committing hundreds of millions of dollars to manufacturing there. The landscape was different in the mid-1970s than it had been in the 1950s. The Japanese were for real. Even if the Big Three weren't taking the Japanese seriously by this time, many at VW certainly were. Many at Volkswagen AG saw the United States as an expensive game to play, squeezed between the deep pockets of the Big Three and the deep pockets of the Japanese, each side willing to spend themselves into oblivion pursuing market share. That just wasn't VW's game. Some members of the supervisory board, as well as the Vorstand, felt that the right course was to go slowly with the new cars and continue to sell the Beetle and the new Golf into developing markets. In other words, go where *they* aren't. It would be more profitable and involve less risk.

The company had secured an unfinished Chrysler assembly plant in Westmoreland County, Pennsylvania, a 4- to 5-hour drive from Detroit, by the time it hired McLernon. The plant was a shell and a dirt floor, but the attraction was that its partially finished state would give McLernon a head start. He had 2 to 3 years to start building Rabbits.

———

Sales for VW had been 476,000 in 1972. By 1976, sales were all the way down to 201,000. The German-made Rabbit sold 112,000. The Beetle sold 27,000. The remaining sales were divided up between Scirocco, Dasher, Microbus, and Karmann Ghia. Soon enough, problems began surfacing in the Rabbit. By the tens of thousands, Rabbits were becoming stricken. Accelerator cables snapped and electrical systems blacked out. They burned oil or lost it entirely. The engines were shutting down, and repairs were costing up to $2,000 per car. Voluntary recalls would affect eventually over 1 million cars. A Federal Trade Commission suit in the early 1980s against Volkswagen of America charged the failure to warn customers of potential high oil consumption in Rabbits built before 1982; it would drag well into the mid-1980s before being settled by VW.

Clearly lacking the Beetle's reliability, the Rabbit called into question the company's whole marketing stance in the United States, grounded on a sound, reliable, unpretentious car—an honest value.

Part of the problem, but by no means the biggest one, was that the dealer service departments weren't adequately trained and prepared to handle a completely new type of car. This would become a bone of contention between the two companies: Volkswagen of America, which handled the sales and marketing, and Volkswagen Manufacturing, which was in charge of building the plant and producing cars. The dealers would be in the middle, firing shots at both.

A design flaw in the Rabbit combined with defective valve-stem oil seals ordered for the Westmoreland-built vehicles that began rolling off the line in 1978 were to blame for some of the Rabbit's problems. The Germans were especially defensive and angry because the problems didn't afflict German-built Golf/Rabbits to nearly the degree they did the Westmoreland-built Rabbits. Regardless, the effect on public confidence in the brand was widely felt. Not only were the problems hurting all Rabbits in the United States, but VW executives were having to defend the quality of Golfs in Europe as well because of it, facing down inquiries from the press at the Geneva, Frankfurt, and Paris auto shows. The Germans were not completely off the hook, though, on the oil problem. The Rabbits had such small oil pans that when an owner got low on oil, and the warning light went on, the driver had almost no time to add oil before serious damage was done to the engine. There was no margin on this problem for the U.S. driver. In Europe, it was not so serious. Cars, for many years, had been built with smaller oil pans, with a low margin for a lack of oil. That's why Europeans typically checked their oil every weekend. It's quaintly referred to as part of a European's birthright. In the United States, it was different. Detroit cars came with larger oil pans and a driver could safely ignore the "idiot light" for a day if need be. The Beetle and its Wolfsburg siblings did not have this problem, but then again, they didn't have oil-burning problems, either. Such glitches, if they ever existed, were long ago purged through the Nordhoff method of constant improvement under the Beetle's unchanging skin. McLernon would eventually order a bigger oil pan.

"The Westmoreland Rabbit got a lot of criticism for quality, but there were serious problems in the design," said of J. D. Power and Associates Chairman Dave Power. "We established the design issues in our research, and Wolfsburg did not make it easy. They fought giving us the access we wanted at every turn." Power's firm in the mid-1970s was becoming well known among automakers for its research into manufacturing quality and customer satisfaction. It was still a few years away from being the household name among consumers that it is today, as car companies did not start using Power ratings in advertising until the mid- and late 1980s.

That the Rabbit came to the United States with problems before VW started building in Pennsylvania is borne out in a J. D. Power and

Associates report from 1975, commissioned by the southern California dealers. Among the problems were that Rabbits and Sciroccos were getting significantly lower highway gas mileage than their Environmental Protection Agency (EPA) ratings indicated. Where VW was advertising 38 miles per gallon on the highway for both Rabbit and Scirocco, owners in southern California who were charting their mileage in the midst of a gas crisis were getting about 30 miles per gallon. This came from a company that had repeatedly advertised their fuel ratings to be honest. Squealing brakes and difficulty in keeping the engine tuned were also frequent complaints of the Wolfsburg Rabbits. Worse still was that only 71 percent of VW owners said they would buy another VW, down from 90 percent in the Beetle heyday.

The materials problem at Westmoreland that struck an unproven (and thus vulnerable) car was exactly the sort of problem that some of the men on the Vorstand had feared, and that is why they did not want a U.S. factory building a car that they themselves had only just created.

"Volkswagen really didn't know a twit about making water-cooled front-engine cars before this, so it was not a huge surprise to us in Englewood Cliffs that there were problems," says Bill Young.

———

Bill Young was a national sales manager in the late 1970s. Whereas many of the Englewood Cliffs staff who needed to coordinate with manufacturing were going to Detroit monthly, Young was going almost weekly. "I had no idea how this plant was supposed to get built and supply cars, so I was trying to make sure I learned," says Young.

In December 1977, Westmoreland was a few months from turning out cars. If McLernon could get the line rolling, his battle for control of the company would be won early. Young, along with the head of distribution, went to the factory to meet with McLernon and Manufacturing Chief Dick Dauch. It was Christmas vacation, and the rest of the Englewood Cliffs staff had fled for the holidays. Young recalls telling the two men that they had a serious problem on their hands. The production run approved by Wolfsburg for the Westmoreland plant involved parts that hadn't been ordered. A logical mix of models had been ordered to start coming off the assembly line based on the forecasted product mix—a certain number with sun roofs, a certain number with automatic transmissions, and so forth. The result was that the factory simply wouldn't have the parts to build the cars that had been approved in Wolfsburg. If McLernon couldn't build the cars on time, he wouldn't get the company. The hope in Englewood Cliffs, and even among a few Vorstand members in Wolfsburg, was for a repeat of what Heinz Nordhoff had seen in the late 1950s: that it was still too early for VW to build cars in the United States, and the plant would be sold.

Upon learning of the situation, McLernon asked Young to spec out 20,000 or so Rabbits that *could* be built from the parts that *were* ordered and would be on hand. This didn't take long, because the range of models that could be built from the ordered parts was so narrow. Young changed the production schedule approved in Wolfsburg, and went on his Christmas vacation thinking he had been a hero.

In January, after everyone was back and settling in, news of Young's so-called heroics began circulating. Young says he did not know until after the holiday that the board in Wolfsburg might have approved the production run with full knowledge that the cars couldn't be built. The inability to meet the production plan would have looked like a botch by McLernon and, thus, would have been an indirect way to sink Schmücker's plan of turning the company over to McLernon. Young's other misstep was in daring to change the production mix at all. Once a production run is handed down from on high, it is not meant to be changed by the U.S. head of sales. Perkins, Young recalls, was livid, which was a departure for the usually mild-mannered Perkins. "He said he should fire me," said Young. "But then I would have been a martyr, and he didn't want that either . . . I truly didn't know what I had done or what might have been in their minds until after it was done."

Production at Westmoreland began on 10 April 1978. A gleaming white Rabbit rolled off the line in front of Schmücker, McLernon, Dauch, U.S. Treasury Secretary Michael Blumenthal, Pennsylvania Governor Milton Shapp, and some 1,200 factory employees. "Quality spoken here" was written on a hand-lettered sign in the instrument panel assembly area. *Quality* was the watchword that day, and Dr. Norbert Kaeslingk made a point of guaranteeing that the Westmoreland Rabbits would be of the same quality as the Wolfsburg Rabbits and the other cars built at Wolfsburg. As it turned out, the comparisons would be distinct and unavoidable.

The rift at the company between Detroit and Englewood Cliffs grew palpable, as did the lack of support from Wolfsburg. Volkswagen of America was saddled with a horrible environment and working dynamic while it was trying to defend its market share just as the domestics were starting to wise up about the small-car segment, and the Japanese were making steady inroads. The Japanese pot of gold, combined with VW's slipping sales, was too much for the dealers to resist, and many VW dealers began adding Honda, Nissan, Toyota, or Mazda to share showroom space with VW. This was, and pretty much still is, unheard of in Germany and the rest of Europe. Even in Canada, dealerships are exclusively VW. Volkswagen for years had been buying out regional distributorships that had been set up in the 1950s. The falling sales and opportunities presented by the Japanese took care of some of the holdouts who had to make a choice between handling Mazda, for example, and VW. By the late 1970s, some distributors just chose the beds of the Japanese.

Quality of the Rabbit was suspect from the start, with a bunch of components that VW was only just getting the hang of, like fuel injection and air conditioning. Without intending to do so, McLernon made it worse. He was a U.S. car manufacturer with U.S. tastes. His people had been building U.S. cars. The nuances and mechanical spirit of VW was lost on his team. They set out to Americanize the Rabbit, or what Volkswagen AG Marketing Chief Werner Schmidt would later call "Malibuing" the car. He dropped the European round headlights in favor of the square ones becoming the norm in Detroit. He sourced out seats and upholstery locally, and it was cheap, awful stuff. The seats lost their bolster supports and became flat. Faux-leather seat covers were so slick that one auto writer said the only thing to offer lateral support to the driver was the door. The dashboard was different than the Wolfsburg version. False-wood trim started showing up, as it had in later models of the Beetle in a desperate attempt to freshen it.

Worst of all, softer springs and shocks were used, thus changing the car's whole ride, the very thing that made it a VW. These changes made the Germans sick. Not only did the changes shred the car of German character and performance, they created more and more quality issues. A list of the most expensive warranty damages for 1979 tells the story: fuel distributor, fuel injector, air-conditioning condensor, battery, alternator, fuse relay board, electric fuel pump, and fuel pump relay. Electricals, it seemed, were not VW's best thing. Advertising was becoming desperate. A 1978 ad showed the Beetle and the Rabbit in the same ad. On the left was a Beetle pictured over the words "Old Reliable." On the right was a Rabbit over the words "New Reliable." It was wishful thinking at best. The claim couldn't honestly be made, and an increasing number of VW owners knew it.

The changes made sense if VW was trying to build a U.S. car. In a way, it was. That, however, shouldn't have been the objective. Volkswagen had come to do interiors very well by virtue of its relationship with the Italian designer Giorgetto Guigiaro, especially seats, upholstery, and interior finishes. These elements of the cars were routinely singled out for praise in the auto buff magazines, and VW had, in fact, set an industry benchmark for seat design.

The Rabbit's mechanical problems persisted. These included troublesome fuel injection systems and accelerator cables, and rattling air conditioners, none of which could be tackled by most VW shade-tree mechanics. Ferdinand Porsche and Karl Rabe had designed the Beetle so it could be fixed easily by low-income wage earners and German soldiers in the field. It was designed to be ultradurable. The Rabbit was none of those things, and was too sophisticated under the hood for many of the people who had learned to troubleshoot their simple VW by tapping on the solenoid with a screwdriver, adjusting the idle screw, or slapping in a new fuel filter. The Beetle had no air conditioner, plus no radiator to overheat. Those kinds of glitches were expected on Big Three cars. Not just a car, the Beetle was a kind of lovable appliance. The Rabbit was becoming just plain unlovable. Devoid of even a design that could be loved, it was becoming just another Detroit econobox with problems.

Despite those glitches, Rabbits were selling as the Beetle was being phased out, down to just the Beetle Cabrio in 1979. With the added cost of Westmoreland, the business plan called for VW to be profitable in the United States with a 5 percent market share. It was going to be a tall order. In the early 1970s, when VW was being squeezed out of the low-priced segment by high production costs, the company responded with one of the most sweeping retoolings in the industry's history, starting with the 1975 introduction of the Golf/Rabbit. It had a new line of precision-engineered, fuel-efficient small cars and priced them at the top of the small-car price bracket. Volkswagen's bet was to make up in profit margin what it would lack in volume. It was risky. By 1980, the Rabbit was priced at $5,700, but could easily climb to $7,000 with the usual options, and even $9,000 for the Cabrio. Toyota, meanwhile, was selling a nimble and reliable Tercel for around $4,500 and GM was charging $5,000 for a Chevy Citation. Still, in 1980, waiting lists for Rabbits ran as long as a year, and people were paying $1,000 over sticker to get the fuel-efficient, five-speed diesel. Gas prices had soared, and VW was lucky to have the only diesel in the small-car segment, a car that would get almost 50 miles per gallon. The burst was short lived, though.

Year-long waiting lists may sound like fat city, but that wasn't the situation. Executives in Englewood Cliffs, as well as in Detroit, were justifiably worried. Westmoreland was up just 2 years and it was very underutilized. Schmücker had already planned on a second plant with McLernon in Sterling Heights, Michigan. Meanwhile, Englewood Cliffs was very skeptical that the Rabbit could keep enough of a technological edge to maintain the price premium that it was charging. Chrysler's Omni and Horizon duplicated the Rabbit in design, and GM and Ford were aiming at the Rabbit as well. With no upmarket cars selling in sufficient volume to produce decent profits, analysts estimated that VW would have to sell close to an impossible 1 million Rabbits and Rabbit derivatives in the United States to maintain its cost and profit structure for long. As fuel prices gradually came down, demand for these small cars declined.

McLernon realized that to get costs in line, VW would have to source or build more parts in North America. He told European suppliers, such as Michelin and Bosch, that if they wanted to supply VW in the United States, they would have to build U.S. facilities. And they did. However, he was blocked from fully pursuing the plan. The U.S. fuel economy law held that VW had to source at least 35 percent of its parts from overseas to still count the Rabbit as an import. Volkswagen needed that to make up for the relatively poor fuel efficiency of its other cars to meet the 27.5-miles-per-gallon average requirement that was coming in 1985.

There have been two vital ingredients for making money in the price-sensitive and notoriously cyclical U.S. car business: (1) volume and (2) integration. Unless a car company could build about half of its own parts, it would never achieve the economies of scale and unit manufacturing costs that were necessary to compete with the U.S. Big Three or Japan. In 1980, VW had neither going for it in the United States. By legal necessity, about one-third of VW's parts in the United States were provided by Volkswagenwerks, and Volkswagen of America had to pay 30 percent more for these parts than if they were sourced locally due to exchange rates and shipping.

By 1980, the Volkswagen of America executives who enjoyed the glory days of the Beetle, Microbus, Squareback, and Karmann Ghia knew that fortunes were slipping away. The Rabbit was to have replaced the Beetle as VW's bread-and-butter car. Volkswagen's total U.S. sales were at 293,000, compared with 569,000 in 1970 and 334,000 as recently as 1974. The Rabbit's problems seemed beyond hope, because as soon as the reliability and quality issues were straightened out, it would be outdated. Besides, they knew a new Rabbit wasn't coming until 1985. Meanwhile, their reputation was suffering, and the other cars in the lineup were not meeting expectations. The move to front-wheel-drive, water-cooled cars was deemed a necessity by VW management. However, it took several years for VW's designers and engineers to perfect the processes and engineering. Moreover, the dynamic that had existed between VW and DDB was missing. The

Rabbit had mangled the carefully honed brand image. The company was divided. The two U.S. companies seemed adrift from the mother ship in Wolfsburg, not to mention from one another.

In 1980, VW brought out the Jetta, a typical Eurosedan—a so-called notchback that the United States had urged them to build. "Americans like a trunk more than a hatch," said McLernon. Auto writers liked the Jetta for its taut driving quality. However, it suffered from conservative styling and pricing problems relative to Hondas and Toyotas, and so was overlooked by the public. In May 1984, a *Car & Driver* magazine review said it perfectly:

> . . . The Jetta will go through life bearing some of the burdens of the new Golf's design. Chief among them is styling, which is more conservative than Ronald Reagan.

The Jetta was so styled because the audience in Europe, still the primary market even though it had been pushed by the Americans, embraced conservative styling. As a performer, it was refined and agile, and represented a legitimate value compared with the BMW-3 series. However, it wasn't being compared with the 3 series by the man on the street. It was compared with the Japanese sedans, which were more reliable, and the domestics, which were cheaper.

Maryann Keller, an auto industry analyst, noted in her book, *Collision: GM, Toyota, Volkswagen and the Race to Own the 21st Century,* that VW demonstrated an uncanny unwillingness to keep step with U.S. consumers' demands. "The company had a generation of Volkswagen lovers and did very little to figure out how they might keep them. They sat by in a kind of strange denial about how the Japanese were seducing a generation of Americans with high quality automobiles that seldom broke. The products that VW turned out to Americans after the Beetle ran its course looked old and out of step."[3]

John Bulcroft, who worked at Porsche-Audi, as well as at VW, said VW's problem in the United States could be traced to simple hubris. Bulcroft recalls being at the Englewood Cliffs headquarters one day around 1974. Some product planners and engineers visiting from Germany brought a Toyota into the workshop behind the office building where company cars were serviced, and some competitive tests were routinely done. With the exception of marketing, notes Bulcroft, most of the service and parts departments were headed up by German nationals. "It was almost like a *New Yorker* cartoon where people slapping their sides and rolling on the floor . . . that's an exaggeration, but not much," recalls Bulcroft, describing the scene of the Germans breaking down the Toyota. "They were pointing out to me how these cars were going to fail, how poorly finished the car was. Opening up the trunk and pointing out how there was just primer paint. They predicted absolutely no future for the product in the U.S."

The Japanese had a totally different mind-set about product quality, says Bulcroft, a long-time auto industry consultant after leaving VW in 1978. "Let's say there is a whine in the drive train. If it's a Japanese product, you'd report back that customers are complaining about the vibration and whine. The response from Toyota would be 15 engineers crawling all over every car they could find, going out to dealerships. And they would do a fix immediately. If you told the Germans the same story, the response would be, 'You stupid Americans don't know how to drive our products.' Then the response would be, we've tested it and we've found no problem. Then they would very quietly make a running change on the production line and fix it, without admitting to any problem. They'd just try to blame it on American drivers."

Divided They Fell

Though none of the VW models were meeting expectations by the early 1980s, the Rabbit was still the main problem. The trouble with the Rabbit, says one-time VW Marketing Director Ray Ketchledge, was that VW engineers took a mandate to build a technically superior car too seriously. "The Rabbit was at the top of the market in terms of technology, unlike the Beetle, which was attractive to its followers and buyers precisely for it simplicity and its timeless quality." The Rabbit was conceived in too sterile an environment in Germany. Then, when the U.S. managers tried to soften it for American tastes, it became a product that no one wanted much, neither VW enthusiasts nor car buyers who had passed over the rear-engine cars all those years. Some customers were coming from both camps, just not enough.

The many miles between Englewood Cliffs and the manufacturing operation in Detroit just got worse, and made it almost impossible for the marketing people in New Jersey to create any meaningful solutions. As stated in a report generated from a Rabbit Task Force in Englewood Cliffs in 1980,

> There is no magic answer . . . there is no one merchandising program or group of television commercials that will turn it all around. We further feel that most of the mistakes we have made have been taking place for a long time and, therefore, corrections cannot be made overnight.

Morale of the U.S. company was down the drain. The Rabbit task force report actually refers to "indifference and low morale throughout our organization." "It was awful," said Ad Director John Slaven. "The politics were thick, much more than usual because of the split organization. It was awfully difficult to get programs together or create any decent advertising when we knew we had a product (the Rabbit) that was our volume car, but was so full of problems. We felt we had to solve at least some of our internal problems before we could transmit a positive attitude to the buying public or the dealers."

A confidential memo from 1980 detailing questions to be put to consumer focus groups spelled out the problems with the Rabbit, and the marketing department's quandary.[4]

Questions to Probe

1. How would a Volkswagen made in the U.S. differ from one made in Germany?
2. Is there a difference between German and U.S. engineering for any product? For cars in particular?
3. How would a U.S.-made Volkswagen rate in terms of price, reliability, ease of service?

4. Which would you prefer to own: A Volkswagen made in the U.S., or the same car made in Germany?

5. How does a U.S. factory worker differ from a German factory worker in terms of: interest in his job; concern for the quality of his work; dedication to his company.

6. If quality is a concern, is it more likely that a German parent company would maintain better quality in the U.S. than a Japanese parent company?

The whole organization, including the dealers, was gripped by malaise. By 1981, sales were dropping with no floor in sight. Interest rates were high and still rising. A change in the sales and marketing management with Stuart Perkins having left and been replaced by Ian Anderson, and the pending move of the New Jersey staff to Detroit, caused more tension and division; a lot of people simply didn't want to move to Detroit. The pressure to sell the Pennsylvania Rabbit was mounting, and the company now had an idle plant in Sterling Heights that was supposed to make the Jetta, which couldn't find an audience.

Betwixt and between, the Westmoreland Rabbit was neither a German automobile nor an American one. Its semi-American styling and design did not evoke German innovative engineering. "We had walked away from being a German car and not quite arrived at being an American one," said Slaven. "The product was neuter."

It was hoped that VW could move to evolve the Rabbit through improvement and repricing before a brand new Rabbit was designed and readied for production in 1985. The task force also hoped that extensive customer clinics should be done to avoid repeating the same mistakes on the next model. It was suggested, too, that styling people from Germany and North America come to the clinics themselves to hear what customers had to say first-hand, instead of having it interpreted for them by intermediaries. Designers in Germany at that time rarely left the studio. They had a mind of their own about what VWs should be for the whole world.

Even small and obvious improvements were met with resistance, such as importing a leatherette seat from Germany that was used on German Golfs, because the cloth seats that were sourced for the Westmoreland plant were chintzy and a frequent target of customer criticism. The fit and finish of the Westmoreland Rabbit was as lamentable as the Big Three, because of poor 1980 standards. Slaven recalled that a buff magazine editor asked him in 1980 if VW could manufacture in the United States and still maintain the German standard. "I couldn't be honest, but I knew the answer was no."

The marketing organization was pushing for a repriced two-door, four-speed Rabbit with a carburetor, not fuel injection, and with a few less options that could be stickered for just under $6,000. The idea was to sell about 10,000 as a value model to drive showroom traffic.

All along, internal communications within the organization were at a nadir. An internal report generated by the marketing department in 1981 opined:[5]

> It is a general feeling now at Volkswagen of America, from middle management on down, that no one quite has their hands on the control of the company. This, in combination with the general feeling of the two separate companies—VWoA Englewood Cliffs and Troy—results in a feeling of confusion and, to some degree, hopelessness. The people who work for the company—those we depend on to get the job done—feel that senior management is not visible at this critical time.

It was a remarkable memo to circulate.

McLernon agreed. "The company couldn't be run by the sales and marketing people. They were of a different mind and work ethic, we believed. It took too long to get things done with the organizations divided, so we shut down Englewood Cliffs. We lost 300 people in the transfer, and I don't believe we missed them. It lowered our administrative costs and made us more efficient," said McLernon.

———

Meanwhile, in Wolfsburg, Volkswagen AG chairman Toni Schmücker was on a rampage, trying to diversify the company into, of all things, office equipment. Schmücker bought into Nuremberg-based Triumph

Adler, a maker of electronic typewriters. Schmucker thought he was buying not merely into technology for the office of the future, but expertise in the area of electronics that would be critical to making cars in the future. Like the U.S. plant was a strategy to hedge against currency fluctuations, the automated office equipment business was meant to hedge against an auto slump. He spent almost $400 million on acquisitions. However, because Schmücker was stuck having to buy German companies because of VW's ownership stake by the German government, these were hardly the cream of the office equipment industry.

Schmücker had a heart attack in June 1981 and wasn't seen again publicly until the Frankfurt Auto Show in September. That month, VW announced its first quarterly loss since 1975. Rumors were swirling that Schmücker didn't have the steam to run the company after his illness and that a successor was in the cards. There was no consensus for a replacement inside the Vorstand or supervisory board, so outsiders were again being scouted as Schmücker himself had been.

By 1981, the Rabbit was no longer the world's most advanced mass-production car, and its chances of regaining a technological edge over the Japanese were shrinking steadily. To understand Volkswagen AG, consider that, unlike GM or Ford, it does not have a huge home market to depend on. It must sell abroad to make any money on long production runs. In the summer of 1981, Schmücker told his staff that "failure to understand or combat the Japanese challenge will place the survival of our company in doubt." He wasn't talking about success— he was talking survival.

Bowing to political realities, Japan was voluntarily limiting car exports to the U.S. market, which meant that the Japanese companies had to turn to the growth markets that VW had been mining: Latin America, the Caribbean, and Africa. The Japanese sales in Latin America in 1980 increased 81 percent, 44 percent in the Middle East, 40 percent in Southeast Asia, and 32 percent in Africa. Kidding themselves that their products were technically superior, German executives had counted on customer loyalty. However, test drivers in the German auto press that year were catching on, and they failed to remain obedient VW shills who would write favorably about the German entries out of national pride. Magazines increasingly gave the Japanese equal or better ratings than the German cars. Munich's Institute for Economic Research reported in 1980 that recent repair statistics of the German Automobile Club showed that Japanese cars caused the fewest problems. All five Japanese brands took the top places; only Mercedes-Benz was able to squeeze into the top six.

Volkswagen's mounting problems in its home market were exacerbated by a malaise in Wolfsburg that hurt its competitive edge. The Japanese had pioneered just-in-time manufacturing, a system in which truckloads of parts arrive at the assembly line precisely when they are needed. Germany could not do this, because its suppliers were far flung, whereas in Japan, the companies are geographically clustered. Frankly, German workers were not as disciplined, either. Nor could VW lower costs by buying Japanese components. Being a combined 40 percent owned by the German government and the government of Lower Saxony, as it was in 1980, meant that it bought almost everything from German companies to help support the local economy. Although VW could not make strategic decisions based on economy alone, its customers could. The decision to build the second plant in Sterling Heights had nothing to do with anticipated consumer demand, but rather with needed market share.

Meanwhile, the wheel had turned in Wolfsburg. Living standards rose above even U.S. levels. On top of each worker getting 1 hour of paid breaks in an 8-hour day, German workers had five times the absentee rate of their Japanese counterparts, and they got 6 weeks of paid vacation. Offices in Wolfsburg emptied by 4:30 each afternoon. More people were marking time until they became eligible for early retirement, receiving bigger and bigger pensions and salaries. Productivity in Wolfsburg was shot.

Volkswagen had a fine, economical, and high-quality car that saw it through the 1960s and 1970s. It was also inexpensive to produce and buy. Now, not only was the quality missing, but so was the low price. The Americans and the Japanese were matching the engineering. Not only did the Dodge Omni and Plymouth Horizon look the same as the Rabbit, VW began selling VW engines to Chrysler to use in them. Whereas the Beetle was a car that no one could copy, the Rabbit had no technological edge that couldn't be copied quickly.

———

In 1981, Volkswagen of America posted a miniscule $600,000 profit on $3.3 billion in sales. That was better than the $40 million loss in 1980, but not even the $10 million profit it achieved in 1978.

In 1982, Westmoreland was unprofitable and Sterling Heights was idle. McLernon publicly blamed the auto slump, but that wasn't it at all. Subcompact car sales were way up. Rabbit sales were tanking, and the pickup truck that McLernon had built off the Rabbit platform was doing even worse. To turn things around, VW cut prices to drive volume and in the summer launched a marketing campaign featuring the sort of reliability and efficiency images that were characteristic of the Beetle's glory days.

Peter Weiher came to the United States in 1981 to be head of sales and marketing for VW and took up residence in Detroit. That dashed any last hopes that Englewood Cliffs could be preserved, especially given McLernon's ongoing quest to cut costs. The New Jersey sales and marketing staff were made offers to move to Detroit, an offer many spurned. John Slaven was among those who opted out. "When the final word came that Englewood Cliffs was closing, it was a logical step because of the terrible divisions in the company. But it was like that sound I imagine a dying bear would make when he breathes his last. Something special was over. It was to weep."

Charlie Hughes recalls a company gathering in 1982 that summed up all the problems that VW was having. Following a "gripe session" about quality problems at Westmoreland, Manufacturing Chief Dick Dauch said, according to Hughes, "Our customers are just going to have to get used to our new manufacturing standard!" "Oh no they won't," responded Hughes, who had just been made marketing director. "They'll just go somewhere else."

A Return to German Roots

Following Schmücker's heart attack and his subsequent resignation in late 1982, Carl Hahn, who had left the company in 1973 after being passed over for chairman, was lured back as Schmücker's successor. Hahn had gone on to be chief executive of German tiremaker Continental Gummiwerke, and he was credited with a dramatic turnaround of the company.

In fairly short order after taking over as chairman, Hahn fired McLernon and summoned South African Noel Phillips to leave his post near Johannesburg, where he had gone to run a VW distributorship, and return to the United States where he had been head of sales and marketing in the late 1970s. Hahn was disgusted that McLernon shuttered Englewood Cliffs, which Hahn had built. He felt the succession of managers that followed Nordhoff in Wolfsburg didn't understand what VW was about. Why should they? They were brought in from the outside. Phillips was a familiar face to the people who had made the transition from New Jersey to Detroit. South Africa was one of VW's training grounds, as well, so Phillips had the confidence of the Vorstand. He was an international man who spoke both English and German. He was, in short, the only man in the system whom Hahn trusted with the job.

Phillips, a burly man who wore expensive suits, had a lot to tackle. Manufacturing, marketing, and dealer relations were all a mess. His first problem, however, was that his wife who had made the move to Detroit with him, absolutely hated southeast Michigan. She went back after just a short time, leaving Phillips behind and in a tough spot to run the company without his family at hand. Phillips had VW, Audi, and Porsche to run, but he put Jim Fuller, who had been running the marketing of Porsche and Audi, in charge of the VW brand, the first time the brand had its own chief since the three businesses had been combined at the company.

Fuller's mission was to try and reground the marketing to where it had been when business was better. He was convinced that the Rabbit, despite its history, could become as lovable as the Beetle. Of course, he was wrong. If there is one axiom in marketing that stays true, it is this: You only get one chance to launch. The Rabbit had too much baggage by 1982. The best that Fuller could do was make it more acceptable and reverse, or at least slow, the sales decline in advance of the all-new Rabbit in 1985. Thanks to some repackaging, the Rabbit now cost less than the Dodge Omni. It was the Japanese, however, who held the cards in the subcompact market. Toyota and Honda could cut prices by an additional 25 percent and still make money if they chose to.

The Americanization of the whole VW brand, and specifically the Rabbit, under McLernon had to be undone if possible. The image of a VW as a European car must be refurbished, Hahn and Fuller believed. To help, Hahn would speed some help to the United States on the product side—the European GTI. It had been a hit overseas since 1977, but hadn't been sent to the United States.

How welcome was the GTI? Consider the *Car & Driver* magazine assessment of the company included in its review of the GTI in its November 1982 issue.[6]

There was no reason to anticipate such a car from VW of America. The cars rolling out of Pennsylvania farm country have been the farthest things from Teutonic boy racers. Since opening its U.S. plant in 1978, VW has soft pedaled its German heritage in favor of an Americanized image. Suspensions turned flaccid, seats became bench flat, and flash and filigree levels rose alarmingly. If you wanted a German style driver's car, you had to choose from one of the imported models on the dealer's floor, like Jetta or Scirocco. That era, we're happy to report, seems over.

Volkswagen AG had a tough 1982, losing money for the second time in 10 years. Profitable but for the problems in the United States, sales of the VW brand in the United States were down a shocking 71 percent from 1980.

The image of the company had dramatically declined as well. In 1982, Jim Fuller wrote in an internal memo: "Volkswagen's importance in the U.S. marketplace has been in a state of decline over the past several years. Besides the sales decline, our own research has demonstrated that unaided awareness of the brand among our target buyers has dropped by half over the last four years." Fuller noted that Datsun and Toyota were outspending VW by a two-to-one ratio in advertising.

Not surprisingly, Hahn and Phillips viewed 1983 as critical. They decided the Sterling Heights Jetta factory would have to be sold. Phillips had been brought in as a communicator, both to soothe an organization that had been divided by McLernon's appointment and the relocation of the company to Detroit, and to rally the beleaguered and defecting dealers. His style, though, could be aloof and remote, recalls Steve Wilhite. "He carved a privileged environment for himself at the company headquarters in Troy," says Wilhite. Meanwhile, Hahn began looking elsewhere for growth, and did a deal with Spanish car builder Seat to become Spain's leading car supplier.

North America was going to take time. "We will fight our way back step by step in North America," said Hahn.[7] Dealers dropped from 1,200 in the late 1970s to 920, and most of those were dualed now. The hard-to-swallow fact that most of them dualed with a Japanese brand was hard to accept, but at least it gave them a window onto the competition through the dealer body. Dealers reported that only one in five of their VW customers were even contemplating another VW purchase. Westmoreland was cut back to one shift in 1983. The compact pickup truck that McLernon had started was killed, as was a concept for a bigger truck. Volkswagen sold the Sterling Heights plant to Chrysler.

Not only inefficient, Westmoreland was outdated virtually the day it opened. By contrast, one of Chrysler's plants that was finished the same year was far more automated with robots and produced 50 percent more cars than Westmoreland. Westmoreland's breakeven was at 85 percent of capacity, according to VW documents, not the 50 percent that most companies planned for. Even so, Hahn said he could run Westmoreland indefinitely and planned to retool it with more sophisticated robots in preparation for the new Rabbit.

Phillips saw his job from day one as marketing cars, rather than producing them. If he could figure out how to sell them, and restore VW's cachet, the plant could build more cars and the problems would dissolve. He set out to fix the marketing strategy with Fuller, and ordered DDB to take a whack at it. A memo from Fuller in 1983 spells out the marketing direction:

> Volkswagen is unlike any other car maker because only Volkswagen offers the character of German engineering, emphasizing driver performance without compromise.

Roy Grace, chairman of DDB at the time, and creator of many memorable VW ads in the 1960s, remembers a meeting called by Fuller at which he showed a reel of TV ads "from the old days," along with a raft of print ads tacked up to the walls. The idea was to look at what VW had been when it was doing things right and ask rhetorically why the company couldn't recapture the clarity and elan of that period. "He asked us in frustration, 'Why can't we create stuff that good?' " said Grace. "I said to him, 'Because you aren't the same company and these are not the same products.' "

Charlie Hughes remembers his first day on the job as marketing director. He asked DDB to create a sign that he could put up in his office. It had the VW lollipop logo with the words "Honest Value" under it. Hughes put the sign up in his office. When he walked into his office the next day, someone had tacked up a sign on top of it that read, "What we used to be. What we aren't. What we have to be again if we are going to survive."

Advertising had been in a muddle almost since the Rabbit was introduced in 1975 as the volume car. All the legendary brand-building, ground-breaking advertising—the stuff that universities used to teach in advertising—had hopped the tracks. Late-1970s ads for the Rabbit and Scirocco foolishly tried to extend the Beetle advertising. It was desperate and ham-fisted. One legendary Beetle ad was actually reprised for the Rabbit right down to the copy points. "The Rabbit: The car the snowplow driver drives to the snowplow." "It was bullshit, and we all knew it," said John Slaven. Ford, Chevrolet, and Dodge routinely scour old reels and print ads for ideas that have worked in the past, and update them. VW ads, however, especially the ones that are commemorated in museums and teaching books as advertising perfection, couldn't be retreaded for a vehicle as dishwater-dull and cockeyed as the Westmoreland Rabbit. It was another example of how Americanized the U.S. VW management had become with so many Big Four executives (American Motors Corp. included) running things. The German character was fading into oblivion. There were the typical ads with a Rabbit featuring a good review from *Road & Track* magazine, the kind of stuff carrying scant weight with the people who were shopping for Rabbits. There were print ads that explained fuel injection and torsion bars to magazine readers, beginning a "German Engineering" theme that would become the actual tagline in 1987. Theme lines such as "Volkswagen Does It Again," "Nothing Else is a Volkswagen," and "It's Not a Car. It's a Volkswagen," seemed to change as frequently as the Rabbit's oil filters.

The marketing director under Fuller, Ray Ketchledge, recalls as a particular low point an ad showing a chicken sitting on top of a Rabbit. "I hated it," says Ketchledge. "It was all wrong. The Rabbit was designed to be a technologically advanced car, and here we were putting a chicken on top of the car, which is something we might have done with the Beetle. But it was all wrong for the Rabbit. We were trying to impart the Beetle mystique on the Rabbit, and you can't do that. Meanwhile, we were having serious quality problems with this technologically advanced car, so putting a chicken on top made it appear that we were setting ourselves up for rotten egg jokes."

By 1985, with a new Golf and Jetta, Hahn was seriously pushing the two-division strategy in the United States of marketing both VW and Audi. Volkswagen had been marketing Audi in the United States since 1970, but support for the brand had been dodgy through the 1970s. Now, with VW flagging and profits fatter with the premium-priced Audis, he was investing more in the franchise. He had also been discussing a joint manufacturing deal with Chrysler full of possibilities, including a joint vehicle between the two and Chrysler taking on some of Westmoreland's capacity. There were even talks about a full-blown merger. Chrysler Chief Lee Iacocca had been to Congress in 1979 to beg money to stay in business, and was not yet out of the woods. None of it came to fruition, though. While Hahn was making serious headway in Europe, the U.S. company was still adrift. In 1984, VW moved up to number three in Europe behind Ford and Fiat. Hahn cut a deal to build cars in China. Despite its miniscule output, Hahn considered the China deal huge for the future and referred to it as being up there with trading for Manhattan with the Indians. Westmoreland, though, was a quagmire, that one journalist referred to as "Westmorelandgrad, as in Stalingrad, considering how it bleeds the Germans." It had cost the company an estimated $1 billion between 1976 and 1984. Hahn didn't want to close it for the same reason that Schmücker built it: He didn't know what the dollar was going to do against the mark, so he didn't want to be without it.

Hahn was very frustrated with the U.S. team's inability to gain momentum. The 1985 Golf was a huge success in Europe, so much so that there was talk of the company being a one-car company again. Two out of three vehicles sold worldwide by VW in 1985 were Golfs, despite the company's four other vehicles. In the United States, it was an also-ran. Even with the all-new model, sales were 8 percent below the previous year's Rabbit sales. The reasons were twofold. First, the name of the car had changed to Golf—no more Rabbit. It takes time for Americans to embrace change. Second, the all-new Golf, though much improved, looked almost identical to the old Rabbit. It made for an odd marketing environment for VW in the United States. Because Hahn had been on the front lines in the United States during the Beetle's rise, he had difficulty with excuses. He didn't have time to micromanage the company.

Tall, trim, and patrician, like most of the men who rise to the corporate upper echelon, Hahn was practically born to the job of running VW, as was Ferdinand Piëch, who would succeed Hahn in 1993. Hahn's father was a cofounder of Auto Union, which was the forerunner to Audi. Unlike Piëch, however, Hahn was a finance and marketing maven, not an engineer. He had worked outside the company twice, first as an economist in Paris before winning a job with Heinz Nordhoff, and again after he left in 1973 when he was passed over for the chairmanship. It was felt that he was too young. He married an American woman, and three of his children were born in the United States. He became known in Wolfsburg for, among other things, tearing around the VW test track on the replica of an antique motorcycle that his employees gave him on his 60th birthday. He was raised near Chemnitz, Germany, in a home that was quite near a test track for motorcycles, and thus wreaked of gasoline as the bikes were tested around the clock.

Volkswagen's U.S. woes in the mid-1980s were soon worsened by the opportunities Hahn and Schmidt saw to build sales in Europe. The task was easier than convincing the silly Americans—lining up to buy Yugoslavian death traps—to pay a little more for a Golf or Jetta. Volkswagen had only a 6.8 percent share of the market in Western Europe. Schmidt saw potential for doubling that through stronger marketing and distribution. The deal with Spanish car builder Seat delivered an advantage in Spain and added 400,000 units of capacity in Western Europe. Hahn had a good year in 1985, boosting earnings by 140 percent to $225 million on more than $21 billion in sales.

Back in the United States, the retooling in Westmoreland County, Pennsylvania, for the new Golf helped quality. Volkswagen rose from 22nd to 8th in the J. D. Power and Associates survey of buyer satisfaction in 1985. *Motor Trend* magazine named the GTI Car of the Year, a legitimate and defendable pick. GTI was getting kudos from everyone. Jetta, an underperformer since 1980, showed life: increasing sales by 120 percent in 1985 to 84,000, thanks to a strong dollar; favorable pricing; and good reviews from the auto press. Dealers were getting happy again, too, as dollar volume was running 25 percent ahead of the Beetle's best year ever. In 1983, the gap between VW and Japanese prices was 20 percent. In 1986, it was down to 5 percent.

The Rabbit had never been the first-time buyer's car that the Beetle was, and the company felt for years that it would benefit from having a car like that. Many misguided college students were turning to the new Korean carmaker, Hyundai, and Yugo. Isuzu and Suzuki were selling inferior entry-level cars as well. Ford had the Escort. General Motors, however, didn't seem to care about the segment, satisfied with buying spotty product from Suzuki and Isuzu and rebadging them as Chevrolets. In 1987, VW would import a new vehicle it was building in Brazil, called the Fox. Priced just under $6,000, the plan was to start with about 50,000 and move up to 100,000 Foxes a year. Said Jim Fuller at the time, "It can be the appetizer for a lifetime of buying Volkswagens."

Can VW Survive?

By 1987, though, fortunes had changed for Hahn, and things were getting worse rather than better in the United States. Supply problems delayed the Fox's arrival from Brazil. The Audi 5000 had been sandbagged in the United States by CBS's *60 Minutes,* which had fallen hook, line, and sinker for cases marshaled by plaintiffs' lawyers involving people who claimed that their Audi 5000 sedans accelerated out of control. The bad publicity drove a stake through Audi's credibility, and the company's responses to the media, including one disaster with *60 Minutes* reporter Ed Bradley, were awful. Recalls that year cost VW $50 million, with more dished out on increased advertising. A whopping $5,000 rebate was attached to the car in the hopes of moving them to astute buyers who might smell a bargain, because there was no actual evidence of any problems with the 5000s (and never would be). No government-directed test done on the Audi 5000 revealed any design defect. Audi America went through four vice presidents in 16 months. Audi's collapse was Acura's gain. Just as Honda had soaked up tens of thousands, if not hundreds of thousands of disaffected VW customers, Honda's brand-new premium division drew the lion's share of Audi owners and buyers. Hahn also uncovered a giant in-house foreign exchange fraud that cost the company upward of $300 million, putting a serious dent in the profits that Hahn had booked the previous two years. Volkswagen of America was profitable in 1986, but sales plummeted in 1987 to 191,000.

———

Jim Fuller was a charismatic leader. Before going to VW, he had put in time at Ford, Renault, and then American Motors. He had run the Porsche-Audi group before taking over the VW brand in 1982. He convinced many dealers looking to desert VW in the mid-1980s to stick with him. He had a way with people, for instance, inviting colleagues and dealers home to cook for them. Dealer meetings weren't just steak-and-martini affairs; he sometimes included a trip to a museum. He'd quote John Kenneth Galbraith to them from memory. Business soured further in 1988 to just 166,000 in sales, but Fuller looked ahead to 1989 when three new vehicles would hit: (1) the Corrado, (2) the GTI Rallye, and (3) the Passat.

In mid-December 1988, Fuller and Marketing Director Lou Marengo, then just 33, were flying back from Germany to the United States when their Pan Am Boeing 747 was blasted out of the sky over Lockerbie, Scotland, by a bomb that had been planted by a Libyan terrorist.

The company that had already been through so much was devastated. Fuller was beloved as one of the old hands from Englewood Cliffs who had stayed with the company. Volkswagen was not a big company in the United States. Unlike Ford or GM, it was a small, close, battle-weary family.

"Jim was a spiritual leader, and very much the right guy to see the company through these troubled times," said VW Public Relations Director Steve Keyes. "A lot went out of the organization that day."

To steady the ship, Hans Hungerland, who had been at Englewood Cliffs in the 1970s and had returned to Volkswagen AG as head of exports, was dispatched to Detroit to run the company. A trusted lieutenant of Hahn's, Hungerland was chosen both for his experience in the United States and his easy way, which would be needed to steady the grief-stricken workforce and ranks of dealers that were close to Fuller. Murphy's Law had prevailed at Volkswagen of America for a decade. Losing Fuller and Marengo was literally a death blow to an already languishing morale.

Volkswagen was the first foreign carmaker to build cars in the United States. Despite the struggle over the years at Westmoreland County, the company had some pride in this. By the end of 1987, however, it was ordered closed. Hahn had said the factory could stay open indefinitely as a hedge against currency swings, but on top of other problems in other markets, the losses became intolerable. Overcapacity, a slump in worldwide demand, and a stock market crash in 1987 were all too much for the Pennsylvania plant to shoulder. The Golf and Jetta never met expectations. Before this, the Rabbit was plagued by inconsistency and serious quality issues. The plant was an orphan from the beginning as far as many in Wolfsburg were concerned. Hahn had inherited it from Schmücker; therefore, he felt no emotional bond to it. Volkswagen Chief Fuller had been among the VW faithful in Englewood Cliffs who thought it a questionable idea from the start; they'd all put in untold hours trying to make up in advertising and marketing what the Westmoreland Rabbit lacked in quality and personality. Meanwhile, Honda opened its first U.S. plant in Ohio in 1981, and has never looked back.

———

Dave Huyett once asked VW Marketing Chief Werner Schmidt: "Hahn started in the United States. Why doesn't he care about us?" Schmidt answered, "He looks at you guys as if you are the child who went bad." Says Huyett, "We would talk to him about what we needed. But it most often wouldn't go anywhere. And of course, Bill Young, while good for the company in one regard, was not so good in another. He was bad in Vorstand meetings, because he would speak his mind. He was not diplomatic. An independent. He was the opposite of the Germans."

Hungerland needed someone to run the VW brand. He needed an American who could steady the troops and dealers at what was already a very tough time. He also needed someone who was part of the family. Bill Young left the company in 1982, opting not to move to Detroit after the consolidation of the marketing and manufacturing companies. Though he loved the brand and the company, he spent enough time in Detroit over the years to know that he really didn't want to live there. He moved to Manhattan Beach, California, with his family, a far cry from the Detroit Athletic Club, and even promised his son they would never move from the beach. Hungerland called and asked him to come back and run the VW brand. Young was running a successful consultancy with another VW expatriate, Steve Wilhite.

Young, however, had loyalty to both the company he loved and to his friend Hungerland. He promised that he would give it 2 years.

When Young took over, the product was a problem as it had been for 15 years. It was competent but mostly overpriced, relative to the competition. The VW brand stood for very little at this point with the U.S. consumer. Golfs, Jettas, GTIs, and Quantums all competed head to head with Japanese offerings, but had neither the price and value or quality to match. Also, a new Corrado, a snappy sports coupe to replace the Scirocco, had just arrived. The Eurovan was a nonissue, despite the rise of minivans, selling just a couple of thousand a year to the VW religious. If there wasn't anything Young could do about the product to enliven it, he *could* attack the marketing.

Young toured the country, visiting dealers to reassure them. Of course, he knew most of them from his previous years at the company. Knowing that he didn't have carte blanche from Wolfsburg, he was careful not to make too many promises regarding what would be done. He avoided touting the upcoming Corrado coupe and Passat models to the dealers, because there was plenty of worry that these two models were going to add to the problems, not subtract from them. It is very difficult to sell and market premium-priced cars when consumers have been rejecting the entry-level stuff. Solutions to the moribund sales of the Golf and Jetta were not around the corner.

Young quickly pulled the plug on VW's "German Engineering" ad campaign from the ad agency now known as DDB Needham after Doyle Dane Bernbach had merged with another agency, but doubled the marketing budget. The money was earmarked for regional marketing programs, allowing dealers to structure promotions that made sense to their individual selling areas. Weary of cash rebates, and suspicious of how the money was being used, Young developed a unique incentive plan that he felt was right for the worrisome economic times in the United States. Inflation was on the move, and the economy was still faltering after the stock market crash in 1987. Young assigned rebates of between $500 and $2,000 to VW models, but he made sure that the money went directly to the lending institution. Why? If customers paid cash for the car, VW would give them U.S. savings bonds for the amount of the rebate.

"The idea was that giving back cash tells the customer that the product is not worth the price you charged in the first place," said Young, a vocal critic of rebating and cash-back incentives.

Young also commissioned a study by J. D. Power and Associates in 1989 to get a reading on VW's market strengths and weaknesses. He wanted an unbiased study about what he had to build on, and confirmation to see if his own instincts about the problems were right. It would also give him the ammunition that he needed in Wolfsburg to back up the turnaround plan that he would devise.

The biggest overriding problem, said the Power report, was the disconnect between U.S. consumers and the designers and engineers in Germany who were building cars. Just after taking over from Fuller in 1988, Young discovered that the new Corrado coupe, a sports car that would cost around $22,000—the most expensive VW to date, other than the Vanagon camper—was arriving on U.S. shores without an option for a compact disc (CD) player. The CDs had replaced LPs and were starting to overtake cassettes in cars. Premium cars were offering a CD player as an option, and consumers buying sports cars showed a strong inclination for an in-dash CD player. Focus groups, too, showed that it could even be a deal breaker with the young male buyers who were the target for the Corrado. Young made overtures to Wolfsburg and was disgusted with the response that he got. He was told by a German engineer that it was pointless to put a CD player in an automobile because the quality of sound provided by the CD would be lost in a moving car. In other words, the Power report was dead-on correct.

This was typical of Wolfsburg, which was filled with people who had spent little or no time in the United States, and who had been resisting adding cupholders to cars as well. "Cars are for *drifink* and *gettink* place to place, not for *eatink* and *drinkink* and *havink* a party," said the typical VW engineer in the 1980s.

Honda was a kind of nemesis for VW by 1989. It was clear in 1989 that Honda would come to surpass Chrysler as the third biggest car seller in the United States after GM and Ford. It was building cars in the United States by this time, though VW had closed *its* plant. From a marketing standpoint, with a highly creative and talented West Coast agency, Rubin Postaer & Associates, it had become the spiritual successor to VW. Both the cars and the advertising were wonderfully likable. It was a painfully familiar strategy to VW veterans.

The paths of Honda and VW show clearly what happens when a car company's first effort is a smash hit, versus one whose first product is an unqualified dud. The Beetle was a carryover vehicle from the 1930s that didn't see U.S. shores until 1949. It didn't achieve any real volume until the late 1950s, more than 20 years after it was conceived on Ferdinand Porsche's drafting table. There was every reason for the Beetle to flop. It was introduced at a time when cars were filled with chrome, tail fins, and the bigger they were the better they were. The Beetle, however, struck a special chord with people, especially young people. Volkswagen milked the Beetle and its technology for so long that the company had great difficulty moving beyond it with success.

Honda's first Civic, on the other hand, was a joke, and of poor quality. It was prone to rust and breaking down. The Japanese responded by adopting *kaizen,* which means constant improvement, an idea that Nordhoff had clung to from 1948 until his death in 1968. It became committed to bulletproof quality and blew by VW in the United States. Volkswagen had been matching rebates with the Big Three. Young thought that this was a disastrous approach. He was fanatical in his hatred of rebate marketing.

While Young had been away, DDB had merged with another agency and been acquired by Omnicom Communications following the resignation of chairman Roy Grace, who went off to start his own ad agency. The agency was now DDB Needham and was based in Troy, Michigan, staffed mostly by Detroiters who had cut their teeth at the agencies in Detroit cranking out ads for the Big Three. Doyle Dane

Dr. Ferdinand Porsche: designer and spiritual father of the Beetle.

Dr. Carl Hahn: master builder of Volkswagen of America.

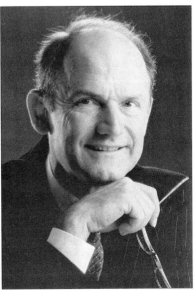

Ferdinand Piech: grandson of the legendary Porsche. Arrogant and frightening. Also, one of the top product development executives of the 20th century. He has motor oil and axle grease in his veins.

Dr. Jens Newman: The most American of the Germans at Volkswagen, his energy and vision, as well as his influence with Piech, have been critical to Volkswagen's recovery in America.

A troubled start: laying a cornerstone for the KdF factory in what would become Wolfsburg after World War II.

Original Beetle: The Beetle did not change much over the years, constantly improving from the first batch that came out of Wolfsburg. Still, no basic design lasted as long.

Canvas: More than any other car of the twentieth century, the Beetle was a canvas to its owners, not merely a conveyance.

Karmann Ghia: The Karmann Ghia may be even more revered than the Beetle. It was pitched as a sports car, but didn't have the horses for that. It was merely beautiful.

The Thing: More than 30 years after the Kubelwagen began production as the German army's favorite jeep, it surfaced as "The Thing" on U.S. shores. Though short-lived, VW was ahead of its time again in the United States with a sport utility. Also, VW's talent for naming vehicles did not desert it.

The 100,000th Rabbit from the Westmoreland plant sold. Volkswagen's American executives were optimistic. The Rabbit was technologically advanced, but it was not nearly as well built as the Beetle.

New Beetle/Concept 1 in Clay: a savior in progress.

The New Beetle gets all the attention. But the new design of the Passat has been a sales success and contributed valuable profits. Its design helped it win Best Family Sedan honors from Consumer Reports.

Lemon.

This Volkswagen missed the boat.

The chrome strip on the glove compartment is blemished and must be replaced. Chances are you wouldn't have noticed it; Inspector Kurt Kroner did.

There are 3,389 men at our Wolfsburg factory with only one job: to inspect Volkswagens at each stage of production. (3000 Volkswagens are produced daily; there are more inspectors than cars.)

Every shock absorber is tested (spot checking won't do), every windshield is scanned. Volkswagens have been rejected for surface scratches barely visible to the eye.

Final inspection is really something! VW inspectors run each car off the line onto the Funktionsprüfstand (car test stand), tote up 189 check points, gun ahead to the automatic brake stand, and say "no" to one VW out of fifty. This preoccupation with detail means the VW lasts longer and requires less maintenance, by and large, than other cars. (It also means a used VW depreciates less than any other car.)

Volkswagen plucks the lemons; you get the plums.

DDB ad: Doyle Dane Bernbach created ads that were art—art that sold cars. The honesty and wit in the ads changed advertising forever.

New Beetle: Sales tapered in 2001, but there is no denying that it has been crucial to the company's resurgence in the United States, and a lightning charge to the brand.

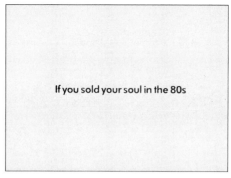

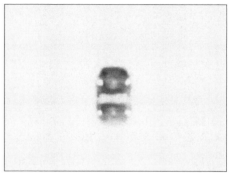

Arnold ad: Arnold may have been a surprise choice, but it has proven to be a worthy successor to DDB in creating the right image for a unique brand.

AAV: A concept for a VW sport utility vehicle expected to debut in 2003. Late to the party with an SUV, VW is hoping that it is fashionably late. It's no "Thing."

Microbus concept: One of VW's icons made a comeback at the 2001 North American International Auto Show. Volkswagen will almost certainly produce it, but whether it lives up to the hype as the vehicle for minivan haters remains to be seen.

Bernbach now had the same problem that VW had in 1982. Few people from New York had any interest in moving to Detroit.

Turning restless again, dealers were blaming DDB for a lack of showroom traffic. A lot of these dealers had come to love the old DDB ads, recognizing how important they were to engendering interest in the brand. Others, though, always thought that DDB's stuff was off the wall and couldn't figure out what the ads were supposed to be saying half the time. Every car company has both kinds of dealers: those who understand brand-building advertising and those who just want endless sell-a-thons.

Say the Word . . . *Desperation*

When Young accepted the job from Hungerland, he did so with the understanding that he could change the ad strategy, and even fire DDB from the U.S. business if he didn't get what he was after. He wanted big ideas, and he took the job thinking the relationship with the agency had run its course—at least in the United States. Hungerland agreed, even though it was going to be a tough sell in Wolfsburg with Global Marketing Director Dr. Werner Schmidt, and former U.S. Marketing Director Peter Weiher, who was now back in Wolfsburg working with Schmidt. Young told DDB Needham Chairman Keith Reinhard that he felt VW had died as a brand after 7 years of rebates. "I told him I'd give him six months to come up with the big idea," says Young.

After 5 months, Young had seen nothing close to a big idea. He notified Schmidt and Weiher that he was giving DDB 30 days. Neither Schmidt, nor Weiher, wanted Young to fire DDB, a move fraught with political consequences. They both had deep roots with DDB, which had VW business all over the world. In addition, Dr. Hahn didn't want a change for the same reasons. If Young was able to fire DDB in the United States, every market in the world might ask for a review. By concentrating all of the business with DDB and making the relationship nearly unassailable, Hahn had at least kept the advertising stable.

He believed very strongly that VW advertising should be consistent market to market, allowing only for small deviations for local customs.

On DDB's deadline day, Peter Weiher flew to Detroit for the meeting. If DDB was going to get fired, he wanted to be there to see if he could talk Young out of it or, at least, to see if there was anything redeeming in DDB's pitch that might buy the agency time. Young was sure that this would be the last meeting with DDB. Wilhite, who was national sales manager, was there, too, and he had pretty much had it with DDB as well.

There had already been a half-dozen meetings trying to find an idea that Young would buy, and each one was worse than the one before. Still, Weiher and Hahn believed that there was no need to fire the agency. The people could be changed. That was always possible, and it was a given part of the ad business.

Keith Reinhard and a team of creative staffers pitched to Young, Wilhite, Marketing Manager Bill Gelgota, and about a half-dozen other people from Volkswagen of America. Then, something happened: Reinhard pitched *Fahrvergnügen*.

Reinhard and his team went through their presentation pitching a campaign built around a German word with which no one in the room was familiar, not even Weiher. Gelgota, says Young, almost threw up. Wilhite was disgusted. Weiher, according to Young, was sitting quietly with his eyes rolling. Young, however, to his own shock, was interested.

Fahrvergnügen, for the uninitiated, is a German word that a DDB copywriter found while going through a German technical manual. Literally translated, it means *the pleasure of driving.* Doyle Dane Bernbach's idea was to use this word, which would get everyone's attention, to explain what makes VWs unique drivers' vehicles, and, from time to time, justify a higher price than a U.S. or Japanese equivalent.

They were all pretty honest with Reinhard and his team, laying it on the line that, yes, it was crazy. Young, however, would be the last one heard from. During the break, Young had seen how his own team was reacting. They hated it, especially Wilhite, and thought it was insultingly bad. Young finally offered his opinion. "Well, we gave the agency an impossible task . . . to break through the clutter with a relatively small budget. And by God, *Fahrvergnügen* is going to break through the clutter!"

"The dealers will think you have lost your mind," Wilhite told Young at the meeting.

Meanwhile Weiher, Schmidt, and finally Hahn, were very happy that DDB managed to win over Young. The Germans were dumbfounded, according to Young and Wilhite, that Young bought *that* campaign, given how combative he could be, and how intent he seemed on firing DDB.

After buying the idea, Young's orders were to leave nothing to chance. The company and dealers were going to get behind this crazy idea with both guns. For 6 months, VW and DDB went into prelaunch mode with ad concepts (TV, print, billboards, magazines, newspapers) and dealer merchandising material (signs, cups, and brochures). "I tried to leave nothing to chance," said Young. "We had been doing the rebates for years and killing the brand. All anyone did when they came into a dealership was ask how much money was being offered. I wanted to stop that cycle. *Fahrvergnügen* looked like a way for us to give the dealer, the salesperson, a way to engage the customer, to have the customer ask a question other than, 'how much?' The dealer's response would be, 'I can't explain it. You really need to drive it to find out what it is.' It wouldn't be for everyone, but if we could change the plane of discussion, I thought we had a chance."

Young had a lot of credibility with the dealers, and so did Wilhite. Wilhite, however, who was friends with Young and followed him to Detroit, hated it. He thought it was completely bone-headed. "It was exclusionary," says Wilhite, still a close friend of Young's. "It didn't address any of the real brand attributes that Volkswagen had built up. It was very gimmicky."

It was such a reach of logic, Young knew he had to have 100 percent buy-in from the beat-up dealer council, so they, in turn, would sell it to the other dealers. Young called Wilhite into his office one day as the advertising and showroom materials were all being produced. It was just days before the dealer council meeting at which the campaign would be presented. Young, smoking a cigar and putting his big-brother face on, put his arm around Wilhite and asked for his support on *Fahrvergnügen*. Wilhite agreed, reluctantly. He knew that Young deserved, and needed, his chance to make it work.

Volkswagen had a string of unsuccessful slogans and campaigns, all backed up by the shoot-yourself-in-the-foot strategy of rebates. Young put all his money behind this one idea. "We pulled rebates and never went back on my watch," says Young. "I always consider it one of the smarter things I did. DDB produced a video explaining to dealers and the media the origin and meaning of *Farhvergnügen*. The TV ads, which cost around $1 million apiece to make, combined film and animation into a look that was unique for the ad business up to that point. The music scored used a European techno rock sound that reminded people a little of the Swedish band ABBA. Radio ads musically repeated the phrase, 'Say the word . . . Say the word . . . Faaaaahrfeeeergnuuuuuugen . . . Say the word . . . Say the word.' As if written by psychologists instead of a songwriter, it was designed to get into the listener's head."

The day after *Fahrvergnügen* was introduced, Carl Hahn was in New York with Young to have breakfast. That morning, The *New York Times* ad columnist Randall Rothenberg had devoted his column to the campaign. The night before, Johnny Carson had talked about it in his monologue. People hadn't talked about VW advertising this way in 20 years. Hahn, recalls Young, was impressed, bemused, and bewildered. It seemed like a hair-brained idea to him, too.

Young says DDB deserved a chance to save the business in the United States. He bore no malice toward the agency. He admits, and longtime VW hand Dave Huyett concurs, that Volkswagen of America was a bad client, seemingly always in transition from the time the Rabbit was launched in 1975. "When you go from five hundred thousand a year in sales to one hundred thousand, the whole world changes," says Young. "I have heard over the years that DDB's creative went to hell in a hand-basket when they moved to Detroit with us. . . . The truth is that everything went to hell in a hand-basket when Volkswagen moved to Detroit."

Six months after *Fahrvergnügen* was launched, all of VW's measurements were up: advertising recall, public relations hits on TV shows and in the newspapers, J. D. Power and Associates customer satisfaction ratings. "People actually thought our quality was up after that, which was bullshit, of course. It was lousy," said Young.

Wilhite thought the campaign did the opposite of what VW needed, and reflected the opposite of what the brand was. "It was a curiosity, but it was not invitational," said Wilhite. "It was foreign. Even though the design and driving characteristics of the cars are German, the brand is as American as Mom and apple pie. The *Fahrvergnügen* executions were cold and distant, which, of course, is very German. But it was bad for us and the brand. When consumers find something exclusionary, they dismiss it, or they make fun of it. The dealers thought we'd flipped out. At that point, the only reason we were in business was the personal relationships between key people at Volkswagen, like Bill and myself, and the dealers. The dealers were saving us more than we were. The media spending we put behind it moved the needle on awareness and the PR value was worth something. But all the key ratings—brand attribute measurements, brand consideration, sales volume—all of the measures of health and vitality of the brand were going the wrong way. That campaign crystallizes the difference between 'awareness' and 'relevance.' People were aware, but we weren't relevant. And if you ask someone to pay between $12,000 and $25,000 for a product, you had better be relevant."

Wilhite's assessment was right, and VW was hurt further by the delay of the new Golf and Jetta. Sales in 1990 were 136,000, down from 169,000 in 1988. In January 1991, Marketing Director Dave Schembri had an idea. The economy was in the dumps. The Persian Gulf War was on. Consumer confidence was shot, and sales were dragging. The new Jetta and Golf weren't yet being produced. All VW had was the new Passat, which was well received by the press; the Cabrio; and the Eurovan.

In consumer clinics, Schembri found that people weren't buying new cars because they were scared of getting stuck with a big loan if they lost their jobs. Schembri proposed to Young: What if we guaranteed their loan payments if they get fired or laid off for up to a year? No one had ever done anything like that, Schembri said. It appealed to Young, who, after all, had approved *Fahrvergnügen*. Young agreed and set about trying to figure out just how it could be done. Volkswagen would have to buy an insurance policy from Lloyds of London guaranteeing to save Volkswagen of America from a disaster if every VW buyer got fired in 6 months. Schembri got together with DDB, and decided to break it during President Bush's State-of-the-Union address; viewership would be swollen because of the Gulf War. Volkswagen bought a network roadblock, which meant all networks would carry the ad, to run in between the speech and the Democratic response.

"We would like to interrupt this recession with this important message from Volkswagen . . ." went the ad.

The next day, every major newspaper in the country called, as well as most of the major networks and many local TV stations. It was getting more notice than the launch of *Fahrvergnügen*. Schembri, one of the more ebullient and personable characters in the industry, was sky high that his idea was paying dividends. The network morning shows called and Schembri flew to New York to appear on national TV with Connie Chung to talk about the program. The only thing missing from the extravaganza were new Golfs and Jettas to benefit from the buzz.

It generated about $80 million in positive publicity over the course of 2 weeks, and there was a 30 percent bump in showroom traffic.

Good stuff, but again, it was short lived. In anticipation of the new Golf and Jetta, Schembri and John Slaven, who was consulting with the company, got another idea to juice the marketing. Infomercials had become popular on cable TV. A company could buy 30 minutes of time very cheaply and show what it wanted. The medium had been used mostly for kitchen gadgets and self-improvement. Slaven and Schembri, though, thought the VW story was perfect to sustain a 30-minute program. Starting with the design of the Beetle by Porsche, through the 1940s and 1950s, Ben Pon and Will van de Kamp, the 1960s advertising and counterculture, and the Microbus and Karmann

Ghia. Slaven wrote the script and got actor Tom Skerritt to host it. He also lured feminist Gloria Steinem to speak about how VW had been the first auto advertiser in her *Ms.* magazine in the early 1970s, and that it didn't have to change any of the ads for the *Ms.* readership. Steinem had never endorsed a product before. Unlike virtually every other car company, VW ads could run anywhere because of their honesty, and she had remembered VW's ad commitment at a time when many advertisers balked at advertising in her magazine.

The program was completed in late 1991 when Tom Shaver was hired as head of VW brand. Shaver had come over from Saturn. It wasn't his project, and he was not in favor of it, so it got only a couple of airings on cable TV. Once Shaver came on board, *Fahrvergnügen* was also on borrowed time, as Wilhite's predictions had come true. Overall brand measurements had shown that *Fahrvergnügen* had stirred some initial interest and brand recognition, but it hadn't served as the catalyst to customer inquiry that Young had hoped for. It didn't help that the Golf III and Jetta III were delayed coming to market because of development delays owing to safety requirements such as airbags and antilock brakes, which had not been built into the designs, but were speeded to the final versions by necessity after the government set new safety standards.

Fahrvergnügen was dead on the heap of other taglines and slogans that had dotted the 1980s. Could the brand, and the company, be far behind?

The German Patient

SIX

In 1991, Bill Young became the president of VW in the United States, running both VW and Audi, replacing Hans Hungerland who returned to Germany. There was no sign of any turnaround at Audi. At VW, though, he could at least look forward to the launch of the brand-new models of the Golf and Jetta. The new and improved A Class (the internal code name for the platform that was shared by the two models) was supposed to bring in new buyers who had passed over the previous version for its poor quality and skimpy amenities. However, he couldn't look forward yet. Because the plant at Westmoreland had been closed, Jettas and Golfs had been coming to the United States from Germany. The new cars, however, would be sourced for the United States from the Puebla, Mexico, plant, which had been making about 80,000 original Type 1 Beetles a year for the Mexican market. Volkswagen sales in 1991 had been just 91,700— the first year that the company had sold fewer than 100,000 cars since the 1950s. The Jettas and Golfs that had previously come from Pennsylvania had been inferior, and the ones coming from Germany were only marginally better. For instance, neither the air conditioners nor the electrical systems were reliable. The radios were of low quality. As usual, the color mixes seemed chosen by a blind person. Volkswagen was down to selling only to die-hard VW fans, the ones who would buy the cars if they came in boxes and had to be assembled in their driveways.

When Bill Young grabbed the reins as president, he saw a catastrophe brewing in Mexico. Until the launch of the new Golf III and Jetta III, the Puebla plant had been just an assembler of Beetles. The cars were all shipped to Mexico from Germany in kit form, and the plant had only to put the cars together according to plan; it was an assembly plant, not a full-blown manufacturer. Puebla did no substantial purchasing of its own. If Puebla did any sourcing or buying, it was just for local content issues, such as upholstery or maybe bumpers that could be bought more cheaply from a local supplier. The new Golfs and Jettas were an entirely different matter. Assembling them required Puebla to become a real manufacturing operation, like the Westmoreland plant had been. The only hitch was that no one at Wolfsburg bothered to train the supervisors or workers in the complexities of making cars from the tires up. No one knew how to order the breadth of required parts. There were no systems in place at Puebla to build cars according to dealer orders or on any forecasted basis. The plant's computers weren't set up for that, let alone the people. In mid-1992, Young went to Mexico and found, to his dismay, about 450 sea cargo containers full of parts, enough to build 100,000 cars. It was all just sitting in the yard at Puebla.

"It was a nightmare," recalls Young. Having worked with VW Manufacturing on a weekly basis leading up to the start of the Westmoreland plant, Young knew something about plant operations, and he knew how cars get built. However, he also knew that there was no way Puebla was capable of delivering cars that would pass even Yugo's quality standards, let alone VW's. Young had himself appointed head of quality for North America. What this appointment meant was that no cars could leave Puebla for distribution to a dealer unless he signed off on it.

"Volkswagen was barely surviving in the U.S. as it was," says Young. "I felt strongly that if we started dumping these cars into dealerships, we wouldn't have a company left with the VW Fox phasing out, Golfs and Jettas were the entry point for our customers. The quality was so bad that word would spread like wildfire, and even the loyalists would stop buying. And it was a pretty safe bet that if Volkswagen went down in America, Audi would follow," said Young. "That really would have been it."

The first thing that Young did was hire about 25 retired engineers from Volkswagen of America, and he took them to Mexico. These experienced men supervised the building of the cars from the cargo containers of parts. If they found 25 visual defects on a car, it was rejected. Every car was, in fact, rejected. These retired engineers weren't working with computers. They had yellow legal pads and pencils, and they tried to make sense of the inventory in order to identify what parts were missing. It was like 1945 in Wolfsburg all over again. Not surprisingly, this caused a major rift between Young and the head of Volkswagen of Mexico, who insisted that Young fly to Mexico every few weeks to restart the production line. Young imagined that it would take a few weeks or maybe a month to straighten out the problems and smooth the flow of vehicles before new cars could ship from Puebla. It took over a year. "I was expecting improvement in the quality, but it kept getting worse," said Young.

North of the border, things were getting rough for VW dealers who were having to get by on Passats, GTIs, Cabrios, and Vanagons imported from Germany. Golf and Jetta were the volume cars that attracted traffic to the showroom. Without them, Young knew, sales would slide to the point where many dealers would simply drop the franchise. And many did just that. By this time most of them had paired VW with Mazda, Honda, or even a domestic make like Buick. For many, VW wasn't worth the floor space and signage it cost them.

Young had worked at VW long enough to know how to get things done. As complicated as a global car company is, it can operate in slipshod fashion. And so it was with the monthly meetings of the operating board in Wolfsburg, known as the *Vorstand*. In the spring of 1992,

Young went to the Vorstand meeting, intending to earn approval of an unprecedented plan, based on the previous year's sales, to pay dealers $1,000 for every car they weren't getting from Puebla. If a dealer had sold 500 Jettas and Golfs the year before, he would get a check or checks totaling $500,000 to help him stay in business. Because he had no Golfs and Jettas to advertise, Young would take the money out of the U.S. marketing budget.

Young surmised that he would need about $80 million worth of dealer subsidies. He put the motion into the board book—an agenda for the Vorstand meeting. Typically about 4 inches thick and "so full of crap," says Young, few if any board members bothered to read much of it. A VW board meeting in the late 1980s and early 1990s was not a well-organized affair. Attending were the 12 board members, plus 4 or 5 assistants and interpreters. There were also runners for each board member, like at a session of Congress or the United Nations. Young's proposal to subsidize the dealers came from his sense of fair play. It also arose from fear, though. He knew Volkswagen AG would never understand this plan or the legal issues in play. Because VW served as its dealers' bankers, actually doing their books for them, as well as supplying them cars, they were subject to certain arcane U.S. laws. Because VW could not supply the cars that they were bound by contract to provide, the company could be held liable, according to U.S. law and regulation, for triple the dealers' losses. It would be responsible not for the $80 million that Young was proposing to hand over to the dealers, but for $240 million after lawyers finished the litigation.

Young waited for just the right moment to have his motion voted on, and it passed with no one paying attention to the vote. It was worded in such a way that veiled its intent. He had approval. His ass was covered. Young returned to the Auburn Hills, Michigan, headquarters building and began cutting checks to dealers. Two and a half months into the program, Volkswagen AG Head of Sales and Marketing, Werner Schmidt, called Young on the phone, rebuked him for 10 minutes, and screamed that the program "would bankrupt the company!" It was Schmidt's worry that every future delay on product would spur a payout to dealers based on cars they hadn't sold. Young took it all in, expressed some surprise at Schmidt's incredulity, and then reminded Schmidt that he had, in fact, voted for the plan at the board meeting. Schmidt slammed the phone down without a word.

There was a peculiar disconnect between Volkswagen of America and Volkswagen AG regarding the quality problems that plagued VWs in the late 1980s and early 1990s. While the performance aspects of VWs had always been first rate, and the drivetrains as tough as any company's, the company had long had difficulty with mundane parts and systems, such as window regulators, sunroofs, radios, and windshield wiper motors and arms. Volkswagen of America executives would complain to Wolfsburg, and Wolfsburg would scoff at the Americans. Some Volkswagen AG executives would go so far, says Steve Wilhite, as accusing American dealers of falsifying warranty claims. "They assumed that if a dealer was putting through warranty forms for five window regulators on the same car, they must be scamming Volkswagen," says Wilhite. "The problem is that certain parts were so bad that it would routinely take five times to get one in that was any good."

As national sales manager in the early 1990s when quality was at its worse, says Wilhite, he would listen to German officials speechify that the problem wasn't poor quality, it was that the sales force did not have confidence in the quality of the product, and thus encouraged problems to occur. "It sounds crazy because it was," recalls Wilhite.

The problem was not much better at Audi, though the German division had been run by Piëch since 1988. In 1991, recalls Bill Young, he discovered some $100 million in Audi warranty claims that had not been paid to Volkswagen of America by Audi AG. These were serial warranty claims made by dealers for repairs made, which were paid to dealers by Volkswagen of America, which has responsibility for Audi in the United States. The way the system works is that after Volkswagen of America pays off the dealers, Audi AG is supposed to pay Volkswagen of America; only it hadn't, and for some time. Young went to Germany to have it out with Audi officials because as it stood, the money was laying on the profit-and-loss statement that he had just inherited from his friend Hans Hungerland. Young recalls being lectured by the Audi controller at the time that the problem with Audi in the United States was not poor quality, it was that there were not enough exclusive Audi dealerships. "That was the mindset," said Young. "It was everything except the product."

Meanwhile, in Germany in 1992, Daniel Goeudevert, deputy group chairman and second in command to Dr. Hahn, declared, finally, that Europe's number one automaker faced a "crisis situation," and was barely breaking even—despite worldwide sales of 3.5 million cars and trucks. It was actually not surprising to VW watchers. The company's cost of manufacturing was between 15 and 25 percent higher than any other carmaker, due in part to the abundance of German workers the company could not lay off when business softened. The Japanese were moving into some of VW's strongholds and the United States was a disaster. Still, the company had cash. Again, as is always the case, no one outside VW really knew how much profit there was, or what was being siphoned off into mysterious reserve funds. German corporate accounting methods made following these companies an adventure even for trained Wall Street analysts. Perhaps most troubling, though timely, given Young's decision not to accept the Puebla vehicles, was a recent public admission by Goeudevert that product quality had "deteriorated."

Because of Bill Young's refusal to allow the substandard Jettas and Golfs to enter the United States, sales nose-dived to 49,533. Many auto journalists were writing that VW might have to abandon the United States because its sales were plummeting, and there was no turnaround in sight for Audi.

Shoot the Agency?

Whereas several Volkswagen of America staffers were fed up with DDB's institutional nature, many of the VW dealers openly hated the agency. Calling for DDB's firing became an annual event at the national dealer convention, and had become a quarterly refrain at the VW dealer council meetings. Doyle Dane Bernbach's ads were still seen as effective elsewhere in the world; they actually won numerous international awards for creativity at this time. In the United States, however, the creative product had suffered along with VW's mechanical product. The old DDB agency that created the hall-of-fame advertising in the 1960s was acquired in 1985 by Omnicom Communications, an enormous ad agency holding company, and was merged with another agency, Needham Harper Steers. The resulting agency became known as DDB Needham. Doyle Dane Bernbach Needham had VW and Audi accounts around the world, stemming from the assignment that Carl Hahn gave the U.S. agency back in 1959. The ads were so successful that DDB opened offices wherever VW wanted them—Germany, France, Australia, South Africa, Brazil, and elsewhere. Werner Schmidt, VW's sales and marketing chief, had deep relationships with DDB and favored a single global advertising resource to keep the brand communication consistent from market to market. The more business VW gave DDB around the world, the cheaper the agency worked. At DDB, John Bernbach, son of legendary ad man Bill Bernbach, was responsible for holding the worldwide VW business together. His relationships with Carl Hahn and VW executives in Germany were crucial to keeping the business in tact.

However, as VW's business in the United States gradually unraveled, so did the relationship between the client and the ad agency. By 1992, DDB Chairman Keith Reinhard was as important to the account as Bernbach, and he tried to stay connected to the U.S. business, despite having a global company to run. As Hahn was replaced in Germany by Ferdinand Piëch, Reinhard eased Bernbach out of the VW business and found a new man, Andy Berlin, to hold the U.S. business together. Berlin, who was president of DDB's New York office, had come from Goodby, Berlin, Silverstein in San Francisco, an agency that he cofounded and one of the best creative shops in the country. Berlin and his partners sold out to Omnicom, just as DDB had. In the 1980s, this was the surest way for executives to harvest paydays from the agencies that they had started.

Brawny and bearded, Berlin was urbane and something of an intellectual; he was considered one of the best strategic thinkers in the ad business. He also was a born leader. Unfortunately, he also could be polarizing. Some thought he was the best thing to come along since Bill Bernbach. Others, however, took an instant dislike to him. Omnicom Chairman Bruce Crawford invited Berlin to DDB to fix what had become a troubled and politically torn New York office. Crawford sold him to DDB Chairman Reinhard as someone who could bring harmony to New York's divisive fiefdoms. Unfortunately, Berlin proved a poor political handyman. He rarely suffered fools gladly. However, many of those fools he tried to strong-arm had tight, lucrative ties to major clients. In the ad business, the men and women who run large accounts are like mother lions protecting their cubs. Power at an agency is directly linked to your sway with the client. John Bernbach, for example, had great sway with VW when it was run by Carl Hahn. As soon as Hahn was gone, Bernbach became expendable. Clients came to depend heavily on effective account chiefs. Often, the greatest power at an agency is not with a president like Berlin. Agency presidents come and go with the tide, especially when they jump in from the outside and lack the insulation of high-paying clients who value their unique contributions. Account chiefs such as Bernbach, though, could stay on the same piece of business for decades. When such an account moved to a different agency, it's not uncommon for the account head to follow the business.

————

At the start of 1993, no Jettas or Golfs were flowing north from Mexico, and VW dealers were starving. In the fall of 1992, Bill Young recruited Tom Shaver from General Motors' Saturn Corporation to run the VW brand. Once on board with VW, Shaver tried to make sense of his new assignments, particularly the fouled-up advertising. Dealers, irked over the lack of product and the steady stream of no-impact advertising, called for DDB's scalp. Shaver didn't want his first move to be the major disruption of an advertising review. Neither did he want it to be the one to cancel a 35-year-old contract that had been responsible for some of the most memorable advertising in history. He hesitated, even though the last great VW ad was 20 years old.

Part of Shaver's hesitation sprang from the fact that he liked Andy Berlin. Shaver saw Berlin as a charismatic intellectual from California with a team of young turks to deploy on VW. And the good feelings were mutual: Berlin saw Shaver as someone with new credibility and the ability to drain a lot of bad blood from the relationship between DDB and VW.

Volkswagen was still pitching *Fahrvergnügen* to the public. In 1989, the *Fahrvergnügen* campaign boosted consumer awareness and stimulated showroom traffic; however, it had no staying power. The execution of the ads wasn't very interesting, and the product problems overwhelmed the idea. The joke became that *Fahrvergnügen* actually meant "the pleasure of driving your car to the repair shop and getting a Mazda loaner car." By this time it was as clever as a Beetle with a rusted-out floor.

Shaver approved a campaign that had been produced by DDB's Detroit office in the fall of 1992. It showed beautifully photographed VWs set to the music of an Irish New Age orchestral group called Clannad. Like *Fahrvergnügen,* the campaign generated a lot of short-term attention. However, Tony Wright, the chief strategist on the VW account after Berlin assumed control, noted the ads did nothing to help the brand. "The Clannad campaign was nice to look at, but it offered nothing to the consumer as justification for paying the premium for a VW instead of a Toyota or a Mazda."

To break the ice and generate some chemistry between his and Shaver's teams, Berlin organized a snorkeling trip in January 1993. This allowed the hands at VW in Detroit to escape the Michigan January. Berlin owned a yacht (that previously belonged to McDonald's founder Ray Kroc) that he offered as the venue. It was meant to be a bonding session for the group in order to chart the next heading for VW advertising. Berlin invited Tony Wright, Shaver, VW Director of Marketing Dave Schembri, and Advertising Director Greg Stein. Also aboard were Mike Rogers and Greg Staffen, the DDB creative team appointed by Berlin to work on VW. They brought along videotapes of VW ads from around the world, and Berlin directed his creative team to present their ideas for the launch of the new Golf and Jetta models to the clients. With antiseasickness bands strapped to their wrists, the sailing party took off for its 80-mile cruise.

They didn't get far. An earlier storm had left the waters choppy, causing the boat to pitch violently. A clock radio flew off a shelf, cold-cocking Staffen. As the bow slapped against the water with each swell, Shaver and Stein queasily watched the video monitor. Schembri excused himself and retreated to the head, looking ashen from nausea. "Good idea, this bonding session," DDB's account executive for VW Tony Wright told Berlin. After 30 stomach-turning minutes, a chastened Berlin turned the boat back to the harbor, where the meeting continued in the calmer waters of the marina.

In truth, the day on the boat was a bad experience for reasons other than the weather. The ad sketches Staffen and Rogers brought positioned the VW brand rather than the new products. "A lot of warm and fuzzy stuff," said DDB creative Mike Rogers, "which, of course, was completely wrong, and they let us know it." Volkswagen was desperate to start selling cars, and while it needed a brand idea, it also needed a retail strategy. Moreover, even though the videotapes showed what DDB was capable of abroad, the work done for the U.S. market paled in comparison. On that fateful trip, they sought inspiration for a new theme line for a new campaign, but got nowhere.

In February 1993, Berlin, Wright, and the DDB creative team traveled to Germany to drive the new VWs and discuss a marketing strategy with Volkswagen AG executives. There were many points to consider. The new Golfs and Jettas that would emerge from VW's problem-plagued plant in Mexico were the first significant upgrades in 8 years. Once the glitches were worked out and the assembly lines were at full capacity, dealers would finally have a competitive product to sell. In addition, VW would launch the cars with the most aggressive incentives in its industry: a 10-year/100,000-mile warranty, 2 years of free maintenance, and a lease deal that was under $200 a month. In addition, VW believed that the new advertising theme had to match the power of BMW's "Ultimate Driving Machine," a slogan that the Germans admired a great deal.

Staffen and Rogers had done a commercial for VW in 1988. In that spot, VWs slalomed around German engineers in white lab coats. The ads were well received by the client and dealers, but they fell flat in the marketplace. Itching for another crack at VW, Staffen and Rogers came back from Germany with the idea that eluded them on the ill-fated boat trip. Their new line for VW: "Happy Driving."

Berlin hit the ceiling. "If you guys think I'm walking down the hall to tell Keith Reinhard that his *Fahrvergnügen* line is being dumped for 'Happy Driving,' you're out of your bloody minds," he bellowed. "Andy pummeled us," recalls Staffen.

Therefore, it was back to work on a new line. Unlike many agency bosses struggling to save a major account, Berlin did not throw a legion of creative teams at the problem; Rogers and Staffen were it. A few hard days and long nights later, they told Berlin they had it. The two had picked up on an oft-mentioned frustration expressed by the client. While Volkswagen had tumbled in the United States, losing the confidence of many consumers, how could the company trumpet its redis-covered solidity and strength and that it was Europe's top carmaker? Set to images of people in Europe and Japan loving their VWs, the tagline that was presented to Berlin; ultimately sold through to Shaver, and taken all the way to the German who was now in charge of Volks-wagen AG's North American business, Jens Neumann; and Ferdinand Piëch was "The Most Loved Cars in the World."

By early summer 1993, Schembri was replaced as VW director of marketing by longtime VW employee Dave Huyett. Huyett was at the Audi division where he took part in firing DDB, which had been doing Audi work from its Chicago office. He then hired McKinney & Silver, a small North Carolina agency. If Shaver was still finding his way around VW at the time, Huyett was a grizzled veteran with the company since the 1970s. Huyett and told Berlin he wanted to fire DDB, and he had the go-ahead from Germany. "At the stage we were at, we needed to be the focus of the top management of our ad agency. We felt like our challenges were bigger than the attention that a big multi-national agency could give us. It was much the same situation at Audi," Huyett told Berlin.

In late July, Shaver and Huyett flew to New York to meet with Berlin and Wright. The four, plus Reinhard, had previously discussed setting up a DDB division that would serve VW alone. No other client distractions. An agency that was completely devoted to VW and its myriad of marketing problems. There would be no more questions of VW getting enough time and resources from the agency's best people. However, when they sat down at P. J. Clarke's over hamburgers, the VW executives said that there was a problem. Volkswagen's dealers had rejected the idea. The dealers wanted DDB gone, and they wanted nothing else. The dealers, in fact, did not like the new advertising, and neither did Steve Wilhite, VW's national sales manager. The Germans, however, liked it very much. So, not only were there deep divisions in the company about the agency, but about the new ad strategy as well.

"We had been pushing for a change in the advertising for some time," said Chris von Berg, a VW dealer in Laurel, Maryland, and head of the VW retailer council's marketing committee. "We had been with the same agency for a long, long time. It was just good business to do it."

It may have been good business, but it wasn't the right time. Staffen and Rogers had just returned from a month of shooting "The Best Loved Cars in the World," TV advertising at great expense. Before Huyett's arrival, Shaver bought into the strategy, which included a carefully managed raft of retail ads, some cleverly focused on the dealers themselves in each market. The floor traffic and sales numbers from the early markets were good. Many dealers, however, still didn't have a supply of new Golfs and Jettas and thus didn't have advertising in their market; they were calling for DDB's head.

Neither Shaver nor Huyett wanted a review yet. The 9-month interruption—4 or 5 months for a review, and 4 or 5 months to get the new agency up to speed—would be devastating in the midst of the launch. However, they had the dealers to contend with. At the same time, with sales trending toward less than 50,000, they needed to shake things up. They liked the idea of a spin-off agency. What's more, they wanted Berlin and Wright. "I thought they had the right energy for what we needed," said Shaver. The question, said Wright, became: "Could they have us without DDB? And the answer became, 'sort of.'"

The spin-off agency solved both Shaver's and Huyett's problem for the time being, as well as Berlin's and Wright's. Both Berlin and Wright

wanted to break off from DDB for the same reasons as the VW dealers. They'd become frustrated with the politics and infighting that
gripped the agency. It was a time-wasting, soul-sapping work environment. Berlin and Wright were ambitious and were getting bogged
down in petty things within the halls of DDB that had nothing to do
with producing advertising. Everyone who wanted an end to the relationship between DDB and VW had valid reasons.

———

Ferdinand Piëch ascended to the chairmanship of Volkswagen AG in
January 1993 and began a housecleaning of Dr. Hahn's disciples, the
likes of which VW had not seen before. Most of the 12 board members would be gone in less than a year, leaving just five of Piëch's
trusted associates.

Among those on the hit list were Hans Hungerland and Bill Young.
Piëch disliked Hungerland immensely because of his close association
with Hahn. Hungerland had worked in the United States in the 1970s
and was president of Volkswagen of America. After Jim Fuller and
Lou Marengo were killed in 1988, Young was on the cut list because of
his close ties to Hungerland. Hungerland warned Young that Piëch
was gunning for them both. Young had already endured two and a half
years longer than he thought possible. He hoped that his stand against
bringing the defective Jettas and Golfs to the United States would be
recognized by Piëch as a courageous act, thus preserving his job.

Shortly after Piëch took over, he appointed Dr. Jens Neumann to be
the board member in charge of North America. Neumann went to
Auburn Hills to meet with Young, Huyett, and Wilhite and assess
where things stood: the Puebla plant, marketing, dealer relations, and
so forth. It was a good meeting. Young had done the right thing by
stopping the Puebla supply of cars. However, Neumann went into
Young's office, thanked him for a wonderful meeting, and then apolo-
gized for having to ask for his resignation per Piëch's orders. Young
expected this but resented it, nonetheless. At first he refused and wondered aloud with the amiable Neumann if there might be another way.
Young had worked hard holding the line and keeping dealers together

when the United States was starved of decent product. Even though he missed the warmth of Manhattan Beach, California, he had become attached to VW—the dealers, the cars, and the brand.

Young was a hero to the people who worked for him and who knew what he'd done to keep the leaky ship afloat. Volkswagen in America would have been a hollow company supplying damn few dealers if it had not been for Young's insistence that the cars in Mexico be delayed and his guile in getting the dealers compensated. Young had made sacrifices for the company. He gave up a nice consulting business in 1988 to move back to Michigan when VW called. He felt that he wasn't through with the work he had started; what's more, Young wanted to leave on *his* own terms. Given all this, he wanted Piëch to reconsider, for Neumann to change the chief executive's mind.

"Mr. Young," said Neumann, according to Young, "I have worked with Dr. Piëch for more than ten years. I can't tell you for sure if the sun is going to rise tomorrow, but I can promise you one thing Dr. Piëch has never done in his whole life, and that is change his mind."

With that, Bill Young went back to Manhattan Beach.

The dismissal of Young for what amounted to personal reasons stung the Young loyalists all the more a few months after his departure when Dr. Piëch made what was for the time stunning admissions about the quality problems that beset the company. In a videotape that was circulated to managers around the world, Piëch admitted that enormous changes had to take place, and had to take place fast if the company was going to avoid ruin.

"In describing the drastic situation the company is in, the purpose is to bring home to everyone the fact that we have to make enormous effort and we haven't much time to do so. Many years have been lost," said Piëch via translation.

The first thing to be attacked, he said, would have to be quality. "The number of defects per vehicle manufactured has increased. Product quality has decreased appreciably over the last ten years. Here the company has forfeited the lead it once had over it competitors. The second area is high cost. Purchasing, production logistics, assembly and labor are all extremely uneconomical. On an international level, Volkswagen is a long way down the list on manufacturing costs. I'm quite aware of the 25 percent, 30 percent cost difference between us and the Japanese."

In addition, he said, the company is hardly competitive when it comes to vehicle per employee. As a result of high costs, profits have fallen dramatically over the past several years. "Quality problems, runaway costs and a negative profit development are the actual causes of our current situation. How can we regain our competitive advantage? In the following order we must address quality, service and profits. I am deeply convinced that the first results in the second. We must work toward goals of quality and service, not revenue if we are to succeed. This concept will work provided the following priorities are observed in implementing it. First of all, the customer. He who best fulfills most of his customers' needs will win. To do that, one must know what the consumer wants. We must change one little thing. We can no longer supply the market with what the individual engineer considers right. But first listen to what the customers really wants. What they are prepared to pay for. And do that. Our second implementation priority—product, not process must be placed first if we are going to manufacture economically. We must concentrate on producing a technically perfect end product, the bedrock of customer satisfaction and far less on the inner workings of our bureaucracy."

Besides being a total vindication of Bill Young's decisions to refuse the poor products from Mexico, these remarks of Piëch's marked a startling change of direction and philosophy for a company that just months earlier had been blaming dealers and sales managers for product defects. "It was really a clarion call," says Wilhite. "That, hey, we have to get this thing going and turned around."

Another of Piëch's priorities as spelled out in this video locker room pep talk was communication. "More communication and individual autonomy. The improvement of communication is of central importance as a means of implementation. Efficient communication processes promote individual decision-making abilities. An excellent means of making full use of the creativity and abilities of those individuals actually doing the work. The prerequisite for this is that management allow the doers to develop their capabilities within this newly established form. I expect from management a delegation of power to ground level to the people who actually do the work. In other words, assigning the production process to the workers and development to the specialists . . . management must be responsible for helping and supporting all levels of the vast system from the bottom up."

"These were massive changes," recalls Steve Wilhite. "This had long been a company that was thick with bureaucracy, and everything in triplicate twice before decisions were made or funds committed."

Piëch's remarks concluded: "The name Volkswagen will once again mean Volkswagen. Die Erfolgreichsten." Translation: The best.

So startled by the words, Wilhite traveled with a copy of the tape for the next 5 years wherever he went. He was going to take the directions to heart. And if ever he was challenged, he was going to play the tape for the challenger so they could see that he was only following orders.

Moving On

The year 1994 was a great and turbulent year in the history of VW. It was a year that people now look back on as crucial to the decision to keep VW in America. The first part of the year was witness to enormous response by the press and public to the Concept 1, the show car that would become the New Beetle. It surpassed all expectations. Yet, it was a terribly painful year for the people who determined that hundreds of people had to be fired, as well as for those who lost their jobs.

That January, 59-year-old Clive Warrilow came down from Canada to lead Volkswagen of America, succeeding John Kerr, who briefly held the position following the departure of Bill Young. Warrilow, South African born, had run the Canadian business since 1988. He'd risen through the ranks in South Africa, eventually running the operation before coming to North America.

Despite the subsidies given to dealers while no cars were being shipped from Puebla, dealers were still going out of business. In some cases, they just abandoned franchises that were then picked up for free by qualified dealers pouncing on an opportunity. Picking up a VW franchise in this way was *almost* like picking up a Kia or Daewoo franchise in the late 1990s. Volkswagen had fallen so far from grace, with U.S. operations running at so deep a loss, that few expected the company to remain in the United States. The U.S. staff was reeling, having seen the much-loved Bill Young get axed by Dr. Piëch, followed only by an interim term from Kerr. Many were familiar with Warrilow, from his frequent visits from north of the border, but the company was awash in as much cynicism as red ink. Yes, the New Beetle had just been shown to incredible applause. Some people were talking positively about VW in a way that they hadn't for a long time. Cynicism from dealers and long-time VW hands still gripped the organization, though.

"It was bad and getting worse," says Warrilow. "We were selling discounts and not product. We had lost the respect of the dealers. Marketing had become very confused. The ads for the individual models didn't seem to go together, and the umbrella campaign, or so-called brand campaign, hit with a thud. It had been campaign after campaign. The flavor of the month. And 'The Best Loved Cars in the World' was as bad as every other. That's what happens when you get desperate, and the situation was desperate," said Warrilow.

Under the guidance and direction of Jens Neumann, Warrilow combined the operations of the United States and Canada. Bill Young had been making staff cuts for years—8 percent here and 9 percent there. As people retired, they weren't replaced. Functions were combined and trimmed as best they could be. With the sales volume decline in 1993 and Volkswagen AG growing tired of writing a check to balance the annual books, Warrilow soon realized that he needed a chain saw, not a scissors. Meanwhile, Neumann was sent to the United States by Piëch to see if there was enough left of the U.S. market to build upon, or rather rebuild upon.

The dealers were up in arms, and about 85 percent of them had brought another brand of car into their showrooms. Some dealers brought in more than one brand. Competing for mind share among the ranks of their own dealers and salesforce became a major hurdle to success. If a salesperson could place a customer into a Honda or Mazda with ease, why should he or she break his or her neck to convince someone to buy a Jetta? If a customer came in with a *Consumer Reports* magazine article, they already knew that VW's quality was down the drain. In Canada, Warrilow had the advantage of a dealer network that comprised exclusive showrooms. Canadian dealers were as enraged as their U.S. counterparts, but they lacked another brand to offset the VW losses.

Warrilow sized things up and established a team of staffers including Marketing Chief Steve Wilhite. Their charge was to reinvent the company—redesign it to make some money now that Golfs and Jettas were coming in. The team was squirreled away for more than a month trying to figure out a comeback strategy. A series of long, hard meetings in Auburn Hills followed, working over budgets until the numbers came out right. There was an endless stream of pizza boxes coming in over the course of weeks, recalls Dave Huyett.

It was a very difficult time. A list was hung on a wall, a catalog of employees who composed each department. Names kept getting crossed off as departments were pared, functions eliminated, and assets sold. "We let forty-seven percent of our people go, because there was no other way to reach profitability," says Warrilow. The team closed zone offices and got the people in the field to work from home on computers. The culmination of months of research revealed one thing to the team: VW was circling the drain. "We didn't need research to tell us that, so we abandoned the research department," says Warrilow. They eliminated the dealer business consulting operation, by this time a bad joke. Volkswagen actually tried to *charge* dealers for company advice, despite having screwed so many of them with terrible product, ineffective ads, and endless, petty battles over product color and equipment. If VW couldn't get that stuff right, how could it justify charging for business advice? It was very radical. "It was also very difficult for our German colleagues to swallow, because they don't do that in Germany," says Warrilow. "They don't have such radical restructuring that results in such dramatic job loss. I never understood the German mindset in this regard. But they saw that things were so bad here that they gave us a free hand to try anything." The group was not unaware that their work paring down the company, for what they hoped would be future profitability, might also be a good way of preparing it for elimination.

Warrilow's team set out to craft a new, lean organizational structure that was unlike any in the industry. The team grew very focused, even as it blasted away with its blunderbuss. Skills and ability alone didn't determine who was let go and who was kept. It was attitude. "We didn't have the sales volumes to support the structure we had," said Warrilow. "And we had too many people that had been with the company too long and had developed a cynicism that was a real cultural problem." The team cherry-picked the keepers based on their own experiences with them and let the cynics go. It was done very subjectively, but the people handling the restructuring knew who the cynics were. "Cynics will kill you, and the company was full of cynics," said Warrilow. In fact, Warrilow had to let half of his leadership go, including Tom Shaver, who'd been brought over from Saturn by Bill Young in an effort to impart some of the Saturn thinking to VW. Saturn had reinvented both customer service and dealership marketing—indeed, the dealership experience. Saturn also had some of the best advertising in the business. Warrilow said Shaver "was a great guy, and valuable," but the dealers tore him to pieces. They were furious over lack of product and lame advertising, and "he was just in the wrong place at the wrong time," says Warrilow.

"It was probably the worst period of my life," says Steve Wilhite, then the general sales manager. "We had to let a lot of our friends go, people who had been with the company a long time and who loved Volkswagen."

Along with cutting overhead, Warrilow knew he had to resurrect the brand image. That meant making the dealers and customers happy and making money. As president of Volkswagen of Canada, he achieved some stability there. He had a reputation for honesty and candor and often told dealers that if they couldn't trust him, he would resign. In return for that pledge, he asked that they be intelligent and trustworthy themselves. Warrilow revamped VW's marketing in Canada in large part by securing approval from Wolfsburg to fire DDB Needham soon after he arrived. For years DDB hadn't offered the Canadian market anything but slightly retooled U.S. ads. Volkswagen's fortunes in Canada were so desperate in the late 1980s when he arrived that when he wanted to change ad agencies, no one, not even DDB, put up much of a fuss.

Despite having grown up in VW's rigid system, Warrilow realized for more than a decade that a management style based on beating people with a stick left much to be desired. Making employees go by the book and forcing them to check, double-check, and triple-check their decisions endlessly up the line was not a good way to manage. It had become all about protecting yourself at VW through wearisome bureaucracy, instead of everyone working toward the overall health of the corporate body. This was typical of German companies; people were not generally empowered to act independently. Get it done by committee, always by committee. Indeed, Bill Young's laudable entrepreneurial approach to problem solving earned him many enemies in Wolfsburg—this and his candor in telling too many Germans that they made really lousy cars.

"Hard drinking and late nights. Up the dealers. Make sure you are covered nine ways from Sunday before you spend any money. Pad the expense accounts. It became a way of life," says Warrilow.

When Warrilow arrived at VW in the United States, though, the red ink was overflowing. Volkswagen AG seriously considered pulling out of the United States. Piëch ultimately didn't want to, but at the time his ambivalence ran deep. If there was no future for VW in the United States, he wanted to know so he could channel the resources into markets with greater potential. He had big plans, and he needed money to accomplish them. If the U.S. section of the company could be rebuilt, he wanted to know that, too. He also knew that no matter what his ambitions were for building up the company, full potential could never be realized if VW abandoned the greatest consumer market in the world. At the bottom, however, the continued losses and disarray could not continue.

After sacking Young, Neumann went to the United States in late 1993 on a fact-finding mission: Were the dealers still committed, and could the U.S. team achieve profitability in the foreseeable future? Neumann hated the idea of leaving the United States. One of Piëch's loyal lieutenants, Neumann also saw rebuilding the U.S. market as an opportunity to shine for Piëch. Turning around the valuable U.S. market could vault Neumann ahead of his rivals back in Wolfsburg.

Warrilow, as well, had no desire for VW to exit the United States on his watch. Warrilow had spent many years coming to the United States, learning and adapting techniques for the South African market. As the head of Volkswagen of Canada, he'd sat in monthly meetings with Bill Young, John Kerr, and Neumann hashing out problems. Over the years he'd made friends with many VW employees and even some U.S. dealers. Enough U.S. managers were committed to saving the company that Warrilow and Neumann believed there was a core team that deserved a shot at making VW great again in North America.

Warrilow took people at Auburn Hills aside in his office and over lunches, and he told them that they had three objectives: (1) sell cars, (2) take care of customers, and (3) make money. He didn't care how they did it, but it was *their* responsibility. If what they were doing didn't achieve all three, they should reevaluate and ask for help. They had jobs to do, and he wasn't going to micromanage them. He also said that he would sign any invoice or expense report put in front of him, but if he caught them stealing from the company in terms of their expense reports, "they should take their jackets and leave." He asked each one to shake his hand, and he told them that he was being held to the same standard. This was a new way of business for VW veterans, used to hierarchies and quadruple signatures. "VW had become like working for the government. . . . I had to change that or we didn't stand a chance of turning things around so we could make some money," says Warrilow. In the past, numerous committees double- and triple-checking up and down the line were expected. Volkswagen executives who were recruited from General Motors and Chrysler enforced the German method of business, because it was the Big-Three way of doing things, too. "We took a sledge-hammer to all that," says Warrilow.

Empowerment

Warrilow had become a devoted believer in individual empower-
ment. He had empowered people to be independent thinkers and
problem solvers in South Africa, and even more so in Canada. At one
time in his career, he was much like the Germans to whom he
reported; after a while he began to resent their way of doing business.
He, like the Germans, had once believed in telling people what to do
and making sure that they did what they were told. Paper trails and
accountability—that was the German way. Warrilow, however, began
to change his ways, first at home with his own teenage children and
then at the office. He recalled sitting at home with his children one
summer, laying out the family's next vacation—the places, the dates,
the routes, and the sights. One of his sons chirped up and said, "Hold
on, Dad. Can we talk about where we're going and if we all want to
go there?" Recalls Warrilow: "I thought, hey, this is interesting. I
found that involving my kids more in family business made for a better family. And I began changing the way I worked with people at the
office in the same way. It sounds awfully basic, but it's the truth."

Perhaps the most dramatic way of communicating his philosophy
to a crew of battle-weary VW executives would come about 18
months into the restructuring in 1996 when Warrilow saw that not
everyone understood what he wanted. Warrilow took three busloads
of VW staffers to a dusty farm in Solvang, California. The group
climbed a circular catwalk and gathered around a corral, hanging their
arms over the fence. The executives had no idea what they were in for.
Monty Roberts, better known in books and the movies as the "Horse
Whisperer," entered the pen with a young, unbroken colt. They
watched for about 45 minutes as Roberts practiced his magic and got
the horse to accept a saddle, bridle, and harness. Before Roberts, the
accepted way of breaking a horse was to break its spirit. It can take
months, even years, with some horses and can involve physical abuse,
even the breaking of bones. Roberts, on the other hand, never even
raised his voice. He developed his unique and natural technique by
watching wild mustangs and observing how brood mares disciplined

their young. Roberts tells of his own father breaking horses with incredible brutality. He was equally brutal with Roberts, punishing him for being too gentle with animals. Roberts noticed that brood mares, in contrast to human wranglers, signal displeasure to irascible foals by locking eyes on them, as a predator would, and angling their bodies away to show forgiveness. Roberts travels the world teaching the brood mare's technique to those who want to train animals, as well as rehabilitate abused animals.

Businesses, however, such as VW and Merrill Lynch also have hired Roberts to demonstrate the method as a metaphor for management— carrots instead of sticks. The idea is to create thinkers instead of automatons. Empower people to succeed, not threaten them with a fear of failure. Neumann said it is the soft side of the business, a side of industry that Germans typically ignore. "At that time, the Germans were still letting us run our own show, and not getting in our way too much, so anything we tried was okay as long as sales volumes and revenues were headed in the right direction," Warrilow said. A *Forbes* magazine article reported on Warrilow's outing and quoted Neumann as saying the exercise wouldn't work in Germany and might be too esoteric.[1]

Lock and Load

In 1994, VW put all of the money it had into a deal on Golfs and Jettas. They were $199 a month on lease with no money down. Virtually all other incentives were scrapped. The organization gave promotion budgets to the zone managers to use as they saw fit, benefiting the dealers who they thought would use it most wisely. Zone managers were to be judged on results and were not to check with headquarters for every dollar they spent. This was the new way.

In mid-1994, Warrilow and Wilhite began squawking to Germany about wanting to fire Berlin Wright Cameron, the DDB Needham spin-off created in 1993. Beleaguered and frustrated, VW dealers never learned to love the spin-off agency. It was still DDB to them, and most of them hated DDB. Berlin Wright Cameron was on thin ice from the start of 1994 when Warrilow arrived. A Passat commercial was the deciding factor that led Warrilow to ask Volkswagen AG for approval to fire the VW ad agency. In the TV ad, a busy office awaits the arrival of the new company president, who happens to be a woman. Colleagues skittishly ask each other who had gone to the airport to fetch her in a limousine. It's then revealed that a geeky junior assistant has gone to pick up the new president in a VW Passat. The office managers are aghast that a limo was not ordered. The geeky young man meets the new president (an unappealing, imperial sort). She soon takes notice of the car, especially its roomy leather interior. She runs her hand over the leather seats and looks up at the driver in the rearview mirror, obviously impressed. The scene shifts to the young man pulled over on the shoulder of the highway calling his office from a pay phone, reporting that the new president wishes to go for a longer drive. He's disheveled and his shirt is pulled out of his trousers.

"It was a terrible ad. The wrong strategic idea. The wrong casting. The wrong message. It was a degradation of the brand," says Steve Wilhite, then the general sales manager. It was that ad that made Warrilow, with support from the dealers and Germans, promote Wilhite to head of marketing. Wilhite was further peeved at Andy Berlin when, during a meeting, the agency president summed up his assessment of the VW brand: "It's a brand that isn't for assholes." Recalls Wilhite, "I was really taken aback that he would boil down the brand and all of its qualities and equities into such an arrogant statement." No stranger to profanity himself, Wilhite didn't object to Berlin's expletive, but to the arrogance in the statement.

For his part, Berlin remembers being painted into a corner. "I was given this potato to save for DDB called the Volkswagen account," he recalled. "The agency had VW accounts all over the world. While the U.S. account was no longer crucial to the agency's financial success, symbolically it was huge. The work of the old DDB was legendary and people at the agency hung onto it as part of their heritage, even though all those responsible were gone. When Dr. Piëch was named chairman in 1992, and the relationship between Dr. Hahn and John Bernbach was no longer a factor, I knew it would be very difficult for us. The dealers wanted us out—they saw us as an extension of DDB, and they wanted little else."

Following the debacle of the Passat launch, Warrilow and Wilhite began lobbying Germany for permission to hold an agency review, to begin the search for a new advertising partner. The experiment with the DDB spin-off didn't work to keep the ad business in the family. In fact, because Berlin's agency was one step removed from DDB, it actually made it easier for Warrilow and Wilhite to get permission to fire them. Still, tradition-minded VW executives crowded the skies between Auburn Hills and Wolfsburg, and sweaty-palmed DDB executives went to Wolfsburg to try to prevent the review from happening. In the end, Warrilow said, "I think things were so bad in the U.S. at that point the Germans were ready to let us do anything we thought could help. When business gets as bad as it was, it's remarkable what your masters will let you do, because there is so little to lose at that point."

Meanwhile, Neumann was trying to clear up snags at the ports and distribution points so that dealers could get the cars they ordered more quickly. Customers who had ordered new cars from the factory were told that delivery would take a few weeks, but that promise turned into a couple of months. The system was so fouled that dealers couldn't give their customers any realistic idea of when their cars would arrive. Neumann went to San Francisco in February 1994 to address the VW dealers at the National Automobile Dealers Association. Everyone was prepared for a blood bath. It was Warrilow's and Neumann's first dealer meeting since he and Warrilow moved in following Dr. Piëch's appointment and Young's dismissal. The dealers were in open revolt, with more threatening to abandon their franchises. Many were still angered over the treatment of Young, who had gone to extraordinary lengths to save the brand and keep committed dealers in business. All were suspicious and feared the South African and the German would put forth nothing but double-talk.

The VW dealers who also had Audi franchises knew of Neumann from his days as Audi's top lawyer. He had orchestrated the company's legal response to U.S. lawsuits charging that Audi 5000s were prone to sudden acceleration. This, however, was his first time speaking to VW dealers as a group. Neumann was tasked by Piëch to see if any of the dealers remained above the creeping cynicism. Neumann was disinclined to return to Wolfsburg saying that VW was dead in the United States. He did not want VW to follow in the ignominious footsteps of Fiat, Peugeot, and Renault. Those companies never achieved anything close to the brand equity—the Beetle-engendered love—that VW had built. In addition, their products and dealer organizations were far inferior to VW's.

Neumann got the job to run the Americas because he had been educated in the United States, and the Germans thought he was best suited to figure out the VW debacle in the United States. Neumann was born in Germany but attended Friends High School in Baltimore, Maryland, in the late 1950s and early 1960s as an exchange student. He graduated in 1962 and loved his time in the United States. He was known as Mr. Energy at school, a tag he still wears today. Neumann was introduced to the dealers by first showing a slide of his graduation picture from *The Quaker*, his high school's annual. He is sitting on top of a VW Beetle, wearing a huge grin. The caption in the annual, which Tom Shaver read: "Born with the gift of laughter and a sense that the world is mad." Neumann was active in music (he is an accomplished pianist and a decent singer) and played varsity football, basketball, and tennis. He also sang in the choir and acted. The point was to introduce him as a German, yes, but a German with more than a few clues about the United States. He was not just another German with a disdain for U.S. drivers and their penchant for automatic transmissions, soft suspensions, and cupholders.

The dealers wanted answers. Neumann was smart enough to know that he couldn't blow smoke and sunshine at these dealers. His plan was to lay it on the line—and he did.

Said Neumann: "We want to get out of this rut. We want to regain our pride in working for Volkswagen. We want success. Yes, for business reasons. But also not to be ridiculed any more by our competitors. Or, and this probably hurts most, by our friends and neighbors." Neumann had visited Mexico and the ports. He had spent time in

Auburn Hills. His mission was to streamline the system so the right cars arrived at port and made it to the dealers. It was also to fix VW's delivery delays, the worst in the industry. (Around this time, Neumann attended a J. D. Power and Associates roundtable and had to endure discussions and slideshows about how VW ranked next to last among the opinions of *all* dealers. Only Alfa Romeo ranked lower.) He impressed on the dealers the need to push Golfs and Jettas because they were finally arriving in force from Mexico. It was vital to rebuild sales volumes, and he thought it possible to achieve a 100 percent sales increase in 1994. Some dealers were enthusiastic, having seen Concept 1 the month before at the Detroit Auto Show. Most, however, thought it was too little too late. Furthermore, they had no guarantees at that point that the New Beetle would ever be built. Many believed it was just a publicity stunt to garner goodwill, which it did. As it was, many potential customers were turning up at dealerships wanting to see the New Beetle. However, many dealers worried that Concept 1 was just setting consumers (and dealers) up for more disappointment.

Despite the dubious dealers, Neumann ploughed on: "I am not going to make big commitments or promises to you. It is your turn to judge whether we are trustworthy by our actions and whether we practice what we preach. Finally, if not, you will make a sound business decision and drop Volkswagen as a franchise. The customer will continue to ignore us. The decline will continue and I'm afraid at the end of the day no decision in Wolfsburg is needed any more. . . . If Walt Disney sells happiness, I propose to you that Volkswagen creates sympathy. Now, this may be a funny word to your ears, but being European, sympathy means positive sympathetic feelings. Like Germans would say 'sympatische,' the Italians 'simpatico,' or the French 'très sympathique.' This is the kind of sympathy I mean when I talk of sympathy. It's some human chemistry thing going on which you cannot really describe in words. So let us create these sympathetic feelings by treating people with responsibility, sensitivity and care."

"That was quite a meeting," said New Jersey dealer Adam Green. "Dr. Neumann handled himself and a very difficult situation and setting as well as I've ever seen. So many dealers were hurting. I have to say I never thought about selling or giving up my franchise. There was too much value in Volkswagen to walk away."

———

Sales climbed from 49,000 in 1993 to 97,000 by the end of 1994. The company's assessment of its place in the U.S. market, however, was still pretty negative. Sales *were* up now that cars were flowing from Puebla, but the figures might just have been the result of pent-up demand from die-hard VW enthusiasts. Overall, though, brand awareness was still down, and new customers were not exactly flocking to the dealerships at the required rates.

The Passat ad from Berlin Wright Cameron that Warrilow and Wilhite—and Neumann for that matter—had hated was the last straw. Wilhite and Warrilow had finally received permission to hold a review for the U.S. account. It would be the start of a new era for VW in the United States when the process for selecting a new ad agency was completed.

The Pitch

SEVEN

We shall not cease from exploration.
And at the end of all our exploring
will be to arrive where we started
and know the place for the first time.

T. S. ELIOT[1]

When hardship is the rule of one's life, it can be difficult, sometimes impossible, to articulate what exactly is missing. It's no different for a marketer trying to save one of America's most beloved brand names, and find what wasn't working. "The decision to hire a new ad agency was all about trying to get centered on our values," says Steve Wilhite. "Something magical had been lost. When you are in a space like that you wonder what was, but struggle to articulate what you're looking for. The words that wind up in a presentation or white paper are inadequate. People talk *around* it. They can't paint the full picture. But when it happens, you know it. When you happen back upon it. It may not *be* the same. In fact it won't be. But it *feels* the same. That's when you know it's right."

Wilhite compares this time of early 1995 as his hope that VW could become *born again,* not unlike the way it happens in the religious context. "When you are a kid, and you go to church and learn all the magical stuff, it's great. But then you get older and get caught up in the institution and the dogmas, and that thing is lost. I was hoping we

could almost recapture the marketing equivalent of a child's innocence."

Wilhite's analogy may seem overserious, but it works to describe
VW's lot in 1994. It was at rock bottom. It is in such human predica-
ments, however, that people turn to God and become *born again*.

Part of the problem between Volkswagen of America and Volkswagen AG was that Wilhite and Clive Warrilow believed that the
image of VW in the United States had to divorce itself from what
Volkswagen AG wanted as the world brand scheme. Volkswagen in
Germany had long been following a brand positioning that loosely
translates to "Volkswagen: You know what you have." There was not
much emotion in the message. The German parent, for example, saw
VW as a car for everyone, and a brand that is grounded in honesty, reliability, and consistency. *Emotional* was defined as *lastingly likable*. Wilhite didn't see that as a viable or logical positioning for VW in Europe,
let alone in the United States where the marketing landscape is far different.

Round Up the Usual Suspects

With Wolfsburg's approval to fire DDB Needham from the U.S. advertising account, Steve Wilhite called Chicago consultant Jones-Lundin,
which had helped Dave Huyett with the review for the Audi account in
1993. The Audi advertising went to McKinney & Silver, a small but creative agency in North Carolina, far away from the Michigan rust belt.
The choice of McKinney & Silver surprised many in the industry, but,
like VW now, Audi had nothing to lose. Sales had fallen to a mere
12,000 in 1991, and the company and brand were still reeling from the
devastating publicity in 1987 when *60 Minutes* reported on Audi owners and plaintiffs' lawyers who charged that Audi 5000 sedans accelerated out of control. The Audi team had selected McKinney for its
creative talents and because the agency was hungry for a car account.
At McKinney, Audi, despite its woes and small sales, would get kingly
treatment and attention from McKinney's best people. Wilhite wanted
the same thing for VW.

There were not many ad agencies available to VW and its $100 million advertising account. Most of the good ones already had car accounts; however, there were a handful of smallish creative agencies that were free of conflicts. Jones-Lundin started out with a field of 20 agencies that responded to its overtures and were capable of handling a car account with its many demands, including: Publicis/Bloom, Dallas, Texas, and New York; Earle Palmer Brown, Richmond, Virginia; Jordan, McGrath, Case & Taylor, New York; Tatham Euro RSCG, Chicago; Suissa Miller, Los Angeles; and Hill, Holliday, Connors & Cosmopoulas, Boston. These were perennial candidates for car accounts whenever one became available. A few had even made it to a final shoot-out among three or four agencies, but they always came up short. The list of 20 was whittled to 8, and then to 5, including DDB. Despite the allure of a car account, a few of the top agencies in the country actually opted out of competing. They didn't think it was worth it. If VW wanted to give them the business, okay. The agencies that passed, however, didn't want to go through a huge, expensive, and consuming process that a car pitch required and then come up empty.

Ad agencies that aspire to grow above $300 million in combined billings from its clients want a car account. It's a high-profile piece of business that generates big revenue. A car account is also a rallying point for employees and puts an agency on a national stage. The four agencies that had cleared the hurdles: (1) Deutsch, a New York agency that had received a great deal of publicity over the previous 4 years, and whose principal, Donny Deutsch, had become the media's favorite sound-bite source on advertising issues; (2) The Richards Group of Dallas, Texas, which also had a charismatic, creative chairman, Stan Richards, and had gotten attention for its work on Home Depot, Motel 6, and some regional Cadillac dealers; (3) Martin-Williams of Minneapolis, Minnesota, having achieved a reputation as a quiet, but highly creative print agency; and (4) Arnold Fortuna Lawner & Cabot of Boston, an agency that was an amalgam of some recently merged agencies.

Doyle Dane Bernbach Needham would also compete. As far as Wilhite and Warrilow were concerned DDB was dead, but because the agency had held the business for so long, and still created most of VW's advertising around the world, VW's German management insisted it be allowed to pitch. Even Wilhite admits that DDB deserved to compete; however, he was reasonably sure they would impress no one. His worry, though, was that, because the Germans would participate in the review, DDB might do just well enough to allow VW AG marketing chief Werner Schmidt to decide at the end of the process that none of the new contenders did well enough to unseat DDB. That would be the worst possible outcome: to go through the process, and have everyone at Volkswagen of America and all of the dealers see that their verdict could simply be set aside by a German judge.

A review for a new advertising agency began simply enough. Volkswagen prepared a briefing package for each competing agency. The packet included a mission statement, market overview, and summaries of how VW viewed its brand and each product. Volkswagen described its four pillars: (1) reliability, (2) build quality, (3) safety, and (4) fun to drive. In 1995, though, it could really only claim the latter two as part of the present-day cars. It had been without reliability and quality since Nixon had been president.

The review was taking place a year after VW had caused a sensation at the Detroit Auto Show with Concept 1 and just a few months after Volkswagen AG announced that it would develop the show car into the New Beetle. Wilhite's briefing, however, was clear: "Volkswagen must find a relevant new way to 'personify' the Brand. This personification, however, cannot solely trade off the Beetle charm. It cannot be nostalgic, but must rather be relevant, believable, contemporary, original and distinctive. Volkswagen must extract itself from the problems of the past and position itself accurately for the future."

Volkswagen listed its good points and bad points for the would-be successors to DDB Needham. On the plus side:

- Good new product on the way
- Groundswell of publicity (for the Beetle)
- Fond feelings toward VW
- Only mass-market-priced European car

On the negative side:

- Limited resources (a small ad budget)
- Poor quality
- No longer viewed as a good value
- Cynical dealers
- Seen as the Beetle company

Among the threats to its future:

- Loss of consumer trust
- Unknown image and products
- Saturn's plan to import Opel cars from Germany, potentially eroding VW's position as the sole Eurocars in the value segment

The limited resources problem was a recurring theme throughout the briefing material. Volkswagen had roughly $80 million to spend in 1995—not much to support a lineup of cars, though Golf and especially Jetta would get almost all of the marketing dollars that year. Volkswagen had an aggressive target goal of selling 98,500 cars that year, an increase of 34 percent from the year before. Whichever agency won the business, they would only be on the case for a maximum of 7 months to help VW ring the bell. The short funding was built right into the "Agency Challenge," which was stated:

> . . . Present a strategy of how best Volkswagen can rebuild its market franchise and image with the limited resources available.

The four ad agencies chosen to compete against DDB were young companies, as DDB had been in 1959. Arnold was included largely on the strength and reputation of its chairman, Ed Eskandarian, who possessed a considerable reputation in the industry for work done at a now defunct agency, HBM/Creamer. The HBM/Creamer firm had been swallowed up by a British advertising company, WRCS.

Eskandarian left that agency not long after the purchase. Starting over, he had bought and then cobbled together a handful of New England agencies into one shop that by 1994 was handling around $300 million in ad billings. Martin/Williams had been formed in the early 1980s. Stan Richards started his agency in 1976. Deutsch had taken over a $15 million agency from his father in the mid-1980s and had grown it to around $300 million by 1995.

———

Donny Deutsch is a huge guy. Not so large in physical stature, but in character and personal volume. He has a presence that few in the ad industry can match. Early in his career, after taking over an agency started by his father, the word *brash* followed him around. And he had earned it. He seemed to be always quoted in the press. He always answered the phone when reporters called, so he was the one getting the most ink and face time on the news. He wore cowboy boots, had questionable taste in clothes, and wore his hair slicked back. He was a fixture in New York at the Knicks games, sitting near Spike Lee and Dustin Hoffman. It all made for a telegenic character about whom the press liked to write. However, he had a lot of substance to back up the *brash* tag. His agency's work was routinely terrific. For the Swedish retailer Ikea, his agency built up the first real brand campaign for a home furnishings retailer in the history of U.S. advertising. Until then, furniture advertising in the United States was all about President's Day sales or static photography of Ethan Allen room ensembles. The Ikea advertising consisted of short films featuring scenes such as adopted kids talking about their bedroom furniture in their new home, or a divorced mother starting over in a new apartment. One TV ad showed a biracial couple, while shopping for new furniture, talking about how they have been trying to get pregnant. Another featured a couple of gay men shopping for furniture. It was groundbreaking stuff that was written about in the business press. Deutsch created *watercooler advertising,* the kind of advertising about which creative people talked the next day with their colleagues. What *Seinfeld* had done for situation comedy, Deutsch's work had been doing for advertising. In fact, a lot of Deutsch's work seemed to carry the same sort of echo power that DDB's had carried in the old days of VW. He had also achieved star status for working on the advertising of President Bill Clinton's 1992 presidential campaign. For the Tri-State Pontiac Dealers in the New York area, Deutsch had long created some of the best car dealer advertising in the country. Dealers, a very no-nonsense lot when it comes to spending their money, had allowed Deutsch to get creative with their advertising, not just run sell-sell-sell advertising. In one memorable TV spot, Deutsch's creative team produced an ad that seemed like the voice-over was talking about a BMW when it was really a Pontiac Bonneville. The voice-over was German actor Werner Klemperer who had played Nazi Colonel Klink in the TV series *Hogan's Heroes*. Deutsch's dealer advertising didn't look like dealer advertising; instead, it was fun, brand-building advertising that happened to have a 5-second dealer tag at the end of the commercials.

All of the agencies had a healthy fear of Deutsch going into the pitch. He had been winning a lot of accounts, had a strong team, was in New York, and was a media favorite. He was "Agency of the Year" in both *Adweek* and *Advertising Age*. If anyone could make VW's $80 million in ad spending look like $300 million, Donny Deutsch could with his flair for public relations and splash.

Ed Eskandarian and Arnold creative chief Ron Lawner didn't really fear Deutsch too much, though. "We were so glad just to be in the review," says Eskandarian, an elder statesman of the business who had seen it all. "We were underdogs all the way." Eskandarian is a business maestro. In Boston, he is in the inner circle of Boston government and society. He even served as the marketing director of the Big Dig—the biggest public works project in history, a tunnel under the city of Boston. His job was to develop a plan to sell the project to the Boston citizenry. He is extremely well respected as a manager of people and agencies. "A savvier, smoother guy you'll never meet," says Kristin Volk, at that time part of the VW pitch team. By 2001, though, she was head of Deutsch's Boston office.

Eskandarian had been burned in his previous agency, and was starting over. After finishing Harvard Business School in the 1960s, Eskandarian worked at Compton Advertising in New York on Procter & Gamble brands like Tide and Crisco. He hated the commute, though, and moved back to his native New England to a small agency, Humphrey Browning MacDougall (HBM). After a few years, the agency's founder died, and Ed, having the greatest pull with the clients, was able to acquire the agency. He then merged the agency with a New York agency, Creamer. He sold the business in 1986 to WRCS, a British agency. Most agencies were bought and sold in the 1980s as many agency founders discovered this was the only way to get cash out of the business and into their own bank accounts. Buyers found easy junk bond financing, which was the favored currency of the 1980s, or they gave stock to the independent agencies they were buying if they were publicly held. WRCS merged the agency with its other U.S. agency, Della Femina Travisano & Partners, run by Jerry Della Femina. Through the 1970s and 1980s, Della Femina had been the media's favorite ad man. The Della Femina name had true brand cachet. Whenever the media needed an advertising expert, they called on Jerry. Della Femina was in those days what Donny Deutsch became in the 1990s: the best-known advertising agency brand since David Ogilvy. So when the British had to choose a management head for this newly combined agency, they opted for the better-known Della Femina and his band, not Eskandarian. It was a decision they would later regret.

Unlike Deutsch, who's known for his forceful personality and management savvy used to build one of the most successful agencies in the country, Della Femina's reputation was for questionable management practices and rank ego. Eskandarian, one of the most sober of managers, wanted no part of the Della Femina clan and asked the British to sell him the Boston operation he had started. Della Femina, not liking Eskandarian any more than Eskandarian liked him, stood in his way and blocked the deal. Eskandarian left. Within 2 years, the Boston HBM office was out of business, and Della Femina's New York agency was foundering.

Eskandarian bought a small ad agency in Boston, Arnold & Company, whose chief executive had died of a heart attack. The agency had no reputation outside of Boston and around $100 million of billings. Eskandarian was shrewd, though. He knew from his time in Boston that the agency was the perfect base from which to build. It was an old-line, stable agency with loyal clients, including McDonald's franchisees and Fleet Bank. He could buy it a reasonable price with money he had made from selling his old agency to the British, and pick up a few other ad agencies in the region to achieve some size and a client base. He picked up clients from his old HBM agency. He would recruit back some of the people he had worked with at the old agency and start over. The process began with the acquisition of Arnold in 1991, and was followed by picking up Emerson Lane Fortuna, the Boston office of direct-marketing agency Rapp Collins Marcoa, and Cabot Communications. By 1994, he had the core group of managers and creative people he wanted to work with. He told Ron Lawner, Fran Kelley, John Gaffney, and Kristin Volk, all of whom had worked with him at HBM, and a few others who came with the acquisitions, to stick with him. He had a plan.

Almost as if advertising consultant Jones-Lundin had read his business plan, the firm called Eskandarian a few days before Christmas 1994. Arnold Fortuna Lawner was invited to pitch VW, the car account Eskandarian knew they needed to grow, though he was dumbfounded about getting a crack at one so soon. Agencies, especially newly formed ones, can wait years before getting a chance at a car account. Some never get asked. Eskandarian had told his own people just months before that he felt the agency was ready to go to the next level. The call from Bob Lundin was like a train conductor calling.

Meanwhile, in Dallas, Stan Richards was running what *Adweek* called that year, "Dallas's foremost creative hot shop." Hardly dizzying praise, or enough to make Deutsch worry, it was like being declared the most promising ballerina in Galveston. But actually, The Richards Group was, and is, a talented strategic, creative ad agency. It handled about $300 million in ad billings, similar to the rest of the field. Like Deutsch, Richards was on a streak of account wins and creative awards, adding business from national clients Taco Bell and Continental Airlines. Stan Richards, an art director by training, is an old-school ad man and is in the Art Directors' Hall of Fame, along with Bill Bernbach and DDB legend Helmut Krone. His agency had almost no turnover, a rarity in the business, even in Dallas. He believes in promoting people from within and training them according to his creative philosophy, not hiring young guns from other shops. He also has been seen as an agency innovator, getting clients to agree on profit targets for the agency. In other words, if his agency comes in under the profit target he asks the client to reduce the workload or increase the compensation. If the agency exceeds the target, it actually gives money back to the client. Richards has been known to give back hundreds of thousands of dollars to his clients under this system. It was an honest way of doing business that appealed to VW and got Wilhite and Warrilow's attention.

Finally, at DDB, Keith Reinhard put together a team of people in the New York office to pitch the business, though he would draw on staffers from DDB's U.S. network of offices as it had never done before. The idea was to contrast the big, lumbering, out-of-favor DDB from the smaller, nimbler, more creative competition by reminding VW of its deep resources and national reach. Doyle Dane Bernbach would try to make its bigness count for something positive. The DDB pitch included a video of staffers from all over the country—Florida, Dallas, Seattle, Chicago, and into Canada—talking about how the media in the different markets had their own unique needs and dimensions, and that only a company with DDB's organization, reach, and resources could provide that.

On the Road of Life . . .

On 19 January 1995, a delegation of nine from VW, including Steve Wilhite, Advertising Director Antony Denham, four regional sales and marketing managers, and two VW dealers went to Arnold's Boston office for a capabilities pitch. This is the first in-person round of any advertising account review. The agency literally tries to show the client that it deserves to be considered and can handle the job. For Arnold, though, it would be more than that. For more than 3 weeks, the team at Arnold had been galvanized around the pitch that it was going to make during this first meeting. Eskandarian told his team, "We're going to treat each meeting like it was our last."

One of the reasons that Eskandarian, Lawner, and copywriter Lance Jensen thought VW was the perfect car account for them was that they all had connections to the brand. Lawner had driven VWs as a young college student. Eskandarian's wife's uncle was a VW dealer, so the family had owned several. He could recall how the midmounted engine in their VW Squareback was perfect for lulling his children to sleep because the car seat sat over the pulsing, vibrating engine. That is the stuff that puts a brand in your blood. Lance Jensen and his wife owned two VWs, a Golf and a Jetta. They didn't have to look very hard for the VW customer. It was them. Eskandarian was in his 60s, Lawner in his 40s, and Jensen in his 20s. Lawner and Eskandarian owned Porsches by this time, but they started out as VW people.

Jensen and Alan Pafenbach set out to work on creative ideas, along with several other creative teams at the agency. Creative inspiration came from a lot of places. Sometimes, creative people at an agency need to use a lot of consumer research and focus groups for ideas and input. It also makes for great advertising public relations to be able to say that the creative team was inspired by hours of listening to consumers. In truth, the creative team went to a bar near the Arnold office and, before the beer was even served, had come up with "On the road of life there are passengers and drivers." Jensen was writing from the gut. In his late 20s, he was a VW customer and enthusiast. He knew why he liked VWs, and why he and his wife bought two of them, despite warnings from *Consumer Reports* to buy Toyotas and Hondas instead.

Says Jensen: "New England has always been a really strong market for Volkswagen. You see kids driving to Vermont with Grateful Dead stickers on the back window. They are young people, or even older people who think young. A little preppy maybe, and with some money. It's a little elitist, but not money elitism. They are elite thinkers and elite livers. It's people who have a lot of confidence in themselves and what they do, the music they listen to, the clothes they wear. Volkswagens are for people whose worst nightmare is to have a job that bores them. That's Volkswagen. The 'passengers and drivers' line just came out of that."

Meanwhile, Kristin Volk, who had the title of Director of Consumer Insights, agreed with Jensen's and Pafenbach's theme and direction. However, she had to make sure that it held together when actually talking to consumers and studying their responses. Alan and Lance's guts were fine, but they couldn't go into the pitch just saying that they feel this is the right way to go. The positioning had to have some basis in the research; Volk had to determine if others felt the same as these guys did.

Advertising research is a tricky craft. By 1995, a model for consumer research had been taking over the ad industry, *account planning*. Its name belies the function. Indeed, the title Volk had cooked up for herself, Director of Consumer Insights, made for a better description. Account planning is a school of consumer research, conceived in London during the 1960s and refined in the 1970s, that says consumers do not tell researchers how they really behave when asked in the artificial setting of a focus group. Talk to eight people in a stuffy conference room over stale sandwiches and warm soda and the answers will likely have little to do with how the consumers actually behave. For example, you can ask a consumer how important a car's safety features are when considering the purchase of a car, and he or she may tell you that it is the most important thing. That consumer is probably giving the answer that sounds best to him and that he thinks sounds correct to the focus group coordinator. If he were truthful, he might say that his decision is influenced most by the car's exterior design or the power he feels sitting high up in a sport utility vehicle that can rev to 250 horsepower. The account planner would rather coax from the consumer how he feels about safety by asking indirect questions about his children, and then deducing how much the person will spend on safety features based on answers to those questions. Likewise, if a clothier wants to know how a woman shops, the research department ought not to ask women in the setting of a focus group. The account planning approach would say go shopping with the ladies and see how they shop, look at what they buy and what they don't buy. Look at what they touch and what they veer away from.

Research is also the most abused discipline in marketing and advertising circles, because there are countless examples of advertisers and ad agencies *reverse-engineering* a strategy. That means an agency comes up with a campaign idea that the client likes for purely political and subjective reasons that have nothing to do with whether it is likely to work on consumers. Maybe the chief executive officer is an engineer, so he wants to load the ads with a lot of engineering information even though the consumer doesn't give a hoot. The agency, with or without the participation of the client, then goes out and conducts focus groups to test the idea, and it designs the research to support the strategic premise to which it is already committed. This goes on all the time. Throughout the mid-1980s, DDB had been infusing VW advertising with a lot of obvious "German Engineering" information and imagery, combined with rebate and price information. This was done largely because the U.S. client felt that it would move the metal, and the German client wanted to see the engineering information in the ads. There was little consideration given to whether this approach was actually effective. Account directors took these ads into focus groups and asked consumers questions about whether they found this kind of advertising informative. They would ask the people if they wanted to read a lot of ad copy about the technical aspects of the cars. People in this setting are bound to say yes to these questions because they don't want to appear as dullards just wanting to be entertained. It's like asking people which TV show they would watch if they had a choice between *Masterpiece Theater* or *Gilligan's Island*. How many who actually like *Gilligan's Island* are going to admit it to a focus group coordinator in a room full of other people, or even one-on-one with someone they can be pretty sure is college educated and chews with their mouth closed? The other kind of reverse engineering is when a creative director becomes enamored with a particular idea, and the research people know that it is politically wise to make sure the focus group results come out supporting his or her *brilliant* idea. Arnold was not that kind of agency, though. Alan and Lance's idea sounded right, yes, but it would still have to be proved.

Though the "On the road of life there are passengers and drivers . . ." theme had come from the guts of two creative men, Kristin Volk's research was objectively supporting it. She was looking for ways to poke holes in it, but her research kept coming back in support of the idea that VW buyers were people who liked to be in control and part of the driving experience when they were behind the wheel. Arnold Creative Director Ron Lawner had several creative teams working on the idea that the agency would pitch, but kept coming back to Jensen and Pafenbach's line, "On the road of life. . . ." Lawner felt that the line was the closest to the brand's bone. Yet, it had been conceived and agreed upon without the benefit of Volk's processes beforehand.

Volk, in her ongoing research, decided to focus on consumers who stayed loyal to VW even when the consumer press and buying guides gave them ample reason to abandon VW in favor of Hondas and Toyotas. Even most U.S.-made cars by 1995 were of higher quality and reliability than VW, so she wanted to zero in on the people who were unshakable in their affection and dedication—the VW religious.

Said Volk, "It didn't make sense to go after people who had rejected the brand to find out why, or even past owners who had abandoned Volkswagen at some point. We felt it was far more relevant to gather VW lovers and see if there wasn't something in their stubborn loyalty that we could leverage. The idea was to find out what made *these* people love Volkswagen. And maybe we could find more people like *them*. Trying to figure out simply how to make more people want a Volkswagen would have been a bad starting point."

Leading up to the first meeting with VW, Jensen and Pafenbach had been working on something that was being referred to as the "brand essence video." Lawner and Arnold President Fran Kelly had talked it over with Eskandarian. The consultants, Jones-Lundin, had said the first meeting was just to show credentials. That normally means that the agency's upper management takes the prospective client through the history and experience of the agency. It would also be appropriate to show a few *hero* case studies—examples of other campaigns produced by the agency that bailed out other clients. There was a problem, though. Arnold had been pieced together with chewing gum and bailing wire by throwing together the staffs and clients of three small ad agencies in the previous 3 years. There were no dramatic case studies with which to bowl over the cautious Americans at VW, desperate dealers, and calculating Germans. Among the brands the agency had handled were Titleist, Nynex calling cards, Stanley Tools, Stihl chainsaws, and McDonald's franchisees (not even national work for McDonald's). They weren't exactly world beaters. They paled against case studies like Deutsch's Ikea and Pontiac work, as well as The Richards Group's Home Depot, Motel 6, and Cadillac dealer work. Martin/Williams had done wonderful print campaigns and was an established and very stylish and creative shop. The hero case that Arnold would put forth was VW.

"We so felt we had nailed this that we had to show them in that first meeting that we understood their problems and their issues," says Lawner. "We knew this brand. We knew the customers because we were them. We decided to use that first meeting to talk to them about their business and about what we thought about their business and their brand. They were coming to meet *us*, but we were going to make *them* the focus of the meeting."

Jensen and Pafenbach had been working on the brand essence video. It featured Jensen and Joe Fallon, with whom Jensen had been roommates at Boston College, driving around in a Jetta. "Wake up. Wake up. Wake up," the words read on the screen as it began. The tone of the piece was all 'tude, as in *attitude*. Not terribly obnoxious, but confident. And it was playful, even about the benefits of German engineering. "I like the fact that it doesn't have too many features," he says as he shows off the control console. No power windows. No problem. "I can roll down my *own* windows." The music pulses, and even turns a little zany in its tempo. The actual song was "I'm a Rock and Roll Star." These guys didn't take driving too seriously. They took their lives seriously, in a positive, sane, and playful way—and they enjoyed driving. Fallon says in the video that VW should have a theme song, and suggests Wayne Newton's "Danke Schoen," and he starts crooning it. Lines of ad copy pop in and out of the video, such as "It's about having kids. . . . Not becoming your parents." "It invigorates. Doesn't isolate."

Wilhite said in the first meeting, "You said what we haven't been able to say for twenty years." In a way, Arnold had won the pitch in the opening meeting. "I knew they had nailed it," says Wilhite. "The question was, would they screw it up between then and the time we completed the review. I loved what they showed us. It showed an amazing grasp of the situation. But a review of a new ad agency is more than just about the idea. There were issues of capability and chemistry." Indeed, though Wilhite wasn't thinking in this direction, there have been many instances in advertising of an agency pitching the best idea, but the client not liking the people at the agency. In some reviews, a client, at the end of such a review, might opt for the agency he or she likes best but tells them to take the idea of another agency and make it work. Lawsuits have been filed over such events.

Meanwhile, Volk had a concern. All of the imagery from the focus groups relayed youth, youth, youth. She was worried that the agency was moving toward a positioning that was too heavily weighted toward youth, the so-called Generation X. It was true that VW's buyer base was younger than its competitors'. She was worried, though, that the work was exclusionary and not accessible to VW owners in their 40s and 50s. Jensen, however, who was Arnold's poster boy for the composite VW buyer, said, "No. The youth is up here," pointing to his head. "It's attitude, not what it says on your driver's license. Volkswagens are for people who are in their 50s, too, but they are people who are burning their own CDs, listening to new music, and going on bike treks for vacations. Volkswagen people are not tour bus people," said Jensen.

Said agency President Fran Kelly: "The brand essence statement captured the rational and emotional benefits that Volkswagen provided its customers. We knew that to be distinct and appealing in a highly competitive marketplace, we had to take full advantage of how people both thought and felt about the brand. The rational benefit of Volkswagen was that it was the only brand that offered the benefits of German engineering affordably. Emotionally, the car presented a completely different driving experience. It keeps you more connected to the road, more connected to the world. And as we thought about our strategy, we gave consideration to not only what we wanted to stand for, but also what we did not want to stand for. For example, we wanted the Volkswagen brand to be invitational and approachable, not exclusionary like some of the other European car brands had been. We wanted to sell our consumers on VW's unique driving experience, not just on the car's ability to get people from point A to point B faster or cheaper. That was the focus of the Japanese."

Volk gathered groups of owners who had owned at least a couple of VWs. She asked them to make collages out of pictures cut from magazines. They made collages that represented German luxury cars like Mercedes-Benz and BMW, Japanese cars, and U.S. cars. The collages for Mercedes-Benz and BMW showed pictures of mansions, expensive jewelry from Harry Winston, Godiva Chocolate, and Pravda fashion accessories. The pictures of people selected for the collages were pretty model types, men and women who hardly looked real. Pictures of actual money showed up in the Mercedes-Benz collages, with words like *cold, hard cash*. The collages for Japanese brands—Honda and Toyota—showed pictures of mid-America, families and kids playing organized soccer and baseball. They showed midrange liquor brands like Smirnoff vodka, not Grey Goose. Cosmetic brands, such as Revlon, were chosen to group with Honda and Mazda, not Lancôme. The collages for VW showed young, youthful, energetic people. Mountain bikes were clipped. Ads for independent films were used. Images of snowboarding showed up. Words such as *Carpe Diem* (seize the day) were assembled on the VW collages.

People who buy VWs like to feel the road, says Volk. They don't like the remote, isolated driving experience of a Toyota or Honda. They don't much like the high prices of BMW and Mercedes-Benz. They feel smart buying a German-engineered car for less than $20,000, "as if they were in on something cool," says Volk. They enjoy driving.

One refrain has been that VW people almost always want to do all the driving on a long trip. It was from this that Ron Lawner, one day after the first meeting with VW, added the words "Drivers wanted" to the board in the war room at Arnold (where all of the visual executions and ideas were posted). Jensen's line was still up, "On the road of life, there are passengers and drivers." Then, Lawner, without telling anyone or announcing it, tacked up "Drivers wanted."

"It was a natural progression from Lance's and Alan's idea," said Lawner. "We needed something that could be a rallying cry. Something that could stand up alone, even without the line that Alan and Lance had written, which was dead on right, but a little long. When you are doing these things, a line is very important and I didn't want to announce that I had put the line up. I just put it up to get their reaction. It was really just one line up with a lot of other stuff. But when they saw it, they adopted it immediately."

———

One of the tried-and-true tactics of an agency pitching a car account is to enlist the help of a "car guy." This is someone who has been breathing the advertising equivalent of engine fumes for a couple of decades. When you go to one of these walking carburetors, you try to find someone who knows *this* client—maybe a former DDB account director or someone who worked at VW. A guy (and they are nearly always male) who knows the client's chemistry and DNA and who can tell an agency whose buttons to push, who to stay away from, who matters, who doesn't, who to spend extra time with at the meeting, and who can be blown off. Arnold drafted no such player.

"This brand did not need anyone's old way of thinking," said Ron Lawner. "We were clear from the briefing we got from Steve Wilhite that the company was in desperate need of an entirely new direction. We felt we had this brand's DNA running in our veins and in our hallways. Had we opted for one of these guys, we'd run the risk of second guessing our own good ideas, or having someone entrenched in the company's old ways infect our thinking or delivery. We talked about it briefly, but it made no sense to us to go that route."

"We had fresh eyes," says Lawner. "We all had a relationship with this brand. We decided to just give it our best shot from the heart."

Says Eskandarian, "We felt we shouldn't be inoculated with all the history and opinions of so-called 'experts.' Later, we thought about hiring a 'car guy' to run the business. But we knocked down that idea, too. We didn't want someone telling us what the company had been or what they had learned five years ago. The world is changing so fast that we were convinced that would be exactly the wrong thing to do."

What helped Arnold the most, says everyone who was connected with the pitch, was the time they spent talking to dealers. "People underestimate the dealers," says Eskandarian. Arnold talked to 600 out of the 700 dealers during the pitch, about 100 in person and the rest by phone. "The dealers helped convince us that our strategy was right," says Eskandarian. When a VW customer walks in the door of a dealership, the salespeople know who is there to look at VWs, versus Mazdas or Hondas that might be on the same selling floor. Says Fran Kelly, "They look like they ride a skateboard even if they are 30. They have baseball hats on, but backwards. The dealers kept telling us that VWs are not for everyone. That is a key part of the strategy and why it has been successful . . . creating advertising that is right for the brand and right for the customer who is most likely to consider a VW. Then, we work hard to put the message where they will see it, and wait for them to show up. I think too many car companies work too hard to convince customers to consider them, and they wind up not being who they are. What happens is that they don't get the people they are chasing, because that's a flawed strategy. And the brand starts looking bad to the people who liked them from the start."

Only about 24 percent of the driving population, by Arnold's reckoning, are even potential VW customers. This may sound like basic thinking, but it wasn't for VW, and it isn't for much of the auto industry. By reducing the target audience to people who will consider VW when reached with the right brand communication, an advertiser can make a $100-million advertising budget look as big as Ford's $800-million budget to the people being targeted. By shrinking the universe of customers, the ad messages can be more focused and will be seen more often. This approach allowed Arnold to be edgier and less obvious in its strategy and communication. Most marketers talk about media in terms of shotguns and rifle shots. A shotgun approach is especially bad, because if a shotgun is fired at a gaggle of geese from 100 yards, the shooter could easily miss all of them. If the shooter uses a rifle, the chances increase of hitting one or two, but then the rest fly away. Arnold's strategy was neither shotgun nor rifle shot. Instead, the strategy went like this: By concentrating on a smaller group of customers, they could create a brand environment for VW—a brand pond—that the geese would want to come to and stay. To take the analogy further, this allows the salespeople and the company to mix with the geese and invite them to buy the car, not shoot the wallets out of their pockets.

The Idea Factories

One major disappointment that came up before the final round of pitches was the decision by Martin/Williams to drop out of the pitch. The agency's top management, following a meeting with Wilhite, decided that it didn't want to proceed. Wilhite told the agencies that he expected the winner to reinvent the way a car account is handled from top to bottom; that included staffing. He wanted the winning agency to forget about what they thought they knew about staffing and running an account. The senior partners at Martin/Williams, a small agency in comparison with Deutsch and the others, were feeling that they didn't have the right chemistry with Wilhite, and they were concerned that the demands of the account would upset the agency's balance. This is not a lack of guts. As a matter of fact, it was fairly courageous. Smallish ad agencies with unique cultures have been ruined, or close to it, by large pieces of business that dominated day-to-day business to the point of creating too many miserable lives. Nike agency Wieden & Kennedy had experienced this with the Subaru business, which kept the agency in near turmoil for 3 years. Mullen, a regional rival of Arnold's in Massachusetts, experienced it in 1992 after winning BMW, which was too large an account that placed too many gritty demands on what had been a stylish print agency. Automotive accounts are not for the faint of heart. They are big industrial accounts that require huge resources to produce both national and regional/local advertising. Most car companies spend so much money on advertising that they lean on their agencies in ways that few others do—everything from dealer ads, speeches, market research, motor sports, auto show support, sales promotion, public relations; the list goes on.

Meanwhile, Deutsch was taking a similar tack as Arnold. Deutsch, a very smart agency when it comes to research and account-planning methods, was finding much the same material as Arnold. "People who buy Volkswagens do not buy cars to get from point A to point B," said Deutsch Business Development Chief Peter Drakoulias. The agency had bought two VW Jettas so that members of the team could drive the heck out of them and form opinions about what made VWs special. They also used the Jettas to take prospective VW buyers out for test-drives, so they could videotape their reactions and thoughts while driving. Maybe this was the big difference between Arnold's team and Deutsch's. Arnold had a dozen or more VWs in its parking garage, driven by staffers, before the pitch began. Deutsch had to buy the cars to get exposed to VW. The Deutsch team had come up with a strategy and tagline for their pitch that centered on the word "Go." It was akin to Nike's "Just Do It," which Deutsch saw as a sympatico brand to VW. It was simple and energetic. Like Arnold's "Drivers Wanted," Deutsch saw "Go" as something of a rallying cry that could be put on hats, jackets, coffee mugs, billboards, dealerships, right alongside the VW logo.

Deutsch Creative Director Greg DiNoto created a film that hailed the return of VW. Deutsch had offered actor Jack Nicholson $1 million if he would voice the video and agree to be the voice on VW ads. Deutsch knew someone who knew Nicholson. However, Nicholson refused. He doesn't *do* ads. Deutsch's backup was Jim Belushi. In the end, it was just one of the Deutsch staffers talking against clips of vintage car and movie clips: "I'm back on behalf of purists like Steve McQueen . . . it's time someone said, 'Go!,' cut the crap, get back to what matters . . . on behalf of Jack Kerouac, I'm back."

Whereas Arnold had reduced its team working on VW to about 12 people after the first meeting, Deutsch had about 50 people working on it for 100 days. Deutsch's Head of Account Management Esther Lee and Director of Account Planing Cheryl Greene crisscrossed the country talking to dealers. One Deutsch staffer worked a week for a dealer as a salesperson. Every executive and dealer met by Deutsch was checked out, from liquor brand and resume to marital status.

Because Deutsch was such a hot property, the agency was pitching other accounts at the same time, each demanding the time of agency Chief Donny Deutsch. Epson Computers, about a $30 million account, and in a category that Deutsch coveted almost as much as cars, was running concurrent to the VW pitch. Indeed, Epson scheduled final presentations 2 days before the VW final meeting, and on the West Coast.

Before Deutsch's team left its New York offices for the two pitches, he showed his people a video clip from the opening scene of the film *Patton*. George C. Scott is against the backdrop of a huge U.S. flag and says, "We're going to cut out their guts and use them to grease the wheels of our tanks." Of course, Patton was talking about the Germans driving around in Kubelwagens, so it's questionable if the metaphor was really appropriate. The guts that Deutsch wanted to use to grease his tank's wheels were Arnold's and Richards's, not VW's.

Deutsch did something else that may have cast bad karma on his pitch. He allowed *USA Today* reporter Melanie Wells to be a fly on the wall during the weeks of preparation for the pitch. Wells knew Deutsch for years, first as a reporter for *Advertising Age,* and then as the advertising reporter for *USA Today.* Another reporter, Randall Rothenberg, while at the *New York Times,* had been allowed by Subaru of America to be a fly on its wall in 1991 when it was reviewing ad agencies. That led to a long article in the *New York Times Sunday Magazine* about the Subaru pitch and a book, *Where the Suckers Moon.* Donny is press friendly and was perhaps a little cocksure to think the VW business was his to lose given his amazing run of new business and industry honors. The decision to let Wells sit in on a lot of meetings and capture the you-are-there element of Deutsch's pitch, though, seemed

to presuppose a win—counting chickens and all that. When Ed Eskandarian and Ron Lawner heard that Deutsch had *USA Today* "living with
them," as Eskandarian recalled, "it made us a little more determined
to win, I think."

The Richards Group, perhaps not surprisingly, was pitching a strategy somewhat similar to Arnold's. Whereas Arnold had summed it up
in two words, "Drivers wanted," Richards's line was "Don't just sit
there. Drive." Like Lawner and Deutsch, Stan Richards drove a
Porsche. Some of the people on the Richards team had owned VWs
when they were young. Texas is especially good Beetle country because the dry heat favors an air-cooled engine, and the lack of humid-
ity and winter in most of the state means Beetles, unencumbered by
rust and road salt, go on forever. Richards pitched his agency to VW as
knowing the United States and knowing the VW customer from coast
to coast.

Richards's research showed that consumers had a remarkable lack
of awareness about the VW models: Few knew what a Passat was;
many had only a passing familiarity with Jetta and Golf; many still
thought of VW as the Beetle, Microbus, and Rabbit. Richards's proposed ads were heavy on the model names and product attributes.
Print ads mocked up for the pitch were friendly and conveyed the driver's spirit. One ad for the Golf GL said, "The shortest distance
between two points is boring." Another headline for the GTI stated,
"The most fun you can have with your ignition on."

———

DDB Needham, meanwhile, had embarked on a strange theme for its
pitch. While grounded in a real strategy, it seemed so far away from
the tone and feel that Wilhite and the rest of the VW crew and dealers
were looking for that, in the end, it was almost embarrassing. The candidates who would run in the 1996 presidential election had already
made themselves known by early 1995. It was early—the election was
almost 2 years away—and the field looked bleak. The news media was
full of stories about how disgruntled voters would be with such a
sorry field of candidates: Kansas Senator and septuagenarian Bob

Dole, right-wing TV commentator Pat Buchanan, and Texas Senator Phil Gramm. Therefore, the DDB team went out on this hokey mission to get people to talk about voting for a fictional candidate named Rob Robbins. He would run for 18 months through advertising, direct mail, and public relations on a VW platform of honesty and good value. In their video, DDB dressed up a VW Eurovan as a campaign van, and got people of different age groups talking about how VW's honesty and values sounded good to them. The slogan and positioning strategy was "Volkswagen. Think about it." The idea was that the line had two meanings for the consumer: The first message was "Consider Volkswagen." The second meaning was intended to appeal to VW's heritage with people who swim upstream and are thinkers by definition. A video meant to convey DDB's understanding of the VW brand and showcase the agency's capabilities contained a collection of DDB media staffers and dealers from around the country talking about the VW brand—almost all middle-aged white men in jackets and ties. The whole video was static and contrived. The TV ad concepts had fictional correspondents trailing after Robbins. One ad had a correspondent announcing a shocking allegation that "rocked the Volkswagen Presidential ad campaign." Robbins then admitted to straying, being unfaithful. There had been another car in his life, and they showed a picture of him standing next to a Japanese import brand. The ad would finish up with a cameo of disgraced 1984 Democratic Party candidate Gary Hart who was forced to drop out of the primaries after it was learned that he, while married, had been carousing on the island of Bimini with a blond-haired woman named Donna Rice. Print ads had the fictional Robbins on the cover of *Time, Forbes,* and *The Economist.* Direct mailings to consumers offering special values looked like letters from the candidate. Some print ads looked like campaign promises. One such ad said, "Term limits—yes . . . Speed limits—no comment." The ad was for the GTI VR6. A Passat print ad read, "Live in the lap of honesty." A Jetta print ad read, "Put your country first, and your Jetta in fifth."

Whether the creative idea had any merit is debatable. There were a few good spots in the effort, like a safety ad that used a Jetta as a wrecking ball to show how the passenger safety cage protected occupants. However, one ad in which the fictional Robbins said, "The Volkswagen platform is for everyone. College students, families, working people, rich folks, even special interest groups," was off the mark and showed a broader lack of understanding about the brand and how to communicate VW anew. The nature of presidential campaigning demands that a candidate appeal to the broadest possible audience. Volkswagen, as Arnold and Deutsch's research had compellingly shown, is *not* for everyone. DDB pitched "Think about it," as the "Just Do It" of the 1990s. The trouble was that no one in the room believed that DDB Needham had the creative culture or firepower to deliver on the creative demands of that claim.

————

The pitches took place on the 23rd, 24th, and 25th of March, from Thursday to Saturday. DDB was up first, followed by Richards and Arnold on Friday, and Deutsch on Saturday morning.

When Arnold pitched its strategy, the team didn't stop at advertising. They felt that "Drivers wanted" was ideal for shirts, hats, jackets, even driving gloves. The agency had a raft of items mocked up carrying the "Drivers wanted" slogan to show the strong legs of the line. Arnold would give the stuff out to the VW executives and dealers to whom they pitched.

Before the final pitch, the day before the team would fly to Detroit, Ed Eskandarian went to the war room at Arnold to review the work that would be pitched. It was all riding on "Drivers wanted." He looked at the work, and asked, "What else?" It was not uncommon for ad agencies to go into a final pitch with more than one idea or campaign. That sounds odd, but it's true. Ideally, the client, if he or she is smart, wants the agency to be committed to *one* idea and *one* strategy. If it's right, there should only be one. It isn't a multiple-choice test. However, depending on the client (and there are many bad ones), it might be appropriate to pitch two ideas. "This is it," replied Lawner. "I don't know that Ed was totally sold on this one idea, but he was sold on letting us pitch the one idea," said Lawner.

By Friday afternoon, the agency already showed the brand essence video twice in previous meetings, and introduced the "Drivers wanted" theme at their second meeting, which was held at VW headquarters on 9 February. They would show it again, along with further refinement of the consumer research and media plan. They would also see a batch of actual ads.

During the pitch, as Kristin Volk was in the middle of talking about how VW buyers are different from buyers of other brands, a young assistant who had set up Arnold's props accidentally kicked the cord out of the wall that was powering the computer driving Volk's Power-point presentation. Lawner and Eskandarian scurried to Volk's aid. Eskandarian was red-faced with embarrassment and anger. Volk, how-ever, would have none of it. She just pivoted as her bosses tried to get the computer back on line and went on with her presentation from memory.

"That impressed the hell out of us," says Wilhite. "It was a great moment," agreed dealer Mike Sullivan who was part of the panel. "The poise and smoothness she showed and the fact that she didn't need her props impressed everyone. It was a pretty intimidating room," said Wilhite. "Dieter Dahlhoff (Volkswagen AG's executive marketing director) had brought along a woman from his German PR agency, and they were having sidebar conversation and translation throughout the presentations. . . . It was very distracting."

"That's an understatement," recalls Volk. "It was this big room, and the four of us were sitting in the front in these little folding chairs in front of this big group. There was nothing between us and them except dead space. Fran Kelly went before me, and I could hear his voice quivering. I thought, holy shit, maybe I should be nervous too. I wrote a little note on the back of my notes and showed it to them. It said, 'Don't forget to breathe' . . . we passed it around and it seemed to take the edge off."

When the Arnold team exited the conference room, they found the young woman who had kicked out the power cord talking on the phone with her parents, sobbing, telling them that she was sure that she was fired. Not hardly. She was, in fact, integral to the agency actu-ally landing the account.

There was a secondary theme to Arnold's presentation beyond "Drivers wanted." The whole pitch had a theme of "Move the metal," which is a theme that it uses even in 2001, six years after the pitch, to introduce its annual ad plans to the company and dealers. "Move the metal," slang for selling cars, was crucial because though some excitement was being generated around the eventuality of the New Beetle, there wouldn't be any truly new product until 1997 when the all-new Passat arrived. An all-new Golf and Jetta wouldn't come until 1999, and the earliest the New Beetle would come to the United States was 1998. All of this big brand positioning was fine, but the agency had to figure a way to make VW feel new and fresh with the existing product in the showrooms.

"New advertising and a new advertising agency aren't always that important for a big company, especially a car company. But for us, it was going to be huge," said Wilhite. "It is not overstated to say that advertising was 'critical' to building this company when you think that the Beetle and its spin-offs were technologically not very attractive. It was the advertising that made the fact they weren't technologically advanced a brand building asset. We needed to get some of that dynamic back into our communications if this company was going to make it in America." Arnold promised it could get VW sales to 200,000 vehicles a year by 1997 and to 300,000 vehicles by 2000. To do so, the advertising would have to be aggressive and powerful. The Arnold team was urging VW not to get skittish about creatively pushing the envelope in order to reach this edgy, young, often irreverent consumer they believed was the heart and soul of VW's customer base.

Media Director John Gaffney also presented a media strategy that would concentrate VW's $80 million in a few key markets, not spread over the whole country. Markets like New England, New York, Eastern Florida, Chicago, Seattle and Portland, San Francisco and Southern California, Minneapolis, and Eastern Texas would get all the spending. One-half of the budget would be put against Jetta. The idea, said Gaffney, was to make VW look big in the markets where it had the best chances of building sales. "It was better for VW to be on *Seinfeld* reruns in six markets than on the Saturday afternoon movie in fifty markets," he said. This was new thinking for dealers and some of the VW people.

The other part of Gaffney's strategy was to be on prime-time television, which is expensive, but on just a handful of programs. Gaffney wanted VW on programs that didn't have the highest overall ratings, but scored high with the VW target. *Seinfeld* and *NYPD Blue*, just starting in 1994, would be two big programs for VW, as would *Buffy the Vampire Slayer*, which had a cult following among VW's Jetta target. Arnold suggested that VW could take sales from Japanese brands and a couple of domestics—Dodge Neon and Ford Escort—that attracted the VW target largely on price. "By making VW hipper and look big to those buyers, we knew we could get some of them back," said Kelly. The strategy also called for luring Saab and some of VW's former Audi buyers who had defected to Honda and Acura down the price ladder by emphasizing VW's European design and great price/value relationship.

Marketing wouldn't emphasize reliability or value. In the segments in which VW competed, Arnold pointed out, those things were the price of entry, not brand differentiators. People expected and demanded cars to be safe, reliable, and priced reasonably. The differentiator for VW would have to be attitude. The consumers whom they were after lived on attitude. The people who had stayed with VW when their rational selves told them not to were jammed with attitude. Reliability was a problem, because VW hadn't licked their quality problems yet. What Arnold presented was "an honest place for VW to live and grow." The focus of the strategy, reflected in "Drivers wanted," and spelled out for VW was, "A more affordable and likable car than overpriced Europeans, and more drivable than boring Japanese."

———

Deutsch was the last agency to present to VW. Donny Deutsch chartered two commuter jets to take his team and about 40 portfolios of work from San Francisco, where they had pitched Epson, to Detroit. It wasn't extravagant and didn't cost that much more than it would have to fly everyone commercially. This way, they were in charge of their own schedule. It was Friday night in California when they were leaving, heading into Saturday morning in Auburn Hills. They arrived at 4:00 A.M. and went to rooms booked at the Hilton Suites near VW's offices so the main performers—Deutsch, Cheryl Greene, Esther Lee, and Greg DiNoto—could get some sleep.

The parking lot at VW headquarters was empty, except for a handful of cars. A few VW executives and dealers had even brought their wives to the Deutsch pitch. People had containers of coffee from Dunkin Donuts that they had picked up along the way because the VW commissary was closed. Dress was Saturday casual. The Deutsch people were wrecked from lack of sleep. At about 8:30 A.M., the main conference room at VW filled up, and Deutsch began pitching with all he had.

Despite Arnold's dead-on strategy throughout the pitch process and Deutsch's reputation, the selection committee, says Wilhite, was leaning toward The Richards Group. Everyone was taken with Stan Richards and his simple, straightforward, and engaging style. They liked what they heard about and from his agency. Deutsch, on the other hand, was a problem. There was a lot of energy, but Donny Deutsch worried them. A huge personal presence, the concern was that the work and the agency were too dependent upon Donny and his direction. He dominated his team. To some, he was a reminder of what they hadn't liked about Andy Berlin. He was too New York. The VW selection team was looking for energy, but with subtler body English than they saw in Deutsch. Doyle Dane Bernbach's presentation was a train wreck. It was so far off-base from where Wilhite, Warrilow, and Neumann thought the brand should be going that it was as if the agency had never worked on the account. "It was total validation that what we were doing was right," said Wilhite. "The agency had truly lost touch with what we were and where we were going." Arnold was always right in there. Everyone liked Arnold and thought their ideas and energy were right-on. The brand essence video had caught everyone's attention from the start. Wilhite had liked their stuff from the first meeting. At the second meeting between VW and Arnold, the "Drivers wanted" was presented for the first time, and Wilhite felt like he had his agency—almost. Prior to each presentation, Bob Lundin hands out a rating card for each person on the review committee to score how well the agency did in meeting the objectives set forth in the earlier briefing:

- Did they demonstrate an understanding of the customer and the market?
- Did they understand the VW brand and product positioning?
- Did they demonstrate an understanding of the strengths and weaknesses in marketing import cars?

and so on. Wilhite hadn't scored any of the sections of the card. Across the middle, he simply wrote, "Fucking brilliant." That was it. Wilhite would later explain that a friend and dealer, Richard Fisher from Evanston, Illinois, who was a member of the selection committee, says that there is a system he lives by in sizing up people. "In school, if you got a D, you sucked," explained Wilhite. "If you got a C, no one was going to beat you up over it. It was okay. B was doing better, but still mediocre. An A was doing better than a B, but still just okay. Then, there was 'fucking brilliant.' Some people and some ideas are just fucking brilliant."

Arnold completely nailed the assignment, and captured the energy and core of the VW brand, turning it into something invitational. *Invitational* was the key, says Wilhite. "German Engineering." "Nothing else is a Volkswagen." "*Fahrvergnügen.*" All those lines had been statements about the brand. "Drivers wanted" was an invitation for people to come *to* the brand, as well as a brand statement.

So why the leaning toward The Richards Group, and what did they do to blow it? The VW selection committee, says Wilhite, was made comfortable by The Richards Group's depth and stability. Stan Richards was engaging without being scary like Deutsch. He was the center of his team, but the team was balanced, and his people came off as empowered and grounded. Unlike Arnold, the agency had been around for more than 15 years. It was established. It had done some very good work for the Texas Cadillac dealers, so they knew how to do a car account. When it came to their presentation, though, "It didn't have the energy that Arnold had," said Wilhite. "Whereas Arnold's presentation seemed to flow naturally from the people to the point where Kristin Volk could just keep going after the computer shut down, The Richards Group's presentation was almost too slick and rehearsed. It *felt* like a presentation. What Arnold brought forth was that, 'Hey, we're your guys! We know this brand! We *are* this brand! We *live* this brand!' It was unambiguous. They just nailed it."

When Deutsch had finished on Saturday, the selection committee met for the last time. It was unanimous, and deliberation was over in 5 minutes. It was Arnold. The only thing that remained was to get hold of Germany to let Dr. Neumann know how it came out, and get final approval before they called Eskandarian to give him the good news.

———

Monday, 28 March 1995, should have been Arnold's Day. However, Melanie Wells spent weeks hanging out with Deutsch, not Arnold. Her cover story on the cover of the "Money" section of *USA Today*[2] had a picture of Donny Deutsch and his team—the losers. Wells had gathered her quotes for the story over the course of several weeks, so her article had quotes from Deutsch during the research process, right after the presentation, and then after he got the bad news. Deutsch was quoted as saying after his final pitch meeting, but before finding out Arnold won, "I think we blew them away. Something special happened in that room." Deutsch came off as a sore loser: "The jury isn't always a fair jury . . . The best work doesn't always win," said a despondent Deutsch, who later regretted his remarks to Wells in the heat of disappointment. Eskandarian, Lawner, and Kelly were dumbfounded. "It was really something . . . to be the winners and to see those remarks in the paper," said Lawner. "But we had the satisfaction of having the account." Eskandarian was miffed, but says he met Deutsch years later and talked about it. "He is a good guy who had a bad day," says Eskandarian. Indeed, Deutsch quipped in Wells's story that he might take the black Jetta he bought for research and "slam it into a brick wall." Ten days before the final pitch, Deutsch had told Wells, "If we don't win, I'd like to see Arnold Fortuna win because that would show the client is afraid of really shaking things up." Full of disappointment and vinegar after getting the news, he also said, "I feel badly for VW because I think they're leaving a silver bullet on the table. We hit the advertising G-spot . . . Now, I'm nastier, meaner. I'm more determined."

Arnold creative partner Michael Fortuna responded, "Donny's work is memorable because it's in your face. Ours is memorable because it's in your heart and soul." It was a good comeback from the winner.

All good things come to those who wait and persevere. Arnold got VW; Deutsch would later win Mitsubishi, an account of near equal size as VW. Deutsch sold his agency in 2001 to Interpublic Group for more than $200 million, pocketing 90 percent of the take.

———

Now that Arnold was chosen, the real work began. Wilhite knew that Arnold's work had to be great from the start. The trade press would be watching, as would the news weeklies—*Business Week* and perhaps *Time*. The advertising columns in the *Wall Street Journal, USA Today,* and the *New York Times,* would all want to write about the first work from Arnold. *Automotive News,* the publication most read by dealers, would give it big play. This was VW. The Museum of Modern Art had a dozen VW ads from the old DDB days in its permanent collection. People were watching. Germany was watching. Every employee of Volkswagen of America was watching. In many ways, opting for Deutsch would have been the easy way out for Wilhite and Warrilow. Deutsch was the hot shop. Arnold did the best work, however, and that's what it was supposed to be about.

The Recovery

EIGHT

After the review for a new agency was over, there was a meeting between Wilhite and the principal partners at Arnold, his new ad agency. He told his new partners, "The whole world is watching." The dealers. Germany. The press. Not just the advertising press, but the general business press. Every employee of Volkswagen of America. All of the DDB offices around the world. Everyone was watching because VW advertising had such a storied past. It must be right. It must be tight. No mistakes.

Arnold's creative strategy was so dead-on right in its final presentation that the first round of ads were practically done. In May 1995, the first ads broke. Despite expectations, they weren't spectacular. Certainly, they weren't as good as the ads would get in 1998, 1999, and 2000. In fact, says Lance Jensen, "Our strategy was showing all over the place." One of the mantras of good creative agencies in the late 1990s would be, "Don't let your strategy show." That means, especially when it comes to targeting young consumers, that ads mustn't be too obvious. Ads shouldn't try too hard to be cool and hip. If they are, the very people being targeted will reject them.

Wilhite knew the first ads were a bit obvious. However, from where the advertising had been—the static "The Most Loved Cars in the World"—to where he knew VW was headed with Arnold, there was a lot of room. It would have been a mistake, Wilhite believed, to jump too far too fast. The opening batch of commercials featured young, hip, enterprising people. They were Nike-wearing, Nike-believing, latte-drinking workers with car payments and mountain bikes. One ad featured a young Wall Street researcher type talking about calling Hong Kong, making appointments, and breaking appointments. He was a young, energetic man in control, making things happen. However, the ad glibly depicted, he couldn't open his office window, despite his intelligence and importance to his firm. Another TV ad featured an African-American woman rattling off several features of a sophisticated security system on her building to keep people from getting in. "So how do I get out?" was her punch line. The people talked fast, and the camera moved fast, as had become the norm with TV commercials since MTV had taken hold of young attention spans. The people were doers and controllers. Phrases popping up on the TV screen were right from the brand essence video that Arnold pitched to win the account: "It's about having kids. Not being your parents." "It's about being connected to the road." There was an energy and intelligence in the TV spots that hadn't been seen in VW ads since the early 1970s. One woman talked about how well her building was climate-controlled, and then she yelled, "So why can't I breathe?!" The tone being set was that VWs offered a driving experience that made up for all of the everyday ways in which we are isolated from real life and real air. It was advertising that bordered on trying *too* hard and being *too* obvious. "But we had to start somewhere to set up a new voice," says Wilhite.

It wouldn't be until the fall of 1995 that an ad would break that most people at VW and Arnold viewed as the turning point. Titled "Cappuccino Girl," it was an ad that was promoting a zero-down, $199-a-month lease for the Golf, but it also clearly advanced the brand message. That was a dimension of advertising that was being restored to VW. Volkswagen had to pitch deals to sell cars, but every deal would pitch the brand as well. "Java Girl" featured a young entrepreneurial woman whose business was supplying cappuccino pump dispensers and other coffee equipment to cafes and coffeehouses. She drove a Golf around town to service her customers. The ad moved quickly, and she was seen as the quintessential VW owner, buyer, and target. She was smart, pretty, and making her own way in life, being her own boss. The creative strategy called for using people whose lives could bring out certain product benefits. She was full of the VW attitude that the agency was looking for, and her use of the car showed off its roominess and utilitarian benefits. One young man featured in an ad for the Passat talked about four-wheel disk brakes, but did so while discussing the technology he developed for toll plazas that eliminated the need to make people stop to pay the toll. That is the kind of job and idea to which VW owners could relate. Touches of VW's German heritage were dribbled in here and there, but in a fun way, as in one TV spot where the couple was using a Jetta to transport their Weimaraners. The woman simply says, "Weimaraners come from Germany."

The press did pay attention when the ads were introduced. Wilhite was right. The *Wall Street Journal; USA Today;* the *New York Times; Adweek; Ad Age;* the Detroit, Chicago, and Los Angeles papers, as well as the newswire services, wrote about it. Some TV stations even paid attention. The reviews were all favorable. All agreed it was a breath of fresh air for the brand.

Advertising would drive the brand and showroom traffic in 1995, 1996, and into 1997, because there would be no new product until 1997 to excite customers. The plan that Arnold laid out was to use 1995 and 1996 to make the brand important again through energetic, fun advertising that reinforced the VW with its customers. The next step, going into 1997, would be inviting new and different drivers to come to the brand through what Wilhite describes as *invitational* advertising. The advertising was meant to be a fresh coat of paint until the new product arrived. Fresh paint made a big difference. Brand measurements relied upon by VW and Arnold to measure progress were going up like they hadn't in many years. Even without the new product, people were associating the VW brand with superior engineering and fun. Measurements of *brand relevance,* which were based on how readily customers thought of VW for their next purchase, were tracking much higher. Dealers were reporting much higher showroom traffic and the right kind of traffic. Volkswagen had a buzz. People were talking about VW in a good way—and more people put VW on their shopping list.

Media Counts

As important as creativity is to advertising, selection of media is as vital. It is a part of the business—both the auto and ad business—that gets short shrift. It isn't very glamorous. To VW, which did not have $300 million in 1995 and 1996 to spend on ads, it was vitally important.

Arnold had not won the business on creative merits alone. Wilhite and dealers liked what they heard from Arnold Media Director John Gaffney about how and where he wanted to spend their money.

When Arnold began pitching VW in early 1995, the agency had only one member of the team who had worked on a car account, John Gaffney. Fifteen years earlier, Gaffney worked in Detroit at J. Walter Thompson on the Ford business. It was experience that would prove almost useless for the VW pitch. Ford and its longtime agency are not known for the hip, creative, energetic advertising for which VW was drilling. When a company has over $1 billion to spend each year on ads, the people responsible for how and on what it is spent have not historically acted as if they have a precious commodity that must be utilized in the smartest, most creative way. Ford has primarily been interested in making sure that they reach the greatest number of people, any people, with the money they spend. Creatively speaking, the agency does a very effective job in marketing big trucks. Thompson and Ford know how to do that very well. Ford trucks are a huge cash cow for the company. As long as they keep the advertising imagery masculine, tough, and full of country music, the truck buyers keep coming year after year. Cars are another story. When it comes to marketing Escorts, Tauruses, Mustangs, and Windstars, media placement for Ford has been all about reach and frequency: How many people can it reach, and how frequently can it reach them for the least amount of money?

Gaffney says the only real benefit derived from his Ford experience during the VW pitch was remembering how Thompson did a very good job of targeting truck buyers. The creative almost took care of itself in those days of the early 1980s, because the truck market wasn't even a family business the way it is today with sport utility vehicles replacing the family car and station wagon. It was an all-male business. That experience also made him familiar with such things as the J. D. Power and Associates market segmentation study, which the research firm tallies for every auto manufacturer. The study delves into who buys a particular brand of car—VW, Ford, Toyota—why they buy it, and what media they consume. A staple of car advertising, it is very valuable stuff. Laughably, Gaffney was the only one at Arnold who was even aware that it existed.

When Thompson presented advertising to then Ad Director Edsel Ford II, in the early 1980s, it was a factory presentation, recalls Gaffney. The agency would typically create six, seven, perhaps eight campaigns, each with a few storyboards for proposed TV and magazine ads. All the concepts and mocked-up ads were put up on the wall of an enormous conference room. Edsel Ford and his lieutenants would poke holes in ads and ideas, and the agency and Ford underlings would watch closely so they could echo the opinions of the boss "and follow the drift," says Gaffney.

While Ron Lawner and the creative team were working on their creative pieces, and Kristin Volk was working on her consumer think-piece, Gaffney was trying to merge the analysis from the Power report and the agency's own focus groups into a coherent media plan. Any advertiser is usually looking for how much weight it can buy for its ad budget, literally how many TV spots, how many print ads, how many outdoor billboards, how many bus shelters? It's called *optimizing the media plan.* The object is to drive down the cost of reaching each consumer as far as possible.

The problem with this approach, as Gaffney saw it, was that the company and its agencies had been doing it this way for years, and had gotten poor results. In fact, Gaffney charted three lines on a single graph that represented 15 years: (1) share of voice, (2) media spending, and (3) sales. Defined simply, *share of voice* is how much of the ad spending in each product segment belonged to VW. This is mostly a function of how many total dollars are spent. In other words, if there is a total of $500 million spent on advertising subcompact cars, and the VW Golf had a budget of $30 million, its share of voice would be 6 percent. Gaffney noted that share of voice, media spending, and sales had all dropped steadily between 1980 and 1995. The lines moved down the chart like shadows.

Media directors are not supposed to be good judges of creative, and they often get short time in a presentation. However, Gaffney thought the work that Arnold was doing for VW was special. "I hadn't seen anything like it in the marketplace. And I couldn't think of any other brand that could pull it off. I knew, despite our lack of auto experience, that we could. And I felt that media could and would play an important part."

Gaffney's team gathered "the typical media junk" (e.g., demographics of the VW buyer and intender, which include income, age, zip code, education, etc.). Normally, says Gaffney, you don't see a lot of useful information in that material. He saw two pretty dramatic things for VW, though: (1) age and (2) mental attitude. Volkswagen buyers were younger than the buyers of the cars against which they competed; however, they also made more money than average Toyota or Mazda buyers. That is an unusual combination. They were also better educated. Almost 60 percent of VW buyers were college educated, compared with 40 percent for the industry. The differences were not slight. They were dramatic. The median age of VW buyers was 7 to 8 years lower than buyers of Honda, Mazda, and Toyota; the median income was $10,000 to $15,000 more. Those are *huge* differences in the world of media planning.

Gaffney began to see an opening that VW executives might appreciate. The agency usually tells the client that it can't expect share of voice and sales to increase without a sharp rise in advertising dollars. Gaffney knew, however, that the budget was set at between $80 million and $100 million, and that there wouldn't be new money to count on for at least 2 years when the new Passat arrived. For 2 years, they had to sell the old product, but keep the upward momentum going that had begun when VW finally began getting a supply of Golfs and Jettas from its Puebla, Mexico, plant.

That VW buyers were so different in age, attitude, and income from their competitors showed Gaffney a crack in which he could insert a strategy to increase VW's share of voice with the existing budget. He reckoned that because VW's whole universe of buyers seemed to be found in only about 24 percent of the population, the media planning (i.e., the choice of TV programs, magazines, and websites) that had been used up until that point by VW and its dealers was all wrong. The prevailing media-buying strategy at VW had long been "Buy the cheapest stuff." They wanted to see the greatest number of TV commercials and magazine ads for their comparatively paltry budget, with no attention paid to whether the ads were reaching people that could even loosely be called VW prospects.

"So we went in and started telling them how much of the market they could write off," says Gaffney. "We had to tell them first who *isn't* buying their cars and who *won't* be buying their cars before we could get into why we were proposing the media plan we had." Gaffney spoke a language they could understand, though. "We know we aren't getting $300 million. But we think we can make your $50 million to $100 million right now *look* like $300 million to the right people." He got their attention.

Gaffney told VW that TV, especially network TV, was going to be key to the plan. This was unusual because most advertisers with a small share of voice and budget go away from network TV shows for other, cheaper programming where they can get their ads on the air more frequently—cable TV, local news, and *M*A*S*H* reruns. Gaffney's plan, though, was that VW would be on 20 prime-time TV shows. That's it. His team found that VW's educated, affluent, young people watched around 15 hours or less of TV a week. They often planned their busy days around being free when *their* shows came on. In addition, they watched the same shows all the time. This gave VW a chance to look big to these buyers who were the right buyers, as well as to get a substantial share of the time that their customers spent watching TV. Arnold would buy slots on programs that were considered risky by most mainstream advertisers, but were rich in viewership among VW people. This made the media buys cheap as dirt because controversial shows, such as *NYPD Blue* and *Buffy the Vampire Slayer,* which were great for VW, were shunned by other auto companies because of their blue content. The networks airing those shows gave VW discounts because having an auto advertiser is a signal to other advertisers who are on the fence about buying time that the show is okay. In 1995, *NYPD Blue* was lucky to get a headache powder to advertise, says Gaffney. The ratings that the shows delivered were not only high, making the media buy cost-effective, the viewerships were hip-deep in VW prospects. "We could buy those shows for a song," said Gaffney. And he bought a 52-week schedule of several programs like that, a commitment that was unheard of, even for advertisers with 5 and 10 times the budget.

At first, Marketing Director Steve Wilhite was dubious, as he often was when Gaffney proposed a media schedule that didn't jog with the company's track record. "Volkswagen had been a company very much led by the belief that a brand reflects the company you keep," said Gaffney. Neither the VW dealers, nor the regional sales and marketing people, wanted to be on shows that were racy or too expensive. They wanted to see reach and frequency. "Why buy one *Seinfeld* spot when we can buy 100 Saturday afternoon movie spots for that money?" went the argument. To this day, though, Gaffney has never made up a reach-and-frequency chart for the VW business that is required by most advertisers.

Even after Arnold had established its media philosophy, it had two battles early in its relationship with VW. In 1995, while Arnold was buying off-center programming to match VW's off-center customer, it recommended buying both a National Football League (NFL) schedule and the 1996 Summer Olympics. "C'mon . . . football? . . . how does that make sense alongside *Buffy the Vampire*," groused Wilhite. While Gaffney was confident of his prime-time buys, he was just as confident in these mainstream sports buys, but for different reasons.

Gaffney liked the NFL because while it was just an okay buy for VW customers, it was a great buy for reaching VW dealers and salespeople. Among VW's 600 dealers, only a handful are still exclusively VW stores. Most have VW on one side, and maybe Honda, Mazda, or Isuzu on the other side. Many have three or four brands. Salespeople often handle more than one line. All any salesperson is interested in is selling a car, any car. Salespeople can size up a customer while he or she is still in the dealership parking lot. Volkswagen, because of the absence of Golfs and Jettas in 1992 and 1993, fell off the radar of salespeople selling multiple lines. Even when the cars came back, the media budget was still small. Following Arnold's new media-planning strategy, few salespeople were seeing VW's advertising. "VW looked small to its dealers. They weren't watching the shows we were buying. We felt VW needed to be bigger . . . in the salesman's face more," said Gaffney.

An agency normally sends a videotape of advertising to the dealers along with the media schedule so they know when and how often VW ads are running. However, salespeople don't key into this material, says Gaffney. Arnold wanted an NFL schedule because VW could suddenly look bigger to this audience. When a company advertises on the home team NFL broadcast, every car manufacturer gets the same number of slots. That means VW could look just as big as Ford, Chevy, Toyota, and the others. And what do salespeople watch on their Sunday day off? The home team NFL game. However, just being on the game wasn't enough. Arnold wanted the salespeople to feel involved in this media buy. Besides watching the games, salespeople are often in football pools. Gaffney worked with Fox to establish the Fox-Volkswagen Sunday Afternoon Football Pool. The salespeople picked their teams. If they won, they would get a big box of football stuff, including jackets and sweatshirts that were from Fox Sports and had the home team's logo. "We could look as big as any car advertiser on the air to them," said Gaffney. "These guys had seen a lot of crap from VW over the years about which they had very good reasons to be skeptical. We wanted them to know 'Hey, we mean business.' " The grand prize for the best record among salespeople at the halfway mark of the season was a trip to Dallas for the Thanksgiving Day NFL game; the prize for the winner at the end of the season was a trip to the Super Bowl.

Wilhite was skeptical of the wisdom behind this program in that it cost several million dollars, or around 15 percent of VW's ad budget that year. He wasn't as dubious, though, as he would be when Gaffney told him he wanted to buy a raft of Summer Olympics spots.

Gaffney pitched the NFL and Olympics programs to about 30 VW executives, all of whom knew Wilhite was skeptical. Dr. Jens Neumann was in on this meeting, though, and would have the final word. It was Wilhite's expectation that Neumann would shoot down the programs as being too expensive, and that he might not feel right about being a sponsor (as a German company) of the Olympics, which were being held in the United States that summer. "Instead, Neumann banged his fist down on the table," recalled Gaffney. Said Neumann with his signature energy, "This is exactly the kind of thing we need to be doing!! This shows the whole world that we are coming back. These are American things, and Volkswagen is an American company!!" All of a sudden, all of the issues collapsed, said Gaffney. "Dr. Neumann saw the idea. He understood better than any of his American executives. He was willing to take a risk. He saw the immeasurable value in being on a big stage. He saw the reach, if not the frequency."

Even with Dr. Neumann's blessing, though, there was great consternation over whether VW should sell some of the spots as the game drew nearer. The mix of vehicles that summer was not what it was supposed to be. There were too few cars equipped with automatic transmissions. May and June of 1996 had been disappointing sales months. Auburn Hills was looking to conserve some of its money for later when they had more of the cars that sold better. Showroom traffic was down as well. The company was coming out of a successful promotion with Trek Bicycles and K2 Snowboards, a program that offered Golf and Jetta buyers the choice of either one on a roofrack as standard equipment. What if ratings for the Olympics were down? Just a few days before the start of the Olympics, Wilhite's team and Arnold were huddled, discussing unloading a bunch of TV spots to another advertiser. In the end, though, they kept them all. Gaffney fought for his plan. None of them wanted to explain to Neumann why they weren't on the Olympics after he blessed the buy as a brilliant plan. Within a few days after the Games began, showroom traffic picked up. It turned out, too, that there was quite a bit of drama at that year's Olympics, especially among the women gymnasts. The gymnasts are as popular as the ice skaters in the winter Olympics. They get the best time slots, and draw the biggest ratings. Gaffney had cultivated the salesman at NBC with whom he had dealt in making the deal. The salesman was in the control truck in Atlanta, deciding what TV ads would go where. At several key, suspenseful moments, VW spots showed up during commercial breaks. Perhaps the most dramatic moment of the competition, when Shannon Miller needed a certain minimum score to win the gold medal for the United States, and she stuck her landing perfectly off the balance beam, the telecast went to a commercial break while the judges tabulated their scores. Up popped a VW commercial at the highest-rated moment of the games. Traffic was roaring at the dealerships in the following days and weeks. Wilhite called Gaffney the day after and asked how he had pulled it off. "I told you it would be worth it," Gaffney replied. "It's about cultivating people," says Gaffney. "If we had just paid the guy our money and walked away, we wouldn't have done nearly as well. We didn't bribe the guy. We just make it a point of doing business with these folks as well as we can, being nice, helping them when they need it, not being a bully. It pays off."

Media had been an important aspect to VW's rise in the 1960s and 1970s. Volkswagen, for example, had been the first car advertiser in Gloria Steinem's *Ms.* magazine. It was also an early car advertiser in *Penthouse,* though DDB had to justify it periodically to furrowed brows at VW. A company memo from 1982, for example, specifically challenged the merits of advertising in *Penthouse.* The note from Brand Chief Jim Fuller stated, "Penthouse doesn't seem to fit our image or that of the customers we do business with." Fuller was worried about being the only auto advertiser in *Penthouse* at a time when religious groups were poised to attack advertisers supporting such magazines. In fact, the men's entertainment magazine, the media research showed at the time, was a more efficient buy than *Newsweek* magazine or *US News and World Report.* It was also the best-rated magazine for import buyers in general, higher even than *Sports Illustrated.* The advertising department made the point to Fuller that the only people who would object were people who were far outside of VW's buyer group, and that VW buyers don't react positively to being told what they should read or buy.

In 2001, VW bought an exclusive network automotive sponsorship of the Super Bowl at a cost of several million dollars. The Super Bowl has become an event for the advertising as much as the game. Advertisers such as Frito-Lay, Pepsi, and Budweiser nearly always debut new ads meant to entertain viewers. *USA Today* and the other major newspapers make a big deal out of rating the ads. In fact, *USA Today* has a score card that appears in the paper the Monday after the game, and the ad columnist for the paper, Michael McCarthy, appears on the morning news shows to talk about it. Volkswagen put three ads on the big game, and none of them scored particularly high in the paper's scoring system. One TV spot featured two young men looking up at a tree, throwing things into the tree to make something fall down. One would assume it was a frisbee or a kite. After almost 60 seconds, a GTI fell out of the tree. In another spot, two guys are in the woods. The viewer sees a camera flash from behind a tree, and then the two men running toward their car. As they speed away, the driver turns to his friend who is holding a Polaroid picture developing in his hands and says, "What happened?" He shows the picture of him holding a bear in a headlock. A third spot was outside the campaign, and depicted a man driving his Jetta to a wedding. He arrives late, just at the time when the minister asks if anyone has any objections. It was a cliffhanger ad because the viewer isn't sure if the late-arriving man was meant to be the groom, or if he's an old boyfriend, or even a late best man. It was a gamble. For one thing, the Super Bowl is expensive. For another, it can be an awful game by halftime. If VW's ads ran in the third and fourth quarters of a runaway game, the ads can be lost in the shuffle unless they are truly breakthrough. Arnold Account Director Jon Castle defends the buy this way: "It was really to show our dealers and salespeople again that we are out there investing in awareness. By January 2001, it had been a while since we had a new product. Sales in the industry were down and consumer confidence was slipping. We have to keep share of mind with our sales force as much as with our customers. And it doesn't surprise me that our ads didn't score big in such a mass-market media venue. We're not a mass-market brand."

There Are Incentives, and Then There Are Incentives

In 1996, VW was 1 year away from introducing the New Beetle and 3 years away from an all-new Golf and Jetta. The zero-down, $199-a-month leases for Golf and Jetta had moved the metal up to a point, but the Arnold team was also trying to rebuild a brand. Arnold had taken an approach to the business from the first day that transcended mere advertising. Advertising working alone is a lousy way to build or rebuild a brand. When Ed Eskandarian was putting Arnold together by buying up small agencies, he hadn't just bought ad agencies. He also bought a direct-marketing outfit, a public relations group, and a sales promotion firm as well. Some call this *integrated marketing.* Others shy away from the term, because it implies to some that the agency is merely trying to sell the client a bunch of different services.

To smart companies, however, it just means that the agency knows that an ad is not the answer to every problem and challenge.

Arnold had seen in its research that VW people tended to be athletic and activity oriented. Two pastimes that kept coming up in researching the lifestyles of VW customers were mountain biking and snow sports—snowboarding and skiing. These interests had dictated some of the magazine titles Arnold was buying in the media plan. However, the agency began to wonder if these interests couldn't be used to attract customers more productively and effectively than mere rebates and subsidized leases.

What the agency had in mind could become a brilliant, if almost too obvious, stroke of marketing. On the flip side, it could be viewed by the twenty-something customer as the most ham-fisted attempt to be cool since the formation of *The Monkees*. Arnold hadn't handled a car account until taking on the VW assignment, so they didn't think like car people—they thought like marketers.

The idea was to find a hip brand of mountain bike and put a new bike on the roof of a new Jetta or Golf as standard equipment. Bought at a volume discount, the bikes could be purchased for $200 to $250. It was hoped, though, that the target wouldn't simply see the bike and roofrack as a substitute for $300 they could put in their pocket. The principle is hardly new. Carnival arcades have been based on it for more than a century. Buy a bunch of attractive-looking junk that costs 75 cents, and then charge some rube $3 for chances to win it. The contestant might spend $8 to win the 75-cent prize. The stroke to the ego that comes from winning something, even if you spend more than it would cost to buy it, is worth the premium. In similar fashion, the mountain bike on the roofrack would appeal to young buyers who would actually want it. The association with the mountain bike would make the customer feel good about buying, driving, and owning a VW. Furthermore, some percentage of people would be drawn to the offer, even if they never used the bike or simply gave it away. Like people who never drive off-road in their Jeep enjoy the feeling that comes from driving an SUV with four-wheel drive, so would people be drawn to the image imparted by a car that comes with a mountain bike on the roof. The same idea could be applied to snowboards. Arnold then went out and signed two of the up-and-coming equipment companies in both categories, Trek mountain bikes and K2 snowboards. To give an idea of just how far the VW brand had fallen, and how far it still had to go, neither company jumped at the chance to be associated with VW. Arnold had to woo them.

"The Trek/K2 promotion came to us opportunistically," said VW Public Relations Director Steve Keyes. "We had a surplus of models with sunroofs, spoilers, and alloyed wheels and we were thinking of implementing an after-market price promotion to push these cars out. But we knew that this price promotion would go against the very image we were trying to build. So, Arnold suggested that we approach Trek and K2 about a comarketing opportunity. In our initial conversations, both Trek and K2 expressed some hesitancy in working with us. They didn't think that Volkswagen had the image they wanted to be associated with. But we finally convinced them, and in April 1996 we introduced the Trek edition of the Jetta and it was a hit. We decided that instead of putting a monetary incentive on the car, we would put a total package around the car that would help reinforce the lifestyle image of the drivers we were targeting."

Customers responded. Sales of Jetta went up 15 percent in 1996, and were up another 6,000 to 91,000 in 1997. The cost of the bikes and snowboards was far less than incentive marketing and did more for the brand.

Da Da Da . . . Buzz

If there is one ad that stands out in the recovery of Volkswagen of America in its new era of advertising, it is a TV ad titled "Sunday Afternoon." It is a TV ad that was special, say its creators, because they weren't trying very hard to come up with it.

Launched in April 1997, the TV spot features two young men in their early 20s, one white and one black. It was conceived, says Lance Jensen, from an idea he had one day about how "just driving around" was a pastime when he was younger, and still is for young people.

Though the title of the ad is "Sunday Afternoon," it is also known by the music track that underscores the ad, a song called "Da Da Da" by the band Trio.

The ad struck a chord with TV viewers because of how utterly "slacker" the two guys seemed. *Slacker* was a term that became hip in the mid- and late 1990s to describe twenty-somethings who were ambition challenged. Slackers didn't aspire to have 9-to-5 jobs; instead, they watched a lot of TV, listened to a lot of music, read a lot of music magazines, and probably didn't vote.

"It was the most boring shoot I had ever been on," said Account Director Jon Castle. "We followed these guys around with a camera for two days. Period." The two were in a Golf and did pretty much whatever came to mind. The guy in the passenger seat displayed a sudden karate move. The driver cleaned a smudge off the dashboard. The black guy held his fingers up and pretended he was squeezing the sun between his thumb and forefinger. Later in the ad, he started playing with a little springy skeleton toy. "Da Da Da" was playing on the stereo. The two spotted an old chair on the side of the road and loaded it into the back of the Golf. After a few minutes of driving, they noticed that it emitted a pungent odor, so they pulled over and unloaded it. "That was to show how roomy the Golf is and how much stuff you can put in it," said Account Director Karen Driscoll. "All day, we just kept asking, okay, what can they do next?" said Driscoll. The voice-over line was perfect, "Volkswagen Golf. It fits your life, or your complete lack thereof."

"I thought okay . . . sure," said Steve Wilhite. "It's all about attitude, but we also show how roomy it is. Fine." Even Dr. Neumann understood it. It turned out that Neumann is a fan of Trio. Some of the other members of the Vorstand, though, didn't get it. And some dealers refused to run it in their market areas. By 1996, however, they had become used to it. Santa Monica VW dealer Mike Sullivan said, "I know the ads are right when I don't really get it." Advertising Director Liz Vanzura made the agency sweat a bit on the line of copy. "Are we saying our buyers don't have lives?" asked Vanzura.

Vanzura would go through many sessions with Arnold discussing whether the right message was coming through in Arnold's edgy work. "We learned to push each other. They would push me. I would push back until we all knew it was right. We never tested the ads with consumer focus groups though. If we were that kind of company, few of them would have gotten on the air."

It turned out that the ad had even more legs and interpretations than the creators imagined. To debut the ad, Arnold bought time on *Ellen*, a sitcom starring Ellen DeGeneres, who had come out publicly as a lesbian. In the show, however, her character is straight. There had been a big buildup in the media, though, about how her show on ABC would have her character come out gay as well. Several advertisers who had been sitting on the fence with *Ellen* ran for the hills, and a few dropped out. Arnold's Gaffney, though, thought it was just the right show for VW, and no one at VW had given him any indication to stay away from it. It was a coincidence that it was "Sunday Afternoon" that would run. For some reason, says Creative Director Ron Lawner, the *Wall Street Journal* and the *New York Times* both drew the conclusion that the two young men were gay. "That was absolutely never in our minds," says Lawner. "But the fact that the guys in the ad stirred so many questions, added to the fact that we aired it on *Ellen* . . . it was great. It was dumb luck. But it was great because that's when advertising stops being advertising and becomes a piece of incredibly valuable brand communication. And I think by having the freedom that we have, and the license we have, those kinds of lucky things are bound to happen."

Some of the dealers didn't understand "Sunday Afternoon" at all, and refused to fund it in their selling areas. They changed their minds later when it officially crossed over into the highly desirable "water-cooler" status when Jay Leno created a parody film of the ad for *The Tonight Show*. Actor Michael J. Fox took off on the ad, creating a parody to promote his network show *Spin City*. Microsoft Chairman Bill Gates and Chief Executive Officer Steven Ballmer created a "Sunday Afternoon" takeoff playing the guys in the car for a company meeting.

Creating buzz with advertising is becoming old hat, but few advertisers do it well, and even fewer have done it as well as VW since hiring Arnold. "There has to be a fearless factor in creating advertising," says Vanzura. "If ads don't get watched or remembered, they can't do much to sell the product or the brand." This philosophy can be traced back to bill Bernbach who taught that the purpose of advertising is not to sell the product, but simply to be read or watched. If the consumer isn't interested enough to tune into the ad, the money is wasted.

———

The launch of the 1997 Passat was the success that VW expected. Not only did it continue VW's momentum, which had begun with the advertising, but it established that no one would question that a VW sedan could be worth more than $20,000. The original Passat launched in 1990 had nice qualities, but it wasn't the refined automobile that the 1997 car would be. Jim Healey of *USA Today* said, "The Passat is at least as much fun to drive as a Mercedes C Class."[1]

By the end of 1997, VW had sold just under 138,000 cars, a 178 percent increase from the nadir of 1993. The stage was set for a genuine comeback.

0 to 60? Yes

The launch of the New Beetle had been anticipated since it was shown at the 1994 Detroit Auto Show as Concept 1. It was huge for VW. It would debut at the 1998 Detroit Auto Show as a production car in January and hit dealerships in the spring and early summer.

"Drivers wanted" by early 1998 had been setting a new tone for VW advertising, a tone that everyone involved was beginning to think could rival some of the old DDB Volkswagen work for status in the ad business. It was inventive and had a unique tone that other car companies were trying to mimic.

The New Beetle would launch first in the United States. Every other car in VW's history had launched first in Europe, it's home market. However, the Beetle was as much a U.S. car as Chevy or Ford. The New Beetle was developed expressly as a lightning bolt to energize sagging fortunes in the United States.

A two-pronged debate was going on in 1997 about how the car should be launched to the public. Should it be launched within the

"Drivers wanted" campaign? Should Arnold launch it? The latter question seemed almost incredible at this point. What seemed more incredible was some feeling in Wolfsburg that maybe DDB Needham should be allowed to develop the launch advertising for the New Beetle for all the markets: the United States, Japan, Mexico, Canada, and ultimately Europe. DDB Chairman Keith Reinhard hated losing any of the VW or Audi business. After losing the Audi business in Canada before losing it in the United States, he wanted to buy the Canadian agency that won it, only to be told by VW that the business would be pulled again if he did. DDB still had most of VW's business around the world, and so it was not outlandish in Wolfsburg that the agency might handle a world launch of the New Beetle.

Arnold was furious at the prospect. Wilhite was furious. Warrilow was fit to be tied that it might even be considered. "I never entertained the possibility," said Warrilow, "but it was possible that I could have had to fight hard over it if they hadn't come to their senses." *They* were Neumann but, more specifically, Worldwide Marketing Chief Dieter Dahlhoff.

Reinhard, says Wilhite, saw the New Beetle as a way to get back in the U.S. game and increase DDB's worldwide standing. As for the launching strategy, Neumann thought it could make sense to launch the New Beetle outside the "Drivers wanted" campaign. He wasn't sure that the nostalgic pull of the New Beetle would fit into "Drivers wanted." Arnold, however, felt strongly that marketing the New Beetle in its own separate ad campaign would be the wrong way to go, especially given that the New Beetle was viewed as elevating the whole VW brand. How could that objective be reached if it was off on its own? Vanzura wondered, too, whether the full potential of the car would be realized if it were sold to such a narrow customer base as VW had been targeting. While Golf, Jetta, GTI, and Passat had been positioned as drivers' cars, research had shown that many people viewed the Beetle as a kind of toy car. To the contrary, the New Beetle, based on the Golf platform, was just as much a driver's car as the others. Making the New Beetle a legitimate member of the product family had been a condition of Dr. Piëch's approval of the project—all the more reason to keep it in the overall "Drivers wanted" campaign. Still, internal discussions revolved around how much of the Beetle's original positioning from the 1960s should be used in the launch of the new car. If the agency went that way, it would be tough to accomplish within the Arnold campaign and make it all seem of one brand family. Vanzura wondered, "How retro should we go?"

———

We'll never know if the New Beetle would have been right for the times had VW introduced it in the late 1980s as many enthusiasts had wanted. What we do know is that 1998 was a particularly perfect time. Baby boomers, many of whom had driven Beetles, or "Bugs," as their first cars, were having a love affair with their youth. It was an affair in which marketers were only too anxious to play innkeeper. Nostalgia was everywhere in the spring of 1998, from a return of Burma Shave to the use of James Brown's "I Feel Good" for Senokot laxatives. Maxwell House coffee brought back "Good to the Last Drop," and Star-Kist tuna resurrected Charlie the Tuna, a commercial icon that was part of baby boom childhood. Hollywood was in the midst of turning out films based on TV shows that baby boomers loved, such as *The Brady Bunch; Mission Impossible; Lost in Space; The Flintstones; Casper; The Avengers; McHale's Navy; Sergeant Bilko; Flipper; Mr. Magoo;* and *The Addams Family.* Baseball stadiums, such as Cleveland's Jacob's Field and Baltimore's Camden Yards, established the model for every new ballpark being built in the United States—the illustrious and romanticized past. Teenagers, to the amazement of their baby boomer parents, brought back their bell-bottom jeans, platform shoes, and Diane Von Furstenberg's wrap dresses. A spokescharacter from the 1940s was given new life by Lee jeans—Buddy Lee. Cracker Jack restored the original packaging design of Sailer Jack and Bingo. The Sun-Maid raisin girl logo was restored as well. Chevy resurrected its "See the USA in a Chevrolet" slogan. Dead celebrities were all the rage in the mid- and late 1990s, appealing, marketers say, to consumers' wistful desire for the simpler and more wholesome past. Film clips of Fred Astaire were used to pitch Dirt Devil vacuums. Lucille Ball clips were brought out to hawk diamonds from Service Merchandise. Ed Sullivan was employed from the grave to launch a new Mercedes-Benz model, as were Gary Cooper, Clark Gable, and Marlene Dietrich.

Some so-called futurists, the marketing consultants with a knack for impressive labels, say it had something to do with the Millennium and our uncertainty with what is going to happen in the new century. Americans have been reaching back for things they know, that they can count on, and that remind them of simpler times. The pull to simpler times has nothing to do with actual simpler times, but perceived simpler times. The past is perceived as simpler because it is part of the baby boomers' youth. In the late 1960s and early 1970s, during the Beetle's true heyday, the country was ripped by a controversial war, a presidential scandal, political assassinations, rising interest rates, and runaway inflation. "The nostalgia craze has had a great deal more to do with a whole lot of people getting old at once than anything else," says Marketing Consultant Dennis Keene, who analyzes demographics and psychographics for consumer product companies, including the automakers. "A great many of those people waited until their mid 30s to start families. Husbands and wives, mothers and fathers are working 12, 13, 14 hour days and wondering what the heck they are doing it for." There is a problem affecting baby boomers more than any other group, says Keene. "Information and connectivity overload. In 1998, people thirty-five to fifty-two have had to learn to be constantly connected by computer modem, pager, cell-phone, et cetera. The ones coming up behind them, the so-called Generation X and Generation Y, have never known anything different, so it's not learned behavior for them. But for the boomers, who have had to evolve to connectivity, it puts a great deal of stress on their systems, minds and constitutions. It makes them yearn for times and places that were simpler, less stressful, less connected. Boomers are an extremely worried lot. Unlike their parents, they are terrible savers, and are facing college education bills for children they had late in life, six and seven times what it cost when they went to college. They are divorced, often supporting two families and dealing in one way or another with aging parents who live into their eighties and nineties."

One of the most appealing and attractive aspects of the original Beetle was its simplicity. The basic design hadn't changed in the more than 25 years that it was sold in the United States. Even the mechanically inept could make some fixes to make a stalled-out Beetle run again, something impossible for most people driving new cars today because of the sophistication of the engines, including the New Beetle. The New Beetle, like the old slogans and logos, offers psychic relief to people by allowing them to tap into memories of simpler times—when they could fix their own cars, take a walk without being paged, send their kid to a baseball game on his or her bike, and buy a decent cup of coffee for less than $2.50. To the oldest baby boomers, who are the ones most likely to have driven a Beetle as their first car, the New Beetle would join their laundry list of youth tonics—vitamins, Rogaine, plastic surgery, stair-steppers, and Viagra. Baby boomers' parents, who reached their 50s in the 1960s, were largely people of their years, listening to Ray Conniff and driving dowdy sedans as they aged. "I am not going to turn into my parents," is practically a mantra for baby boomers, who, in their 50s, are going to Rolling Stones and Bruce Springsteen concerts and have given rise to a boom in motorcycle and sports car sales. Boomers with money have also been fueling a boom in Victorian and Craftsman homes, restoring them, as well as building them new from antique blueprints. They are driving a surge in Art Deco and Art Nouveau antiques and designs, even prompting appliance and electronics designers to renew the old designs in their newest wares. Cigars and port wine are back. Generation X is drinking gin. The past rules!

There is another benefit to retro for the baby boomer mind. Consumers equate the past with quality. The Beetle is no exception. The return of the Beetle fit perfectly with a solution for one of VW's biggest problems dogging it since the late 1970s. Despite German pride in engineering, quality not only lagged behind the Japanese by a wide margin, it was barely above the lowly Koreans by the early 1990s. Despite its lack of amenities and safety features, the original Beetle was viewed as an extremely high-quality product. The New Beetle was introduced at a time when VW had fixed most of its quality problems, so it was an ideal product with which to showcase the improvements.

Many marketers question going overboard on nostalgia and worry that it is a substitute for coming up with a truly sustainable marketing position. The New Beetle, however, is different and more sustainable than, for instance, a *Mr. Magoo* or *McHale's Navy* movie that disappointed at the box office.

Volkswagen's engineering strategy of building many cars on top of a very few mechanical platforms means that VW has to sell far fewer New Beetles to earn a profit than if it had built an entirely new car from the ground up. Beyond that balance sheet reality, though, is the simple truth that the New Beetle is serving as a magnet to a brand of cars that has been substantially improved and updated. In short, says Dr. Neumann, "If we had built the New Beetle without having made the vast improvements to the Passat, Golf and Jetta, we would have been very foolish to bring the New Beetle out. We would have been giving our customers dessert before we gave them their dinner. But the Beetle is so special that it works as a kind of amazing advertising for the brand, attracting more people to the brand than we have had in some time. If people come to the showrooms to look at a Beetle, but wind up buying a Golf, we are still very happy. Indeed, that has happened many times. So, clearly, there are many people buying Jettas and Golfs who would not have discovered them if they hadn't been attracted to VW by the Beetle. This is really central to why we fought to bring the New Beetle back. And it is something that is very American."

Arnold crisscrossed the country again, as it had done in the pitch for the account in 1995. This time it was to find out how people felt about the Beetle 20 years after the last new one was sold. "We conducted man-on-the-street interviews with men and women, young and old, rich and struggling, highly educated to life-educated, hip to conservative—a very diverse group of people," said Arnold's Fran Kelly. "Our conversations centered on exploring the relationship people had with the original Beetle and the potential relationship they could have with the new one. In our quest to learn more about the

New Beetle, we also interviewed industrial designers and sociologists to capture multiple perspectives about the car."

The research turned up polarizing opinions about the car. Many saw it as a toy. The New Beetle, though, did have its share of fans. Targeting was going to be tough because the interest in the car ranged from the 18- to 34-year-olds that had been the target of "Drivers wanted" on up through baby boomers. It was far more a psychographic than demographic challenge. No matter the age or income, the people who liked the New Beetle and said they would definitely consider buying one, were confident individualists who had a desire to be the center of attention. These people often welled up with emotion when interviewers got them talking about their connection to the Beetle.

"Through the research, we uncovered people's love of round shapes in our world," said Jon Castle. "Circular shapes, sociologists and psychologists told us, represent human forms, such as eyes, faces and heads. Unlike squares and triangles, circles are inviting and friendly due to the fact that no sharp edges exist."

One sociologist tapped by Arnold for the Beetle launch told them: "In the sixties, it took on added meaning that the Bug was seen as the counter-culture car. One of the things that emerged from that time was 'small is beautiful' and the Beetle was seen as a beautiful car. Today, in American society, on one hand there is this move to standardize everything, and on the other hand you have this quest for individuality. For many drivers, this car will enable them to express themselves. The Beetle is no longer about being the 'people's car,' but rather the 'personal car.' "

Public relations was key to the launch of the New Beetle like no VW before it. The reception of Concept 1 in 1994 by the press was overwhelming and an important factor in the decision to build it as a production car. In December 1997, a select group of journalists were invited to Wolfsburg to meet with VW's American and German managements and preview the car. It was a trip intended to give auto writers insight into Dr. Piëch's platform strategy, and in-depth exposure to the New Beetle's development so that they would see that it was a car as serious as the Golf or Jetta, not the toy that consumers perceived it to be. Following the auto show in January, VW's public relations staff had the idea of allowing journalists to drive the New Beetles in different communities around the United States, so they could not only evaluate it as a product, but see how the public responded to it.[2]

Automobile Magazine Editor-in-Chief Jean Jennings went a step further, driving the New Beetle from California to Michigan. An excerpt from her report:

> Out on the highway people are letting us change lanes. They're letting us charge off exits we see at the last second. They're smiling. They're waving. They're letting us out of gas stations in front of them. They're giving the thumbs up. The Culligan Man pulls up next to us at a light in Pasadena. "Is it for sale? What platform? Front-drive?" he shouts from his truck. "Those Germans," he shakes his head. "The Bug. They really did it right." . . . We pay a surprise visit to the Art Center College of Design. Every kid going by on the sidewalk stops and turns toward our Beetle as we pull up along the curb and park. Amazingly, one student opens her portfolio to reveal her senior project in product design. It's a line of accessories for the New Beetle. More kids come out of the building and don't go anywhere. I head for the bathroom and when I return, there are twice as many people, and now all the doors (and hood and trunk lids) are opened up. Transportation-design student Art Osborne, "What's the curb weight? Is it 150 horsepower DOHC four or is it the engine that's in the SEAT?" . . . Some suggestions? The front door is hitting the front fender. And the hood prop is at the wrong angle. . . . Jonathon Duncan, "What's the record for stuffing one?"

Advertising, of course, would be vital as well. There was one argument in the company pushing for targeting baby boomers and their love for nostalgia. The decision, though, was not that easy. Consumer trends among baby boomers showed this group opting for larger vehicles—sport utility vehicles, sedans, and pickups. There was a trend toward vehicles like Toyota Camry and Honda Accord becoming larger and roomier. Meanwhile, VW's "Drivers wanted" campaign was aimed at twenty-somethings and thirty-somethings who were young thinkers. Thirty-year-olds felt like 20-year-olds; 40-year-olds felt like 30-year-olds. The tie-dyed and peace sign nostalgia imagery might play with older baby boomers in their late 40s, but not with the younger crowd. Volkswagen wanted some younger buyers for the New Beetle.

Whereas other companies might well have $100 million to launch a new vehicle, Ad Director Liz Vanzura had about $25 million, and even that was in question. If Beetles jumped off the dealer lots, some of Beetle's budget would be moved to support Passat, and public relations would have to pick up even more of the burden.

As with the launch of the "Drivers wanted" campaign, Arnold put together a brand essence video for the New Beetle launch. It was meant for dealers, the media, VW clubs, and VW employees. Arnold seemed to understand perfectly not only what the old Beetle meant, but why the New Beetle was timed so well. The original Beetle, the Type 1, the video noted, was meant to be the people's car. Instead of the people's car, though, the video pointed out correctly, the Beetle became the *other* people's car. Without trying, Volkswagen of America was selling the unofficial car of people who had an idea about changing the world: social workers, teachers, college professors, people trying to discover their calling in life . . . "their place in the universe," the video pointed out. The brand essence video carried a line of copy that couldn't have been truer of the original Beetle. "Built in Germany. Made in America." Indeed, the car had been designed and built in Germany, but the car's legend was made in the United States. It was for that reason that many of the Germans running the company never really understood or wanted to acknowledge the significance of the Beetle in America.

The video glibly noted that people aren't people any more. "Everyone has become a target market. Generation X. Generation Y. Yuppies.

Empty Nesters. Baby Boomers. Guppies. Early Adopters. Whites. African Americans. Cross Culturals. Neo Pagans. Lost Souls. Hispanics. Pessimists. Late Bloomers."

The *New* Beetle was positioned to a customer target that only slick advertising people could identify: people trying to escape being tagged and targeted by advertisers and marketers.

To position the New Beetle, it was critical to pay homage to the original. Volkswagen and Arnold were after a tricky market, both people who had been enamored with the Beetle and those who were not old enough to drive or own a car when it was popular. Somehow, the advertising and public relations heralding the arrival had to make the car credible to those who loved the old original (which this car clearly was not) and spark the interest of younger people. It was like casting a 60-year-old Burt Reynolds or a 70-year-old Paul Newman in a movie aimed at Generation X, but with the hope that their parents would buy tickets for the early-bird show.

Arnold's advertising for the New Beetle kept the car small in the frame, whether it was on a TV screen, print ad, or billboard. The car had equal billing with the ad copy. One ad read: "The engine is in the front, but its heart is in the same place." Another read, "If you sold your soul in the 80s, here's your chance to buy it back." Another: "If you were really good in a past life, you come back as something better." Another said simply: "Optimism is back." Another: "Hug it? Drive it? Hug It? Drive It? Hug It? Drive It?" Still another, "0 to 60? Yes." In a way, it paid homage to the original DDB ads, but at the same time it was all its own, just like the product itself. Though Arnold Creative Director Ron Lawner says that he was well aware of the original DDB ads, he was never tempted to invite one of the old DDB hands, such as Bob Levenson or Roy Grace, into the agency to work on the campaign. Copywriter Lance Jensen was aware only of some of the more famous ads, such as "Lemon" or "Think Small." "They were big footprints," says Jensen. "But this car had to find its own voice in *our* campaign. It couldn't rip off the old classic stuff."

One of the most ironic lines of Arnold's brand essence video was that the New Beetle had arrived after 20 long years "to save us from sameness." The point was that car designs, by 1998, were static. Honda Civics, Mazda Proteges, Toyota Corollas, Mitsubishi Galants, Ford Contours, and Dodge Neons all had very similar rounded profiles. In a crowded parking lot, if there were enough forest green cars, some poor devil would have trouble finding the one that belonged to him or her.

When it comes to sameness, the Beetle defined it in its own way. Going through only cursory changes between 1949 and 1980, and reincarnated with more pronounced arches in its profile, "The Beetle was back," said the Arnold video, "to save the world."

Arnold understood the ironic quality of the Beetle that DDB had understood and conveyed so artistically in its advertising until the mid-1970s: *understatement.* The car's magic was that its design did all the talking. Unlike mistakes made by a latter-day creative team at DDB who tried to use the same ad copy for the Rabbit as it had used for the Beetle, Arnold knew it could be original and still tap into what made the original advertising so special and right. One ad that perfectly exemplified how Arnold got it right was a print ad for a lime green New Beetle, with just the word *Lime.* It was brilliant to anyone who remembered the classic "Lemon" ad for the original Beetle. The two ads had nothing to do with one another, yet were connected. The original "Lemon" ad, which was groundbreaking for its use of the word that had become synonymous with poor-quality cars, showed a Beetle that was rejected by quality inspectors in Germany. It looked perfect but was not up to VW standards. The "Lime" ad, on the other hand, was created just to push a color and celebrate the return of an old friend.

Unlike the Golf and Jetta, the New Beetle was never photographed on the road or in any kind of environment until 2 years after the launch. For the launch, it was shot against a white background, as if it had been created on a canvas. There were also no voice-overs talking about the car and no people in the frame.

"That was an element of the original Beetle print ads that was incredibly right, and we felt it was still right for the New Beetle," said Ron Lawner. "The New Beetle's design is the star, but it needed to be understated in the art direction, so it wasn't beating its chest. The Beetle has never been a chest beater, and it never should be. A lot of advertising makes that mistake of making the product too large and too prominent in the ad. There are always people at the company asking, 'Why isn't the car bigger?' You have to hold the line against this. You want people to come to your brand. You don't want to hit them over the head with it."

The New Beetle sold 56,000 in 7 months in 1998, and 83,000 in 1999, its first full year. Sales were 81,000 in 2000. Sales slacked off during the last half of that year, along with the rest of the industry. Dealers reported in early 2001 that interest was falling, but that they were still glad to have it in the showroom. "There is no question that it has been a great attraction," says New Jersey dealer Adam Green, who bought his dealership from his father in 1991. "The product we have now is so superior from what it had been that people are really turning on to the whole lineup, especially the Golf and Jetta. But the New Beetle is a showcase and makes people feel very good about Volkswagen. It is an ambassador for the company."

New Beetle buyers skewed a bit older than the median age for the VW brand at 42. Gender was split, 53 percent men and 47 percent women. Average transaction price in 1999 was $19,400, owing in part to the availability of a higher-priced turbo version that came out late in the year. Silver proved to be the most popular color, as was the case with the rest of the auto industry in 2000.

Bread and Butter

Clive Warrilow had accomplished a lot during his 5-year reign as head of Volkswagen of America. Although he was a positive change agent for Volkswagen, he could be polarizing. A gifted manager and fixer, people had a pretty good idea where they stood with him. "You are either out or you're in with Clive . . . and he can be very tough on you if you are out," said one staffer. He had a similar impact in Wolfsburg. Warrilow did not like to be told what to do or how to do it.

By early 1998, VW's and Audi's fortunes were looking better. Sales in 1997 were 136,000 for VW. The days of Wolfsburg not caring what the Americans did were over. "It's amazing how much *help* we were getting," said Warrilow. His independent ways were grating on Wolfsburg, notably Jens Neumann. Warrilow, a fan of culture building in a way that is foreign to most Germans, especially in the fear-dominated culture created by Piëch, had a scheme that would play a part, say staffers, in his final undoing. It would create a situation that would unfortunately mean he would exit North America not quite on his own terms or timeline.

With the launch of the New Beetle at the Detroit Auto Show in January 1998 expected to cause a sensation, and the product slated to roll to dealers in April and May, Warrilow wanted to create an event that reflected VW's comeback. He wanted to make a statement to dealers, salespeople, parts managers, employees, and even vendors. He also wanted to bring the Canadian and U.S. organizations together, something that had never been done. Canadians have a general inferiority complex about the United States and are never keen on being lumped together in business situations with the Americans. The New Beetle would be the unifying force.

His idea was to have a huge blowout at Disney World in Orlando. His choice of Disney was made when he learned of the Disney Institute, an extension of the company that teaches visiting companies something about how Disney's service culture is applied daily throughout the organization. The theme parks were one thing. And there would be a special parade and celebration of the New Beetle at Disney World, as well as test drives in hundreds of Beetles supplied for the event. The public relations staff had some concerns that Disney would send the wrong message, possibly indicating that the company was looking backward instead of forward. It was Disney, after all, that had signed the Beetle to a three-picture deal for the *Herbie the Love Bug* films. It was for that reason, plus the fact that Disney became uncooperative because of a sponsorship deal it had recently struck with General Motors, that the press introduction was held at The Ritz Carlton in Atlanta and not Disney.

Some 5,000 people were flown to Orlando and billeted at Disney's resort properties that month in two waves of about 2,500 each. Each wave was 3 days and 2 nights. Dealers and company personnel who attended were encouraged to go to the Disney Institute for a half-day session. There were events for driving the cars and an evening parade of Beetles and fireworks. Spouses and children were invited. Each dealership could bring four people. It cost a fortune—millions of dollars—and Wolfsburg wasn't amused.

Neumann had furrowed his brow when he first heard of Warrilow's plan, but back in Germany, no one on the Vorstand could understand why Warrilow was committing such funds for something they viewed as frivolous. Again, Warrilow saw the need to invest in what the Germans saw as the "soft side" of the business.

"When we first met with the Disney people there was all this talk about how many podiums, slide projectors and screens we would need. I said, 'No!' No more of that stuff. I want magic. We've had enough podiums and projectors. That's why we wanted to go to Disney."

The Germans have no real knowledge or appreciation of Disney from a business standpoint, according to Warrilow, who doubted that any members of the Vorstand had ever bothered to go to EuroDisney in France, let alone Disney World in Orlando. To them it was kid stuff and the wrong environment in which to launch what they considered a serious machine. "Disney is a business benchmark in customer and employee handling and in just how to do things in general," says Warrilow. "I wanted our entire organization to see how Disney did things—customer handling, focus on the customer, customer experience, customer delight."

A lot of the people had certainly been there as patrons with their families. Warrilow, however, wanted them to experience Disney in this VW context, so they would make the connection between how precisely everything is done at Disney and what he was trying to get across to them at the company, all the way down to the salespeople and service managers who were employees of the dealers, not of VW: It was a new era at VW, and that meant a new way of working. It was a broader application of the horse whisperer experience that he had done in 1996.

At the moment when the Beetles were introduced to the crowd at Disney World, everyone was told to look up to the sky, so that when their eyes came down their senses would be greeted by this dazzling site of hundreds of New Beetles of all colors, illuminated by fireworks and lights.

Dealers, salespeople, and parts managers who were there with their families all on VW's coin had died and gone to heaven. Staffers say the event was "genius" on the part of Warrilow. Dave Huyett said that what Warrilow understood was that the dealers, parts managers, salespeople, and their families had all been part of the suffering that VW endured in the 1980s and early 1990s. Warrilow understood that these people would remember being included in the celebration. The dealership staff didn't just have VW to look after. They also had Mazda, Honda, Nissan, GMC, Jeep, or whatever brand was dualed with VW. Warrilow felt strongly that the Disney trip was not just a reward, but an important step toward inclusion, reinclusion, of the people on the front lines with the customer. They needed to know that it was a new beginning and that they were part of the family, and that headquarters looked upon them as part of the family.

"This is a uniquely American view of the business," says Huyett. "It's very much a disconnect for the Germans."

Just as Warrilow had a few too many run-ins with Wolfsburg, Steve Wilhite was, after a while, too much his own man to function in an environment where the Germans were now more involved. He did most of the heavy lifting in sales and marketing for a decade and enjoyed the lack of oversight and involvement. He had been key in choosing the new agency and in wrighting the marketing and advertising. He liked neither second-guessing, nor having too many masters. About the same time that Warrilow was winding down and getting ready to give way to Gerd Klauss, the first German to run the U.S. company since Carl Hahn, Wilhite took the summer of 1998 off to ride a bicycle across country with his son who was about to start college. His wife had already moved back to San Diego where the Wilhites lived prior to Steve's return to VW. Wilhite would dodge rumors for much of 1998 that he was on his way out as Liz Vanzura, whom he had hired from General Motors to be director of advertising, assumed a more prominent role in what had become a huge success story. Wilhite, though, had been the architect and the bridge between Bill Young's tenure of holding the company together with spit and chewing gum and Clive Warrilow's era of making it over so it was able to make the most of the new products developed by Dr. Piëch.

Wilhite would leave in late 1998 to be the head of marketing for an upstart motorcycle company, Excelsior-Henderson. A call came, however, from an executive recruiter who wanted him to meet Apple Computer Founder Steve Jobs. Wilhite would go on to be chief marketing officer at Apple during the company's renaissance under Jobs. That left Vanzura as the head of advertising, while Dave Huyett took one more turn at being the marketing director under Gerd Klauss.

Volkswagen's recovery continued into 1999 when the new Golf and Jetta were introduced. The cars had been successfully introduced in Europe, and would be extremely well received by the auto press in the United States. Piëch's influence on the new vehicles was in evidence. Even tighter, tauter, and more refined than the 1997 Passat, VW now had showrooms of truly refined drivers' cars. *USA Today* Columnist Jim Healey said this about the new Jetta: "Gorgeous. . . . artful. . . . Jetta sets a new standard for attention to visible detail in a compact car."[3]

In 1999, teaser ads were created by Arnold for the new model year. Usually teaser ads are created for a single, all-new model as a way of tickling interest in some presumably *socko* ads coming later that would introduce an all-new creation.

The agency sold VW on a series of ads that featured no cars, just little vignettes about how people who represented their target customers were preparing for the new VWs. One TV spot showed a goofy-looking guy at a backyard barbecue sticking a chicken leg in a pile of mashed potatoes and then pretending that the drumstick is a stick shift, making revving sounds. The voice-over in the ads simply said, "Get ready. The new Volkswagens are coming." It was like a throwback to when dealerships in small towns kept the drapes closed on the showrooms until they were ready to show the new models. The townspeople would walk downtown on a Friday or Saturday night to look in the windows. Another spot showed a woman working out in a gym, but she was only working her left leg on one of the machines. A man walks up to her and says, "Clutch muscle?" She says, "Uh huh." Again, the simple voice-over said, "Get ready. The new Volkswagens are coming." Another ad showed a dog in front of a fan, as if preparing for when it can hang its head out the window. In still another ad, an office worker pushed his desk over next to an open window so he could hang his arm out the window while he worked. In each ad, the voice-over was the same: "Get ready. The new Volkswagens are coming." It all works to create a mood around the brand, as well as anticipation. Although no cars are shown in these ads, all the ads work to creatively reinforce all VWs as cars for people who love to drive.

Aversion to the crowd is a big part of the VW customers. They don't want flash. People in their 40s don't want the cars their parents drove. "Drivers wanted" is an invitation rather than a statement about the car. "People who drive Volkswagens are different and proud of it," says Account Director Jon Castle. "The objective then becomes to stimulate, surprise and delight."

Volkswagen forgot how to speak for itself in the 1980s. Maybe it was a combination of having the wrong cars for the wrong times. Clearly, however, in the late 1990s, the taut, redesigned, sleek, and well-constructed VWs were the right cars for the times.

A TV ad in 1999, entitled "Synchronicity," shows the "Drivers wanted" strategy most clearly, but it was so well executed that it didn't matter if, as Lance Jensen says, the strategy was showing. The ad was meant to reflect that people who buy VWs view the world differently, and that different view extends to the view from inside the car. A man and woman riding in a Jetta on a New Orleans street observe the people on the street: construction workers, workers unpacking boxes, a guy with a basketball. The couple notices that everyone is moving in sync; everyone is moving to a beat. It lasts for 30 seconds or so, at which point the man driving turns to his wife and just says, "That was weird." Again, the ad is not about the car. It's about the brand.

"Synchronicity" was a tough ad to sell for Arnold. Volkswagen of

America President Gerd Klauss criticized it for being too obscure. He didn't feel that the synchronized action in the ad was obvious enough, that people wouldn't "get it." Vanzura and the creative team at Arnold argued that it was an ad that had to be seen more than once to appreciate. This was a dangerous argument. A really effective ad, most marketing gurus would argue, should deliver the message in one viewing. This was a spot that would also challenge the team's practice of not pretesting commercials with focus groups. "It always just came down to a couple of people at Volkswagen and a couple of people at Arnold, usually no more than three or four people who were deciding on what ad was going to make it," says Vanzura. Later, David Letterman spoofed "Synchronicity" on *The Late Show,* with Letterman putting himself in the ad behind the wheel of the Jetta. "More buzz . . . our stuff just kept getting more buzz, and that's how we knew it was right," says Vanzura. Gerd Klauss, too, later on, admitted that he had misjudged the commercial and has not asked the agency to go to any pretesting.

If a TV spot does present problems, it is quickly pulled off the air or changed. This has happened a few times. In one, a couple is driving home from the video store in their Jetta. The husband turns to the wife and says, "You know that video we made of us in the bedroom? . . . I think we just returned it." The brakes screech, and the couple heads back to the store. The camera cuts to the video store where the patrons are apparently watching the home video on the in-store monitors. Something missed in the editing and scripting was an adolescent boy in the store watching the video, which was clearly inappropriate. The ad was yanked off the air, and the kid was digitally removed from the ad. "I would still rather fix those kinds of mistakes than go to pre-testing," says Vanzura. "If we pre-tested all the ads, there would be constant second guessing and we would lose some of the creative risk taking that has gotten us where we are."

The car in these ads is used as a conveyance for the brand, and what the brand is about is reinforced in a slice of life. There is very little dialogue in VW ads, requiring the action on the screen to hold the viewer's attention. One TV ad, titled "Milky Way," focuses on a group of young people in their early 20s in a Cabrio driving under a shimmering night sky. Reaching their journey's end, which is a loud party, they look at one another. The driver throws the car into reverse and heads back to the open road. *Adweek* Columnist Eleftheria Parpis commented about this spot, "We've all been there, and freedom is contagious."[4] They are not so much ads as they are short films with a brand idea at the center. It is the difference between selling and marketing.

In the 2000 model year, a campaign was launched that focused on how much VW owners love their cars. This is a dodgy idea, because if people watching the ads can't see themselves in the ads, they don't work. In one ad, called "Shopping Cart," a new Jetta is shown in a parking lot. The viewer hears a shopping cart's wheels rolling, and then the cart enters the picture, heading toward the car. Out of the side of the screen comes the owner, running, and then throwing himself at the cart to save his car. In another TV spot, a Passat is shot from above entering a parking lot. It's a wide shot, and the car is seen being driven around in search of a space, hesitating in front of a few open spots, finally settling on one that is not the closest to where the driver needs to go, but rather several rows away from the rest of the cars. In another, a young man is seen taking great care to wash his VW. Then, another man comes out of the house to pick up his newspaper, and we learn that it's not the first man's car at all. He was washing it for the love of a VW. The man in his bath robe—the real owner—looks at him and says, "What are you doing?"

It's the difference between the direct selling (which most of Detroit does) and the indirect marketing (which the best marketers do). In 1993, VW began pitching its cars as "The Most Loved Cars in the World." In 2000, Chrysler was advertising "Engineered to Be Great Cars." Dodge was advertising "Dodge Different." Chevrolet was advertising "We'll Be There." Ford was advertising "Built to Last." These slogans exist only because the companies believe in and follow *quantitative marketing,* the idea that a company can create awareness and recall in its advertising, no matter what they say, as long as they throw $500 million, $600 million, or $700 million against the ads. They don't work, though, to create unique brand impressions. Customers don't want to be told that a brand is "different," or that it is "built to last," or that it's "engineered to be great." What else would they be? Being *told* that a brand is "the most loved" may have been the worst violation of this rule. Mercedes-Benz in the mid-1990s came close to marketing its cars around the slogan "Simply the best cars in the world." Wiser heads prevailed, though, and the company began advertising its cars with no slogan at all, leaving viewers with just its enviable tristar logo as the last word in every ad.

Adweek named "Drivers wanted" the best overall campaign of 1999. The magazine noted:

> Since its first work introducing Volkswagen's "Drivers wanted" positioning—a frenetic spot called "Cappuccino Girl," featuring a salesperson amped up on coffee—Arnold has made Volkswagen a cool, popular car again. Along the way, it has created some of the best advertising the industry has to offer.

Seven of Arnold's VW ads that year were rated "Best Spots" of the month in *Adweek*.

Just as DDB's original ad campaign has been held up as a benchmark for all advertising, Arnold's "Drivers wanted" campaign has proven to be a worthy successor. Mazda, the brand to which many VW dealers defected in the 1970s and 1980s, extensively benchmarked VW's positioning, with many of the internal documents related to its "Get In. Be Moved" marketing strategy and ad campaign showing VW's "Drivers wanted" campaign as a target. The "Wake Up and Drive" campaign produced for Mitsubishi is arguably based heavily on "Drivers wanted." In fact, the words "wake up, wake up, wake up" opened the brand essence video that Arnold created for VW during the pitch for the business in 1995, notes Arnold Creative Chief Ron Lawner. Oldsmobile, before it announced that it was going out of business in 2000, said it had begun a review for a new ad agency, "hoping to come up with a campaign like 'Drivers wanted' to save the brand." In 2000, an executive at Saatchi & Saatchi, advertising agency for Toyota, told *Adweek* that its new campaign was meant to be "Volks-

TABLE 8.1　Evidence of Success in America

	1995	2000	Results
Sales	115,167	355,479	+208%
Unaided brand awareness	11	31	+181%
Conquest/defection	0.5	5.6	+1,020%
Brand loyalty	31	50.8	+63%
Unaided purchase consideration	4	13	+225%
Aided ad recall	37	78	+111%
Brand buzz*	Low	High	Way up!
Dealer enthusiasm†	Low	High	Way up!

Source: *Allison-Fisher, Inc.: Prepared for Volkswagen of America.*
*Added by VW of A.
†Added by VW of A.

wagenesque." Ford's advertising for its Focus model aimed squarely at customers in their 20s and early 30s, has been very reminiscent of Arnold's early work for VW. In an industry that is maniacal about denying that ideas or strategies are lifted from competitors, it was a remarkable statement.

If imitation is the highest form of flattery, VW and its "Drivers wanted" strategy is the most flattered marketing of the new millennium. (See Table 8.1.) Although that presents a challenge for Arnold to keep the campaign fresh, there is a definite advantage to being the original.

The Prince

NINE

Visionary. Conceited aristocrat. Obsessive. Driven to extremes. Dangerous. Ultrafocused. Chauvinist. Rottweiler of the motor world. Belligerent street fighter. All are possible descriptions of Dr. Ferdinand Piëch. Known by many. Familiar to very few. Friendly to fewer still. He is obstinate, frustrating, dismissive, perhaps, but he is also like no other auto executive of his era.

Piëch is probably the last of his kind—scion of the founding family of an automaker who actually runs the company. Yes, William Clay Ford is the chairman of Ford Motor Company, but he is a non–executive chairman, meaning he influences but does not run things. Piëch does it all, sometimes to the detriment of the company that was conceived of by his beloved grandfather, Ferdinand Porsche, and Adolf Hitler. Mostly, though, Piëch succeeds. Indeed, he did nothing short of save the company in the 1990s after a decade of complacent and overly politicized management left the company weak and enfeebled by the time he ascended to the board and the top job in 1993. By 2000, he put VW firmly on track to be one of the few surviving world automotive powers in an era of rapid global consolidation, a process that saw companies like Chrysler, Rover, Jaguar, Volvo, Saab, Nissan, Seat, Skoda, Mazda, Mitsubishi, Isuzu, Suzuki, Fiat, Hyundai, Kia, and Daewoo give up their independence to the few remaining Goliaths.

Piëch is passionate about cars, like few auto chieftains left in the global industry. Unlike the leaders of General Motors and Toyota, he has little interest in building a great diversified company of automotive *and* financial/communications services. He likes automobiles. In fact, he loves automobiles. He is obsessed with cars. He wants VW to lead the world in designing and building automobiles while he is still alive to see it. He is satisfied to let other automakers diversify into communications and financial services. He can design, engineer, and, if pressed, assemble a car himself. He can work the tools himself. He can drive a car or listen to an engine like a mechanic and tell the engineer working for him what is wrong with it, why it won't work, and how it can be improved. He knows when a product design isn't right for the market, or when the brakes being procured are wrong. It is unthinkable under Piëch's watch that VW would bring a truly poor design to the marketplace. When he sees a company, a factory, a brand he wants to add to the VW portfolio, he buys it. Does he care what the shareholders think? No. Nor does he ever seem worried about paying too much. He pays what he must to get what he wants. Does he ever worry about getting fired? Not bloody likely. His net worth is pegged at well over $1 billion, depending on the condition of the financial markets. Ask him what philosophy or system of management he subscribes to, and he'll tell you: "Mine."

"He can take a mature man of 40 or 50 years who is secure in his marriage, career and health and reduce him to a puddle of quivering jelly with just a stare," says one longtime VW hand. "He is crazy, a real unrelenting bastard, and I thank God for him," says another. Adds a third, "I'd go through a wall for him, but somehow I don't think he'd ever ask me . . . he doesn't need to . . . he seems to be able to break the walls down on his own and just expects you to follow."

"Terrifying," states a former Audi executive. "My week was joyous if I knew I was not on his radar in any way." Few VW employees, past or present, will talk about Piëch on the record in anything but matter-of-fact or blindly complimentary terms. "Whether you are working for him now or not, he isn't anyone you want to anger . . . I'd hate to be on some list of Ferdinand Piëch's," says a former VW executive now working for a rival company. "And the way he is going, I could find myself working for him again next week," he adds. Even his loyal lieutenants, such as Dr. Jens Neumann, won't talk about him to describe his style of management or tell a story that might illuminate his boss to a reader either on or off the record. "That is off-limits," says Neumann. Why? In 2000 and 2001, when much of this book was being researched, Piëch created great uncertainty about who will succeed him in 2003. There is no officially annointed vice chief. So, all the candidates, Neumann included, are stepping delicately, fearful of saying the wrong thing.

Piëch has the kind of license to lead VW that only a man of his lineage and personal wealth can attain. There is virtually no one who can take his toys away. Those who might try are simply too afraid of the retribution that would come their way. He is powerful, swift, and relentless. "If he was just another CEO, he wouldn't inspire this kind of fear or apprehension, but when you add all that wealth and power and the whole family dynasty thing to the mix . . . he's not a man you want to cross," says one former Volkswagen of America executive.

Reaching age 63 in 2000, Piëch had just 2 years remaining on his contract, which is granted by the company's supervisory board. He surprised many by recruiting his one-time rival and nemesis of sorts, Bernd Pischetsrieder, former head of BMW who was ousted by the Quandt family in 1998 after BMW's disastrous and costly acquisition of The Rover Group. Piëch, unconvinced that any of the existing internal candidates are worthy to succeed him, and not having any of his reported 14 children experienced or old enough for the task, seems to be backing Pischetsrieder. Piëch has also tapped Pischetsrieder because he has been eyeballing BMW for years, hoping to take it over and add the brand to VW's global footprint, further assuring its place well into the twenty-first century as an independent and dominant auto producer. It is a known goal of Piëch's to surpass Toyota as the world's third-largest auto producer before he retires, or at least before he dies.

Anyone not of Piëch's inner circle permitted to ask a direct question of Piëch is met with silence returned. It's like hitting a tennis ball across the net into the void, and waiting a half-minute for a return volley of uncertain speed or direction. He's not being obtuse or deliberately difficult. He just has the rare trait of composing his answer before responding. Most men of his stature shoot back answers during an interview, rather than appear searching for an answer. Piëch's pause-and-volley style applies whether the questioner is German or English. It is a style that has unnerved many an interviewer and subordinate.

Though by no means the whole story, Piëch owes his position of strength in part to the company's resurgence in the United States. That resurgence, of course, is due in no small part to the decision he made in 1995 to follow through on the whimsy of a couple of U.S. designers in California to do what VW had refused to do for a decade: make a New Beetle.

———

Piëch is the grandson of the Beetle's sire, Ferdinand Porsche. The Beetle, known originally as the Type 1, runs through Piëch's veins like diesel fuel. His grandfather conceived the car, designed it, and brought it to being all while being Hitler's pet auto designer. Both Porsche and Piëch's father, Anton Piëch, Porsche's son-in-law, served time in a French prison after World War II for their roles in the Third Reich. Their chief contribution to the war effort had been the development of the Type 1 car, the *Volkauto,* and the Wolfsburg factory that would turn it out. The factory, in reality, didn't turn out any Beetles before the end of the War. The few that were built were produced by Daimler-Benz. The factory did, however, produce tens of thousands of derivative military vehicles based on the Type 1, as well as produce munitions and parts for planes, tanks, and other armament. That the factory relied on a large slave-labor force was key to Piëch's father and grandfather serving prison time at the hands of the French.

German journalists and those who have worked with him over the years say Piëch sees the VW brand as his lineage and the company as his clan. He leads and lives according to an aristocratic mind-set that he inherited from his parents and grandfather along with his great wealth. Those not with him, by default, must be against him. His wealth allows and motivates him to take great risks with the company, risks that men who fear for their livelihood and position would not, and have not, taken. He has said that he would very much like to have met Napoléon. The complete commitment to risk until the bitter end is what he finds fascinating about the ultimately defeated French emperor. Adding to his power is the fact that the government of Lower Saxony owns 20 percent of the company, a peculiar holdover from the company's formation after World War II. This has allowed Piëch to consolidate support by maintaining jobs in Germany, rather than worrying excessively about quarterly returns. He spurns stock analysts and institutional shareholders like no other CEO can in the twenty-first century.

Piëch's embarrassments since taking over the company's top post in 1993 would have had many a chief executive tossed out on his ear. He fought for the hiring of General Motors' infamous cost cutter, Spaniard Ignacio Lopez, in 1993, only to have the decision blow up in his face with allegations (later proven) that the renegade and irascible Lopez fled his job at GM with computer disks full of confidential and proprietary information. It was further revealed that Lopez and Piëch had been meeting clandestinely, planning Lopez's arrival at VW while he had been assuring his masters at GM that he was staying. In fact, used as a dangled carrot to get him to stay, Lopez had accepted an offer from GM Chairman Jack Smith to become president, thus making him a candidate to succeed him as chief executive. On the morning that Smith had scheduled a press conference to make the announcement that Lopez would become president, he got word that Lopez had instead fled to Germany to take the post at VW. Smith was embarrassed before the media. The head of the world's largest car company was left at the altar with a gallery of reporters to face. It was terribly bad form, and it embarrassed Piëch as much as Smith. The affair led to the ousting of Lopez, legal wranglings that were still going on in 2001, a $1.1 billion payout to GM and a couple of years in which Piëch was hardly seen in the United States because of the tension over the inci-

dent. When Piëch found it necessary to come to North America during the imbroglio, he'd fly to Canada, making the U.S. executives fly
north to meet with him. In separate incidents, VW has been fined
more than $100 million in 2000 and 2001 for illegal price fixing in
Europe. In 1998, Piëch wildly overpaid for Britain's Rolls-Royce. His
overpayment looked even worse when it became clear that he bought
the company without the rights to sell Rolls-Royce-branded automobiles. Rolls was able to sell those rights separately to BMW, which had
been bidding against Piëch for the company. This was tantamount to
bidding for an apple pie and then finding out that you got only the
crust. Piëch has since said that his real aim was acquiring the Bentley
brand, which came with the deal, but no one is buying that cover
story. It's true that he'll be able to reach a sales target of 10,000 vehicles more practically with Bentley than Rolls-Royce, but the deal still
makes him look like a rube for not securing the rights to the Rolls-
Royce marque. Piëch, however, doesn't seem to care what stock analysts, shareholders, dealers, or journalists think of his moves.

What was not embarrassing was the fact that Piëch increased the
German market capitalization in the 5 years from 1993 to 1998 by 400
percent all while new-economy stocks such as telecommunications
and dot.coms were the rage, not old-economy car companies. Volkswagen employee sick days dropped from 12 percent to 3 percent, and
not because of any cure for the common cold that Piëch whipped up
in his garage. Piëch evidently has the support of both the market and
the troops. And why not? Under the leadership of finance, sales, and
marketing maven Carl Hahn, VW had piled up billions in losses
because of horrendously inefficient product programs, which led to
cars that were expensive to build, of poor quality, and dowdy design. A
trifecta of failure.

Investors and employees alike believe in Piëch's ability to deliver the
right products—a knack that contrasts sharply with Hahn's inability to
do the same or to crack through VW's byzantine political structure.
"Hahn is a terrific man, and did a lot of good things for Volkswagen,
but he obviously had lost his interest in the American market by the
time he came back in the 1980s based on the lack of attention the

American division got," says David E. Davis, longtime editor of *Automobile* magazine and himself an early VW dealer in Ypsilanti, Michigan, in the 1950s.

Hahn diversified the company away from being the one-car company, made acquisitions such as Spanish carbuilder Seat and Czech automaker Skoda, and opened up China and Eastern Europe to VW. However, he had no capacity to control manufacturing and development costs, and it caught up with him. Bill Young, the former president of Volkswagen of America, puts it this way: "Dr. Hahn had a lot on his plate in the 1980s, and an organization that he was not suited or equipped to turn upside down the way Piëch did. . . . he also had to deal with all of the issues related to the Iron Curtain coming down, which were many for a German company five miles from the border." Hahn served his tenure as chairman of Volkswagen AG like a diplomat. Colleagues who describe him invariably use the term *statesman* to describe his style. It is not a term that anyone would use to describe Piëch. Of course, when you have his personal wealth, neither statesmanship nor diplomacy come easy. "*Compromise* is not even in his vocabulary, I think," says former VW North American Chief Clive Warrilow.

"Great product does not come from change. Change comes from great product. It is a mistake that many have made in trying to turn an operation around," says Piëch.[1]

Piëch is right. A terrific example is General Motors. In the 1980s, GM had built and designed itself into the sewer by running an operation that, while seemingly efficient, turned out awful products, many of which were identical across its brands. Not only were products poor, they were identical, no matter if you went to a Buick, Oldsmobile, Pontiac, or Chevrolet dealership. Throughout the 1990s, GM has been restructuring its operations, and although profits have improved, product still lacks respect. Product design at GM is by committee—a committee that, sadly, is not made up of designers and car people, but of marketers, financiers, and manufacturing mavens. General Motors' market share has fallen precipitously, so much so that by 2000 it had to kill off the Oldsmobile brand (the oldest marque in the United States) because its dwindling market share could not support so many different brands. Piëch, on the other hand, believes VW's fortunes would only turn around with great products; only then would profits kick in and change occur in the rank and file. He proved this at Audi, which he rebuilt in the 1980s, and he's demonstrated it at VW since taking the wheel.

Piëch's strategy at VW has been to have very few vehicle platforms. A vehicle platform is the underpinnings of the car. To many, it seems risky to manufacture so many vehicles on so few platforms, but it has been done profitably and successfully by both Honda and Toyota. He has taken the number from 16 to just 4 since taking over. In past eras, numerous platforms helped car companies justify the price differences among their cars. It would be ridiculous, for example, for Ford to manufacture a Ford Taurus and a Lincoln Continental on the same platform. General Motors tried this with disastrous results when it manufactured a Cadillac, the Cimmaron, on the same platform as Pontiacs and Buicks that cost less than $20,000. Piëch, however, has demonstrated that remarkable product differentiation can be achieved, even while getting cost efficiencies out of using the same platforms. Remarkably enough, the Golf, Jetta, New Beetle, and Audi TT are all built on the same platform, though prices for those vehicles range $25,000 apart. Piëch refers to this as *putting different hats on the same bodies*. While this strategy has been achieving tremendous cost-effectiveness in the late 1990s and early 2000 and 2001, some analysts are dubious, doubting that consumers will put up with this over the long haul.

At any other car company, it is more than possible that a CEO would fire a designer or production chief after a series of poor products or falling manufacturing quality. This would be difficult at VW because Piëch acts as head of product and manufacturing. Yes, there are others below him who hold senior titles in those areas, and they get demoted or banished. However, a vehicle would never get so far in development without Piëch's hands and decisions being so much a part of its bones and skin that he could so completely blame someone else. At GM, for example, which operates much differently, a series of ill-designed vehicles could come out and the chief designer be criticized apart from top management. If the VW Passat, Golf, New Beetle, or Jetta was a flop in design or quality, the blame would be laid at Piëch's feet. He is chief designer, chief vehicle tester, chief procurer, production chief, and quality control meister. He is, in short, in charge of the product. Piëch takes personal ownership of the strength of a B column in the Golf, the selection of brakes in the New Beetle, a body panel in the Polo. "I have seen him review a dozen headlight designs in a conference room, and in rapid fire dismiss the ones he didn't want and select the ones he did . . . this is a unique man in the business today," says current Volkswagen of America Chief Gerd Klauss. He is also willing to admit that other companies do things better, and he lets his staff know that he knows this. During a meeting at which deficient windshield wipers were being discussed, some of the engineering staff present were hemming and hawing about what do. Piëch, says one who was present at the meeting, simply said, "I am driving a Cadillac right now and its windshield wipers are excellent. Why don't you just find out who manufactures them and copy it." Such a suggestion spoke volumes about what the old man was really saying about the inability of his staff to solve the problem.

Piëch says his knowledge of engineering is the main thing that separates him from his predecessors who let costs run so wild. He puts engineers into the purchasing process so they know what the costs are. When he tells an engineer to do something that is a cost saving, no engineer in the system can tell him it's impossible. Dr. Hahn was a prisoner, in a way, of the engineering people that worked for him. Piëch loves to point out to an engineer how 10 cents can be saved on a component, because he understands the math. Ten cents multiplied 1 million times adds up to a lot of cash for next year's product development budget.

This is the mission and style of a man who is a shop rat at heart. Some like the extreme accountability of the Piëch system. Others find extreme shortcomings with the concentration of decision making. His autocratic system can lead to dangerous delays. Too often to suit many a VW manager, decisions that are critical to a project get held up until the last minute. These late decisions then have ripple effects, increasing costs, as well as risks: that quality assurance required repairs; that tools were missing; that production flow in the factory did not begin at the right time. These are the dangers of Piëch handling so many decisions personally and concentrating so much power in his office and his ever-present notebook.

The company has had slow starts with new products, as it did in 1998 when it was short by 100,000 Golfs of the number of orders placed. Analysts noted that some Golfs were costing more to produce than a Mercedes E Class. Serious cost overruns resulted from Saturday overtime that was required to get the cars right, and by flying parts and pieces into Wolfsburg by helicopter when it was necessary to complete an order of vehicles.

How can Piëch defend it? "No car leaves the factory if it is not right," says Piëch.[2] "If the tools are not correct, and as a result the parts do not fit, then we do as much finishing work as is necessary to make everything fit correctly. This costs time and volume, but not customers." That is a good attitude, of course, but it does not address the problem that, many times, it may be the tools are not correct because of Piëch's somewhat autocratic system. In 2001, despite VW's resurgence in the United States and abroad, Piëch's Volkswagen still lags the industry average for quality. The United States has higher quality standards than Europe. At the start of the new century, VW is well below the industry average in defects per vehicle, as measured by J. D. Power and Associates. Germans still feel that the Power ratings are misplaced, highlighting differences in quality between VW and its rivals that are largely insignificant in the context of actual vehicle ownership and customer experience. Who cares if a few more things have to be fixed if the customer prefers the totality of the car over a Toyota or Honda? This is dangerous thinking for VW. In the United States, VW is most popular with young customers under age 35 among whom word of mouth counts for more than traditional marketing and advertising. Word of mouth spreading subpar workmanship or substandard reliability can catch up to a company in a hurry, and it can happen in a lot less time than it takes to make major quality fixes at factories. Despite the huge sales gains of VW in the 1990s, Piëch has not delivered everything he promised in product quality and getting cars to market in a more timely fashion. Volkswagen won't have a convertible

New Beetle to sell to a clamoring public until 4 years after the New
Beetle arrived at dealerships. That is a ridiculous lag. It will be last to
market with a sport utility. Its customer satisfaction ratings, as measured by J. D. Power, are well below industry average at both VW and
Audi.

———

Piëch's intimate inner circle includes Dr. Jens Neumann, the lawyer
who oversees North America; Dr. Robert Buchelhofer, the sales director; Dr. Peter Hartz, the personnel director; Dr. Lothar Sander, the
controller; Bernd Pischetsrieder, CEO-in-waiting; and Martin Winterkorn, corporate executive director of development, who is known as
Piëch's idea man.

It is a dangerous and destructive trait for a chief executive to think
he can do everyone's job in the organization better than they can. In
fact, many a successful executive believes the sign of effective leadership is to hire people who are smarter than they are. This means
nothing to Piëch. He has taken over many functions himself as they
relate to product development and purchasing, and he makes it his
business to know at least as much as every department head in the
company, according to executives who have worked for him. "I would
never want to know more about a subject than Piëch does," one long-
time executive told me. "I wouldn't know what to do with the information or knowledge and I wouldn't want to know." Piëch bothers
himself with going to manufacturing plant meetings where budgets
and production details are sorted out—the sort of thing that few, if
any, CEOs of multi-billion-dollar companies personally attend to,
except in a summary report or after a plant posts a poor report. He
makes his own quality checks on assembly lines. He extensively test-
drives vehicles in summer and winter, in all kinds of weather conditions. Every 6 months or so Piëch travels to Finland, Poland, Brazil,
South Africa, or China, any place where VW has a factory or does
business, taking some two dozen people along for the ride. The cars,
not to mention the executives who are along for the ride, are tested to
within an inch of their lives, from predawn to early evening. They
drive in a convoy, all the way exchanging cars and driving partners.

The atmosphere, say executives who have been on these trips, can be like a hazing during pledge week at a college fraternity. Pecking order of the attendees is established based on who Piëch chooses to ride with him. Careers are made and broken on these trips. "I have seen men leave these trips more dejected than if their dog had been killed on the trip," said one executive. "All because Piëch didn't talk to them in the way they hoped for. He has that kind of power. To many, he is like a father or older brother whose favor you are desperate to win. But if you can't, you can't." Piëch can be cold and exacting with his power. Men who said or did something to displease Piëch on these trips can find a return plane ticket unceremoniously left on his breakfast place setting. Once, recalled one VW department head, Piëch saw to it that one out-of-favor participant, Heinrich Holtmann, a close associate of the ousted Ignacio Lopez, was pulled out of the convoy in the middle of the day like an outfielder being replaced in the middle of an inning in a baseball game. The "old man," a moniker frequently used to describe Piëch among employees, loves these games of ritual dismissal. Employees routinely lose parking privileges for transgressions, and more than a few have returned to their desks to find a security guard ready to supervise the cleaning out of their desks. Just the sight of the guard was their notice that they had been sacked without benefit of a meeting with a supervisor.

Piëch's system of product improvement is simple. At the ride-and-drives, executives who are present make notes about their impressions, good points, and bad points of the car. The notebook stays in the car. At the end of the day, the notes, usually multilingual, are shared with the group. The engineers are present, and Piëch is the last word on what changes will be made based on the sessions. Piëch might bring back another group in 6 or 7 weeks to drive the cars again, assuming the changes dictated by him have been made. If the engineers haven't had time to accomplish the changes, they had better have a good reason why. If they tell Piëch they have made the changes, and either the change did not address the problem sufficiently or was made badly, "God help the poor bastard," said one frequent convoy participant. "It's hard to be in the same room and watch someone get torn to pieces the way Piëch can do." One of the positive by-products of this style, though, is that the finance, legal, and marketing executives working for the company must become "car men" if they are to survive and advance in the company. They must become intimate with the machinery if they are to hold their own with Piëch.

He cows people in public settings, another trait not seen much in modern business. When Piëch announced in 1993 that he planned to reduce the number of engineering platforms from 16 to 4, an engineering executive asked how he was expected to keep costs down on VW models if he was being forced to use parts that were designed for the more expensive Audi vehicles. Piëch simply glared at the man and said, "I am going to remember your name." Questions that are considered important, even critical, say VW managers, often don't get asked for fear that the wrong query could cost a career.

In late 1994, Piëch had caused so much upset within the organization that managers, in a remarkable gesture, sent an open letter to VW Supervisory Board Chairman Klaus Liesen, stating, "This company is run by a man with psychopathic traits." This extraordinary measure would hardly be found in U.S. business. It was a testament to both peculiar German business practices and customs, and the brink to which Piëch can drive men.[3]

"Because Piëch is so rounded, so completely a car man, it does not do for a man merely to be a good engineer, a good lawyer, a good sales or production analyst," says one former VW executive. "You can't just do your thing well to succeed in the company, or succeed with Piëch. You have to do your thing very well and in a way that he likes. You have to love the company, love the brand, love the car, love the engine, love the success of the company, hate failure and fear it like the devil. That's what he looks for in people."

"I don't care to have someone on the board just because he is clever. One must be taken with the thing, and with the products," admits Piëch. He not only pours over engineering plans and processes to make sure that the product he envisions is being delivered, he explains to an engineer how one Deutschmark or a few pfennigs can be shaved off the cost of the cigarette lighter.

Perhaps Piëch wouldn't extend so much of himself into running the company if he didn't consider it the family business. He equates loyalty to him to doing good for the company. Disputing his position or challenging him in the forum of the supervisory board is not something to be done glibly. "If someone places his ego above the good of the company, than I am harsh and cruel," admits Piëch about his own management. He has referred to himself as only a ruling family member can—as the company's "moral watchdog." Morality in Piëch's world, though, has more to do with what is good and right for VW and Piëch than it does with what is good and right for people, or with their behavior toward one another. He treats people in a way that is unacceptable to most men, say several U.S. and European executives who have worked for him, and only a very small number of people put up with it for long. The people who remain on the Vorstand are among them. These are smart men who have had to literally suppress their intellects and spend inordinate amounts of time figuring out the old man's mood on a given day before opening their mouth or making a suggestion.

When Piëch ascended to the top post in 1992, he began cutting down dead wood and settling acounts. A record (for a German industrial company) 25 senior executives found themselves out on the street in Piëch's first 5-year term. In a company that was out of control and had a clubhouse brand of loyalty, Piëch saw loyalty as only a one-way street, and it ran from bottom to top. When a reporter asked him how he felt about cutting ties with a long-time VW executive who had close ties to Carl Hahn, Piëch's respone was curt and honest: "I have no feelings." Says auto industry analyst Steve Haggerty, "He is driven, single-minded, self-confident and fearless." Piëch cut down the operating board from 12 to 5, tightening his grip on the company. He saw from his Audi post in the 1980s how the company could get bogged down in its own politics. Hahn, say associates, was loved and respected as a father figure, but he allowed board members to run their own fiefdoms. The loss of focus on product and costs levied a heavy toll on Hahn's legacy. "He (Piëch) got rid of a lot of people who needed to be gotten rid of, but also, I think, some people he would be better off today for having kept," said retired Volkswagen of America Chief

Clive Warrilow. "His weakness, I think, is not wanting people around him who have different points of views than his own."

Surprising to analysts and many VW insiders has been Piëch's recruiting of Pischetsrieder, who may leapfrog both Porsche Governor Wendelin Wiedeking, a Piëch favorite, and Robert Buchelhofer as Piëch's successors in 2002. Prevailing opinion at VW and among analysts has been that the two long-time lieutenants might share the top post for a time, with perhaps the younger Wiedeking taking over solely after a few years. However, Pischetsrieder's arrival after his ouster from BMW throws all that thinking out the window. If Pischetsrieder, who is reportedly still close to the Quandt family that owns BMW, could help engineer a sale to VW, he would be a lock to succeed Piëch. As of early 2001, though, the Quandts seem content to stay independent, and worries that it would have to sell out have been dampened by the unloading of Rover and the still relatively robust market for luxury cars. BMW is, in fact, one of the few automobile companies in the world that earns a consistent profit. As for Piëch, he conveniently reaches mandatory retirement age in 2002 at the same time as Supervisory Board Chief Klaus Liesen reaches mandatory retirement. That ensures that Piëch will continue to influence and lead for an additional 6 years though Pischetsrieder or Wiedeking. Another hypothesis is thrown around by Piëch watchers to explain the hiring of Pischetsrieder. Piëch has surrounded himself with men who, while intelligent, have not had an opportunity to flower under Piëch. They have been as close to Piëch as anyone gets for many years. They got to be close to Piëch, though, by not asserting themselves too forcefully. They are wise and strategic thinkers, especially in the case of Neumann and Wiedeking, but have had to rely too much on Piëch's strong and dominant character, thus not allowing their own management traits and muscles to properly develop. Some VW insiders hypothesize that Piëch, down deep, doesn't have faith that any of his lieutenants can follow him. The worry of analysts is that he has trained them into inferiority to suit his own needs and ego. Yet, as a Piëch and a Porsche (on his mother's side), he wants there to be a strong-enough man coming behind him to lead the company after his time is up on the supervisory board or if anything happens to him. That's where

Pischetsrieder comes in. Having been raised in management outside
of Piëch's shadow and run BMW, he has a mind of his own. It may
seem disloyal to the men who have taken Piëch's brass all these years.
Piëch, however, is not a stupid man: He obviously feels that new blood
is needed.

———

Piëch was born in 1937 in Vienna, Austria, and received his engineering degree at the Swiss Federal Institute of Technology in Zurich,
Switzerland, in 1962. Despite his love of cars, he had aspirations of
going into either aeronautics or, and this is hard to imagine, the hotel
business. That interest may account for why Piëch, after taking the
helm at VW, began negotiating with Ritz-Carlton, the premier hotelier
in the world, to build a first-class hotel in Wolfsburg. Piëch, like many
others, had long tired of the lack of excellent lodging in VW's home-
town. Visiting executives were most often put up in the Rothehof, a
lodging owned and operated by VW, which had not been updated
since the early 1960s. Even though it was out of date, many VW veterans liked it for its simple home-away-from-home quality. It did not
suit a billionaire, so Piëch subsidized the construction of the hotel
with VW funds as part of the building of the Autostadt, a $400 million
VW–Audi–Rolls-Royce/Bentley auto theme park and museum.

In school, Piëch was not very good in languages, so he was advised
against going into the Austrian hotel trade. At Swiss boarding school,
he honed an interest in math. He began exploring aeronautics, wary of
going into the car business with such a hard act to follow in his grandfather and Uncle Ferry. He loved studying the inner workings of
engines. At the end of his studies, though, the last prototype of a Swiss
aircraft crashed into Lake Constance, giving the Swiss aircraft industry
a poor postwar future. After World War II, Austrians had difficulty
traveling to France, the United States, or England, where the aircraft
industries were. So, he succumbed to family pressures to go into the
car business. He began his automotive career in 1963 as a clerk in the
engine-testing section of Porsche. Piëch developed the first flat-six
engine at Porsche; he soon became head of research, where he over-

saw development of the Porsche 917. That car gave Porsche its first win at LeMans. Piëch says he read a lot about family dynasties: that the first generation builds a company, the second keeps it, and the third destroys it. Piëch was part of the third generation at Porsche AG. In Ferry Porsche's book, he writes: "The kind of cooperation one might have hoped for between my children and those of my sister (Louise, Ferdinand Piëch's mother) did not materialize."[5] In 1971, the children divided the company's shares among the 10, including Ferry, Louise, and their children. Ferdinand Piëch went to Audi in 1973, where he was main department manager for technical development. In 1988, he became chairman of the board of management at Audi and was made chairman of VW in 1993. Like many men of Piëch's wealth and upbringing, he is secretive about his personal life and declines many more interviews than he grants. German press accounts have chronicled his marriages and his fathering of more than a dozen children. That kind of attention to Piëch's personal life leaves the Piëch family leader bristle and shy from the media. But he didn't make things easier for himself when he told a German interviewer that he fathered so many children to increase the chance of passing on his own unique qualities to a new generation.[6]

Interviews with people who have known him over the years in the European and U.S. media yield a profile of a man who is fierce but insecure, driven by a need to be seen in the same league with his legendary grandfather and his highly respected uncle. He saw himself as being underestimated for years while he toiled away at Audi, and he opposed the appointment of Hahn as company chief. One of the biggest disappointments of his life was when Uncle Ferry and his mother decided that no family members would be able to run Porsche AG.

As a student at Zurich's Swiss Federal Institute of Technology in the early 1960s, Piëch immersed himself in his automotive engineering studies. He drove a Porsche and was often seen modifying it, either under it or with his head buried in the hood. Once, over Christmas vacation, he had completed a modification to the engine, but omitted the heater. He drove some 500 kilometers from his family's estate in

Austria to Zurich. He almost froze to death. Asked why he didn't put the heater in, he simply responded that there was no room.

A split between the Piëch and Porsche families dates back to 1943 when Anton and Louise Piëch negotiated a pact with Ferdinand "Ferry" Porsche, and Ferdinand Porsche, Sr., to let the Piëchs take over Porsche's engineering businesses in Austria. The carbuilding and design businesses based near Stuttgart stayed with the Porsches. After World War II, Ferry began designing sports cars based on the Type 1 VW, cars that would again make the Porsche name renowned the world over. In succeeding years, the Porsches and Piëchs agreed to joint ownership of the companies. Rivalries between the two clans have burned over the years.

Piëch joined Porsche's engine department in 1963, and by 1968 had become head of research and development and racing programs. His goal: to win the coveted Manufacturer's World Championship and the 24-hour LeMans race. Piëch invested millions of the company's money into the race programs, honing the Porsche 908 for competition and building a new 350-kilometer-per-hour Porsche 917. His initial results weren't good. The 908 had taken the Manufacturer's Championship in 1969, but the 917, while fast, was dangerous on the track. The first buyer of the car died on his opening lap at LeMans when he lost control and burst into flames, a chilling event that might have undone other executives. Piëch went back to the shop to refine the 917, and the car won 8 out of 11 races in 1971. In his mid-30s, it seemed apparent that the family rivalry and his own lack of tact would prevent him from being CEO of either Porsche or VW, so he went to Audi. There, he eventually became CEO in 1988. Along the way, he developed the first full-time all-wheel-drive system, known as Quattro. Quattro and the revolutionary rounded designs that Piëch developed are credited with transforming Audi from the German equivalent of Buick to a sophisticated line of premium cars worthy of comparison with BMW and Mercedes-Benz. He had the idea for the revolutionary aluminum space frame now being used at Audi in cars like the TT. Piëch reportedly got the idea 20 years ago on a trip to Colorado where he saw Coors beer cans being recycled. He decided then that he wanted a car that could be recycled in the same way. It took 17 years to develop the technology.

Focus and relentlessness are two characteristics most often brought up to describe Piëch. When introducing the all-new Passat to journalists in 1997, the first VW developed from top to bottom on Piëch's watch, he personally drove some 60 cars readied for the press introduction to make sure there were not any obvious quality flaws. This kind of focus and obsession isn't found among executives of his stature, mainly because they have too many plates in the air worldwide to spend that kind of time driving cars. "He is absolutely the most focused individual I have ever come across," says Clive Warrilow. That focus can make for almost comical scenes. Former Volkswagen of America Advertising Director John Slaven recalled attending a dinner in the 1980s at which Piëch was the main speaker. During the dinner, Piëch got to talking to his dinner mate about design. Hardly touching his food, Piëch had ordered his plates taken away. He pulled out a pen, and began using the table cloth as his drawing table, making sketches to explain an engineering principle. Yammering away in his halting English, he was oblivious to all that was going on around him, including the fact that he had become the center of attention. The emcee of the event tried to introduce him as the speaker two or three times, then resorted to tapping him on the shoulder. "I still wish I had hung around to snatch the table cloth," said Slaven.

He is known for getting his way, one way or the other. Like many people, Piëch hates hotel rooms and offices that have windows that can't be opened. Instead of putting up with it, or ordering hotels to have a room for him where he can open a window, he is known to travel with a tool kit that enables him, if he wishes, to unseal the window himself. He hates not to be in control. An ad produced for the United States by the Arnold agency unknowingly paid homage to this Piëch story by suggesting that VW people are the type that hate not being able to open the window in their office.

In 2001, Piëch's acquisition appetite remained unsatisfied. Besides BMW, Piëch is also known to covet Renault, which had an aborted marriage to Volvo in 1997. Renault's huge stake in Nissan, purchased in 1999, makes that unlikely. Renault Chairman Louis Schweitzer deplores the notion of a VW-Renault tie-up. "A combination of Renault and Volkswagen would be a disaster . . . the two companies have such vastly different cultures," says Schweitzer. However, no one really doubts Piëch's ability to acquire what his will wants. Piëch would want Renault or Peugeot to increase VW's mass and to virtually make the company takeover-proof. The addition of either company would put VW's annual vehicle output at around 6 million units, the same territory as GM and Toyota. "Piëch is set on making sure that VW doesn't become a monogram on someone else's shirt pocket," says auto analyst Rod Lache. The way he has been going, it's difficult to see his plan not being realized. When the smoke of industry consolidation clears, there should only be GM, Ford, DaimlerChrysler, Toyota, BMW, VW, and perhaps Honda left supplying the world's appetite for motor vehicles, with everyone else being a unit, affiliate, or division of one of those giants. Honda and Fiat may survive as independents, analysts say, but with significant stakes held by one of the giants. Already by 2000, GM owned a large chunk of Fiat, though not enough to put the company on its balance sheet. Honda, clinging fiercely to its independence, may have to sell a stake to GM as well in order to share product development costs and tie up with a partner that will leave management alone. Only GM has that reputation among the global giants. Piëch is aware that he was given a piece of the industry by his grandfather and mother, and he says that he wants to give his descendants a *bigger* piece than he was given. The pie should be bigger when they inherit it, not smaller, says Piëch.

Tall and thin, with buzz-cut stubble on a bullet-shaped head, Piëch exudes a fearful aura. "He is an imposing presence," admits Arnold Worldwide Chief Executive Officer Ed Eskandarian. Piëch's eyes are an almost unnatural electric blue. They become like lasers when he is meeting people or being interviewed. He possesses little small talk. "He is also hyper intelligent, instinctive and a visionary," says Tony Gott, head of Bentley and Rolls-Royce, who had extensive time to get to know Piëch when negotiations were under way to sell to VW. "He isn't scary," says Gott, who even goes so far as to refer to Piëch as a "people person." And he isn't referring to his diet. "But if he asks you a question, you had better know the answer." Gott, an engineer by training, has had an advantage over many others, as Piëch gets along with engineers better than any other group of people.

As head of VW's Audi division, he had seen collapse in the division's largest export market, North America, due to rumors that the flagship sedan, the 5000, was prone to accelerating out of control. Audi of America had botched the public relations response to the accusations, coldly insisting that there was no problem with Audis. Jens Neumann, the Audi lawyer at the time, said, "We didn't understand the vastness of the problem and how wrong our responses were." Indeed, it would be proven that there wasn't any flaw in the design of the 5000. In the United States, more than any other business environment, perception and heresay is ten-tenths of the law when it comes to public relations. The trial lawyers didn't have to be right. They had the inept Germans, who admit they were wholly unprepared to deal with such a crisis, working for them. Though Audi was never found to have a problem leading to sudden acceleration, every car sold in the United States now has a shift-lock mechanism on automatic transmission vehicles that requires the driver to depress the brake before shifting into drive or reverse.

Said Neumann: "We never lost a single case, but we totally mishandled the public relations. We learned a lot from that experience—that the customer is right. You can never blame the customers. We said in 1993 that we have to regain the hearts of the customers. Capture them with emotional, moreso than rational, arguments and messages."

Even in 2001, with both Audi's and VW's recovery well along, Piëch frustrates his U.S. managers and dealers with a short supply of automatic transmission vehicles. Cars should be driven with manual transmissions, believes Piëch and most serious German engineers and designers. Even more distressing to the Germans is that more and more automatics are being demanded in Europe, owing to more congested city driving where the constant clutching is as tiring to Parisians and Londoners as it has become to New Yorkers and Los Angelinos. It is strangely an affront to Piëch and his managers that so many auto-matics are demanded by Americans, and that Americans do not want the speed-rated tires with which he would like to equip all his cars. "We had to fight every year for these things," recalls Warrilow. "We didn't ask for soft suspensions, which would be an affront to VW design, but we had to keep asking for tires that were more suited to going over the awful roads of Michigan," said Warrilow. A headline in a 12 February 2001 issue of *Automotive News* reporting on the National Automotive Dealer Association convention in Las Vegas, had to pro-claim "VW Promises More Automatics."[7] It is a headline that could have been written 20 years earlier.

At the 2001 Detroit Auto Show, VW introduced yet another icon reincarnation, the VW Microbus. Ever since the New Beetle got the go-ahead, there has been speculation about what other stars of the past could be brought back. The Jetta wagon, which arrived in 2001, answers questions about a vehicle that attacks the same market seg-ment as the old Squareback. The Microbus, though, is a concept, and hadn't (as of July 2001) yet received final go-ahead from Piëch. George Peterson, president of AutoPacific, an automotive research and con-sulting practice, recalls giving a presentation to a group of VW design-ers and engineers at the company's Hannover, Germany, facility as the Microbus concept was being developed. "I was asked by this one fel-low if I thought the Microbus should have sliding doors or sedan doors that open on a hinge. I said. . . . well, Volkswagen set the trend for the sliding door with the original Microbus. But I think the trend now is to sliding doors on both sides of the car. Chrysler has done that, and now Chrysler sets the trend in minivans in America. The fellow responded, 'Dr. Piëch has decided that Americans only need a door on one side of the car.' " By the time the Microbus was shown at the Detroit Auto Show in 2001, though, doors on both sides had been integrated into the design. The feedback from consultants about the one-door plan was too negative. Moreover, the design of a sliding door on each side of the minivans has spawned a design change that is, in 2001, making its way into the concept cars being shown at the auto shows—the dis-appearance of the center column. Engineers discovered new ways to design extra rigidity into the frames that was lost when one side of the minivan was no longer stationary. Mazda, Mitsubishi, GM, and DaimlerChrysler in 2001 all showed cars, big and small, that had no center support column, and yet were stiff and rugged enough to stay crashworthy. The aesthetic design advantages of this were not lost on Piëch. It shows that he is not as hard to convince about U.S. driving tastes as he once was. While he was chief engineer at Audi in the late 1970s, it took hours at a meeting, recalls one staffer, to convince him that Audis needed both air conditioning *and* a sunroof. He has even listened in bemusement at the design studio in Simi Valley, says one VW hand, about how Californians are apt to drive with their windows open, or the top down on a convertible, with the air conditioning on at the same time.

———

It seems Piëch is not driven by money. It's respect that he is after. Had he been running VW in the 1980s, the company would already have a full line of cars, from the entry-level Polo, up to the superluxurious Rolls-Royces, Bentleys, and Lamborghinis. He wants to take on Mercedes-Benz, which itself has been going down-market into VW territory. Not only is Piëch attacking Mercedes at the high end with his acquisitions, but he introduced a 275-horsepower, eight-cylinder Passat in 2001, followed by a sedan that will cost between $70,000 and $80,000, equipped with a 12-cylinder engine. Many inside and outside the company believe it is folly, especially in Europe where it might make sense to introduce such a car as an Audi but not as a VW. Piëch wants respect for the VW brand, though. "Rivalry means nobody falls asleep," says Piëch.[8]

Piëch supports rivalry within the company and sees it as a critical component of continued success. He refers to the other divisions of Volkswagen AG, such as Audi and now Bentley, as "daughter divisions." He discusses "sibling rivalries" between them. He may take Bentley, Audi, and Bugatti cars to LeMans, rather than choosing to support just one. His decision to take VW upmarket to the $75,000 level with the D1 concept has Audi's designers and engineers on notice. His decision to go that far up into the $40,000 to $50,000 segment with a car based on the Passat platform is about profits. The higher you go in price, the more profit there is to make. VW Ad Agency Arnold believes that for the same reason people are opting for VW Jettas and Golfs instead of Hondas and Toyotas, enough younger luxury car buyers—5,000 a year in the United States—will choose the $70,000 VW over the BMW-7 series and Mercedes S class. Its "Drivers wanted" advertising campaign appeals to people who do not much like the remote and insulated ride of an Acura or Lexus and who believe that the Mercedes S class is too big and pretentious. Its real rival will be the BMW-7 series. People at VW would not be surprised if Piëch himself phones anyone who trades in a BMW for the new VW to chat about why they did and invite them to stay at the Ritz-Carlton in Wolfsburg and tour the Autostadt. VW Marketing Chief Frank McGuire admits, though, that the plan to get 30-something VW enthusiasts to trade up to a $75,000 VW looked a lot better before all of the air and money drained out of the Nasdaq stock market and the economy.

No one will ever confuse VW with being a one-car company as it was from the 1940s to the 1970s. Under Piëch, VW has fully recovered. As Daimler-Benz proved, however, it doesn't take much to undo several years of careful planning, as it did when it acquired Chrysler in 1998, only to have the acquisition eliminate almost $50 billion of market value of the combined companies in just 2 years.

Piëch is making sure that VW not only survives, but thrives into the next generation. As he says, it would be wrong to eat the pie that was given to you. The right thing to do is make the pie bigger—and tastier.

Curves Ahead

TEN

As VW begins the twenty-first century, the question arises: Has it recovered in the United States, or is this just a momentary surge? The answer has to be yes to both questions. Just as VW fell to depths in the early 1990s that were almost unimaginable in the late 1960s when it was selling close to one-half million cars in the United States, a long-term slide in the future is not impossible. It is unlikely, but not impossible.

Together with Arnold Worldwide, Volkswagen of America is in a zone with the right products and the right marketing. It's a tough combination to achieve. Few auto companies have managed it. None has managed it as quickly. Demographics and psychographics (cultural attitudes and lifestyles) seem to be in the company's favor as well. The 20- to 30-year-olds of 2000 are confident individualists for the most part, independent thinkers who don't necessarily aspire to the BMW, Mercedes-Benz, and Lexus that their parents lusted for through the 1980s and 1990s. Not that those brands are going to suffer in the early twenty-first century, but it means that there are plenty of people to consider VW as long as product excitement and brand marketing stay on course. Volkswagen is making nimble, fun-to-drive automobiles again. Baby boomers are looking for vehicles that make them feel younger than their driver's licenses show.

In 2001, the New Beetle, which was so much the star of VW's resurgence in the late 1990s, is lagging a little sooner than the company would have hoped. Many dealers report that sales in 2001 are off as much as 30 percent from 2000 when the New Beetle sold more than 85,000 units during a record sales year for the U.S. auto industry. Also, the car has not attracted younger buyers in the numbers that VW had hoped for. Baby boomers, feeling nostalgic, have been the main takers. A turbocharged version, the company hopes, will be more attractive to twenty-somethings and thirty-somethings. A 180-horsepower New Beetle S, which comes in the fall of 2001, and the 2003 New Beetle Cabrio should boost sales, too.

The 2002 Passat clearly marked a pricing move that will test VW's brand elasticity. The Passat has come a long way since 1990 when it made its debut in the United States. In 2000, *Consumer Reports,* for example, named the Passat "Best Family Sedan," topping such stiff rivals as Honda Accord, Toyota Camry, and Ford Taurus. The basic Passat starts at $21,000, but the GLX V-6 Passat with 4Motion (all-wheel-drive) tops $31,000. Volkswagen is betting that there will continue to be enough buyers of midsized cars with a little extra disposable income who are willing to spend a little more for zippier German engineering without jumping to a BMW-3 series or Mercedes C class. The Passat can stand wheel-to-wheel with its richer German brethren, especially since the Mercedes C class has been cheapened, reviewers have noted, as DaimlerChrysler has tried to wring additional profits out of its Mercedes brand.

It's the 2003 Passat W8, an eight-cylinder sedan and wagon to be launched in the United States during the first quarter of 2002, that will really test the price waters. The 4.0-liter car will generate 275 horsepower, and it will serve as a bridge between the Passat line and the D1 luxury car that VW intends to launch after that. The price of the W8 will be around $37,000.

Long overdue in the VW stable has been a sport utility vehicle. That will be solved in 2003, however, when it launches a premium SUV that it has developed jointly with Porsche. In fact, Porsche has taken the lead in developing the vehicle that it will sell as the Cayenne, as well as the SUV to be marketed by VW, possibly as the Colorado. There is enormous competition in the SUV segment, and VW is late to the party. But having only around 35,000 to 40,000 units to sell in the United States should mean that it will not have to fire-sale them. Rather than cutting into sales of other VW models, the expectation is that every sale will be incremental, as VW buyers have always had to go to another brand for an SUV.

All this investment and good news is enough for Volkswagen of America President Gerd Klauss to ask dealers to start investing in dedicated real estate. Starting in the 1970s, many VW dealers began adding other brands to their showrooms, so now only about 15 percent have dedicated VW showrooms. Klauss is campaigning dealers now, and wants to get 50 percent of the U.S. dealers to comply by mid-decade.

Another Icon Cometh

At the Detroit Auto Show in 2001, Volkswagen dipped back into the retro well, showing a concept sure to be built. Seven years after Concept 1, and 3 years after the debut of the New Beetle, VW showed the new Microbus. Like Concept 1, the Microbus had its supporters and its foes within the company.

In early 1999, a few Volkswagen of America staffers began working on a case for the Microbus. Americans who had been through the depths, and now the recovery in progress, feel that there are three icons of the VW brand that have to be addressed in some way: (1) the Beetle, (2) the Microbus, and (3) the Karmann Ghia.

Arnold did a video in support of bringing back the Microbus. The video, reminiscent of the video produced by Freeman Thomas and J Mays to make a case for Concept 1, showed how VW buyers don't have a vehicle that addresses their yearn to *explore*. The idea behind the Microbus concept is to give people a multitask environment. All of this may be marketing semantics, but there is little doubt that an unserved niche may exist for VW people that is met neither by minivans, nor by SUVs. One consumer interviewed for the video said she is looking for a vehicle that is both "functional and responsible." The Microbus symbolized the open road, said the video, while the minivan symbolizes the end of it. There is no question that minivans have taken on a housewife image in the United States. What remains to be seen, though, is whether the Microbus that VW has in development can deliver on this lofty ideal of transcending both the minivan and SUV segments. Just because it will have VW's 4Motion all-wheel drive, a cool stereo, a pop-up roof, and a built-in vacuum doesn't mean that it won't ride and drive like every other minivan or SUV on the market. Encouraging to VW, though, is that there seems to be interest in the idea of a Microbus among Generation X, as well as baby boomers. In a 2001 MasterCard TV ad, for example, two college-age men are depicted touring all of the baseball stadiums in America in a vintage Microbus, not a modern-day sport utility.

The Microbus will have to sell only about 50,000 to 60,000 in North America, and another 30,000 worldwide. To keep it economical to build so that unrealistic sales volumes do not hinder its success, it shares a platform with the Eurovan, as well as a pickup truck concept being worked on. There is much anticipation that it will be priced around $30,000 when it finally arrives. It figures to be the first minivan to deserve a rock concert tour to help promote it. If there is another Woodstock, or LilithFair, look for the Microbus.

Neumann told the Microbus champions at Simi Valley, including Concept 1 cosire Freeman Thomas, that he didn't want a concept developed if it wasn't truly buildable. There were engineering problems with the B pillar as far as the early sketches were concerned. Those were based on building it off the existing platform that was supporting the Eurovan, not the new one. Also, to be a true Microbus, the nose had to be flat and stubby. This presented enormous problems in the way of making the van safe. Neumann said—and this was Piëch's philosophy as well—that the Microbus should not only be the best vehicle in its class, but as safe or safer in crash testing than the leaders—Chrysler and Ford.

Though the Simi Valley studio has produced sketches and models for a modern Karmann Ghia, it seems unlikely that VW would resuscitate the classic KG, unless it became an outright replacement for the New Beetle in the future. In North America, VW is already slicing the Golf platform among Golf, Jetta, GTI, New Beetle, and Jetta wagon. What might be logical for the future is that a new-generation Karmann Ghia could replace the New Beetle when the company feels it has run its course. The two models could alternate being a VW brand magnet. More likely than a Karmann Ghia marketed at the same time as the New Beetle is the introduction of a true entry-level car to the United States, such as the Polo is in Europe and Latin America. The margins are so thin at that level of the market, though, that not even that is certain. Volkswagen marketed the Fox in the late 1980s and early 1990s, but it was withdrawn by 1995.

Sustaining the Magic

Volkswagen's relationship with Arnold is evolving just as DDB's relationship did, and truth be told, current developments have a few people concerned. Since winning the VW business in 1995, Arnold has been sold twice, first to Snyder Communications and then to French advertising company Havas. Havas had a weak global agency network called Campus, which it is merging with Arnold. The offices are being renamed Arnold in each market, an unlikely move before Arnold won VW and made such a success of its advertising. So, just as DDB grew globally on VW's back, so is Arnold.

Because Volkswagen AG favors uniformity and streamlined operations where it can achieve them, it has Arnold challenging DDB's hold on the international advertising accounts. Even before the competitions started taking place in Germany and elsewhere, Arnold's campaigns and brand strategy were being adapted by DDB offices abroad at VW's behest. Some VW staffers, though, both past and present, look at these developments with great trepidation, recalling how the magic created by DDB in the early 1960s dissipated as DDB got bigger and broader and then was acquired in the mid-1980s. It was, after all, with incredulity that some midlevel Volkswagen of America executives learned that conversations had taken place between Arnold's Ed Eskandarian and DDB's Keith Reinhard about a merger as early as 1997. Volkswagen executives had gone so far as to threaten some of DDB's business in Europe and Australia when DDB chairman Keith Reinhard made overtures to buy VW's Canadian agency that had replaced DDB in the late 1980s.

There is worry that Arnold will lose the qualities that made it stand apart from DDB in 1995, as well as its other small, independent competitors in the hotly contested review for the VW advertising business. "I don't see that happening," says Jon Castle. "Our commitment is to the American market first. Winning overseas business is nice, but we are in close communication with Dr. Neumann to make sure that our priority remains the American market." Havas in early 2001 was also in talks with Audi agency McKinney & Silver, going for a consolidation of VW business just like DDB.

History has a tendency to repeat itself. Although VW's current products are the best VW machines ever built, their uniqueness relative to the Japanese and some domestics has a great deal to do with how they are marketed. Styling of the Golf and Jetta are not so unique that they can speak for themselves.

The team that chose VW and fixed the marketing has completely turned over, with Steve Wilhite having moved on to other industries altogether, and Liz Vanzura departing at the end of 2000 for GM, where she will work with "Drivers wanted" cocreator Lance Jensen to relaunch the Hummer brand for GM. Jensen left Arnold to start his own agency. The glue seems to be provided by the special relationship that has developed between Arnold Creative Chief Ron Lawner and Dr. Neumann. At the 2001 Detroit Auto Show, Dr. Neumann, in the presence of his wife, looked in Lawner's direction and said, "He is the only one who understands me." It was a testament to Lawner's commitment to keeping the advertising special, and Neumann's dedication to keeping the U.S. marketing pure and separate from political wrangling in Wolfsburg, which tends to want to see more rational than emotional advertising behind its cars.

The launch of the D1 luxury car has a lot of VW managers nervous. In 2001, Volkswagen AG selected a small German agency that impressed Dr. Piëch with a plan to launch the car to aristocrats, rather than as an "alternative" luxury sedan for people who eschew the luxury imagery of BMW and Mercedes-Benz.

After Dr. Piëch moves to chair the supervisory board in 2002, leaving the chairmanship of the Volkswagen AG, in all likelihood, to Bernd Pischetsrieder, the hope is that Dr. Jens Neumann, who has been in line for the top job, will still be around to guide North America.

Good Financials Make Good Products

In March 2001, shares in VW fell to a 6-month low based on skepticism that the company could keep profits rising in the midst of a global economic slowdown. Dr. Piëch pledged to cut costs by more than $900 million in 2001 to offset the down market. Volkswagen's net debt of 3.4 billion euros was worse than analysts expected. Volkswagen has been investing heavily in product development and factories to support Piëch's luxury car strategy, trading at 22 times its operating free cash flow compared with between 8 and 12 times the cash flow among its rivals. Its profit for fiscal 2000 was not bad at all, but it's the future that analysts and investors look at. Indeed, Volkswagen AG's profits in fiscal 2000 were $1.88 billion, more than double the profit of 1999. North America contributed 20 percent of that, almost twice what it had kicked in the year before.

The 20 percent ownership of VW by the state of Lower Saxony can frustrate any chairman's ability to run the company on a globally competitive basis. In March 2001, for example, after Dr. Piëch declared his intent for a 1-euro-per-share dividend, the supervisory board—made up of employees, management, and Lower Saxony representatives—overruled him and declared a dividend of 1.20 euros. Analysts noted that the move was undertaken because of the slowing German economy and high unemployment rate and the wish to impart the extra cash to shareholders. It was a unique event in VW's history.

Dr. Piëch is running out of time to meet goals that he had set when he took over in 1993. He promised shareholders then he would achieve a pretax profit of 6.5 percent on revenues by 2000. He fell dramatically short: Volkswagen earned just 3.5 percent in 2000. That is not terribly surprising, considering that the original pledge was unexpected coming from a man who has never demonstrated much concern for shareholder value and is not exactly working for incentive pay. Even French automaker Renault earned 6.3 percent. Such a jump to Piëch's stated goal before he retires seems unlikely. It could, however, be attained while he is chairman of the supervisory board, a post he is expected to hold until he is into his 70s.

The company's age-old problem is labor. Piëch has been slow to shift a greater percentage of production from high-cost Lower Saxony to cheaper labor markets. About one-half of VW's workforce of 324,000 is in Germany. Volkswagen's German workforce kicks out just 40 vehicles per worker annually. Its Spanish workforce manages to build 79 per year. Nissan's Sunderland, England, plant manages 112, and British autoworkers don't exactly have a reputation for burning up the industry's measurements of efficiency. Ford's Taurus plant in Atlanta produces 105 cars per worker per year. Volkswagen's profit per vehicle in 2000 worked out to just $373 per car, compared with Renault's $571.

Consider that while Volkswagen AG sells five times as many cars as BMW, it had roughly the same market capitalization. That is a reflection of both VW's dependence on low-margin vehicles and its high cost structure. This explains, in part, Piëch's facination with leaving the company a legitimate competitor in the luxury car arena, where profits per vehicle are a lot higher than they are with Golfs, Jettas, and Polos.

Maybe Piëch tends to turn a deaf ear to investors and analysts because he knows that he cannot compete with his global rivals on an even playing field. The government in Lower Saxony is Social Democratic, and it places a much higher premium on jobs than share price or profits. Goldman-Sachs auto analyst Keith Hayes says, "Wolfsburg is almost an arm of the German social security system."

Piëch's strategy of building many cars on few platforms looks brilliant on one level: The cars do, in fact, look remarkably different. Who would believe, for example, that the VW Golf, Jetta, New Beetle, Audi A3, Audi TT Roadster, SEAT Toledo, Leon, and Skoda Octavia are all built off the same mechanical platform? Consumers do read, however. Over time, knowledge that the cars are so similar under the skin has been absorbed by the marketplace, and some cannibalization of models has been taking place. In the United States, while many come to a showroom to see the New Beetle, many leave in a Golf. In Europe, trading down to less expensive vehicles that are mechanically the same as the more expensive ones is more prevalent.

Dr. Piëch is refining his platform strategy, planning on increasing the number of platforms by 2005, but designing the vehicles so that groups of cars extensively share systems. Piëch says there will be 11 groups of cars sharing brakes, transmissions, and the like, which will save the company billions in operating costs going forward when his successor is managing the balance sheet.

There are costs to rid though scale, and Piëch understands that the bigger VW can become, the broader he can spread costs. By 2001, he had largely tabled his hope of acquiring BMW, but he still holds out hope to absorb either Italian maker Fiat or Peugeot. The latter seems more likely than the former, because Fiat appears to have cast its lot with GM, which now owns 20 percent of the Italian carmaker and seems content to leave management in place.

One significant change for VW, which analysts and investors, even scholars, are watching closely is Piëch's decision to adopt international accounting standards. Volkswagen's financials, even more than other German companies, have long been something of a mystery. The Germans are well known for having secret reserves, which materialize on rainy days before quarterly reports when the share price is slipping too fast and too hard.

The Rich People's Cars

Piëch's luxury strategy is being closely watched, too, and has led many critics to suggest that he is overstaying his usefulness to the company. He has dedicated time and resources to acquiring Rolls-Royce and Bentley (though not the Rolls-Royce brand), as well as Bugatti and Lamborghini. His plan to launch a VW-branded vehicle to compete against Mercedes S class, the D1, is viewed as an exercise of his ego rather than a sound business idea.

At the end of 2000, Piëch stated that he plans to introduce 67 high-end models in the next few years, which includes all of the body and engine variations on the vehicles. He has allocated $18.6 billion in development costs to build the models and $102 billion for factories.

Piëch has given up, for the time being, trying to convince the Quandt family, who owns 46 percent of BMW, to merge with VW. However, he will be watching closely from his perch as supervisory board chairman, hoping for enough weakness in the company's financials that the Quandts will have to seek out a big brother.

Bentley is his upmarket baby. After acquiring Bentley, one of the first things Piëch did was to go back to putting Crewe, England–built engines in the cars. Before that, BMW had been supplying engines, and few buyers wanted a Bentley with a German engine. The first model in VW's resurgence plan is the medium-sized Bentley (MSB). It shares many characteristics of traditional Bentleys, but has a steeply angled hood and will be closer to the ground, according to sketches. The MSB is aimed at a younger buyer (as all cars seem to be these days), and the hope is that women will take to it. Ninety-eight percent of Bentley buyers are men. The price will be something around $140,000 to $150,000. It should land on well-heeled driveways in 2003. Piëch expects the car to take Bentley's annual production from less than 2,000 a year to almost 10,000 after a car to be priced around $110,000 comes out after the MSB.

The Bugatti EB 16.4 Veyron is another story, with not nearly as reasonable a business plan. A production model of this 8.0-liter, four-turbo, 1,000-horsepower, 750,000-euro-plus car is set to debut in late 2003. About 100 of these are expected to be made per year for the people who buy such toys. In the long run, says Piëch, Bugatti can replace what he lost in the Rolls-Royce/Bentley deal when he failed to secure rights to market the Rolls-Royce name after 2003. Bugatti, he believes, can replace Rolls in the super premium segment.

Quality Is a Job Still to Come

There is no doubt that VW is pleasing its customers. Strategic Vision, a research firm that measures what it calls *Total Quality*, ranked VW number one among full-line automakers in the $21,000 to $35,000 segment in 2000, which was based on customer data gathered in 1999. Strategic Vision's Total Quality Index measures customer satisfaction as consumers define it: the whole experience of buying, owning, and driving a new vehicle. Volkswagen topped every category in which they had a model entered, said the firm, "by clearly exceeding buyers' expectations." Volkswagen's score bested not just GM and Ford, but Honda and Toyota as well. Its scores were more in line with luxury brands like BMW and Mercedes than the mass-market brands. Indeed, it posted a higher score than Honda's premium Acura brand.

On the other hand, even though VW has done much to improve quality, it has many miles to go before it can begin to sleep. According to J. D. Power's 2000 IQS study, VW improved by 20 points from 1999, but was still ranked above only Hyundai, Kia, Daewoo, and Suzuki with 203 problems per 100 vehicles. The industry average was 158 problems. BMW, Porsche, and Mercedes-Benz all ranked in the top nine brands. Volvo and Saab, VW's European rivals, both ranked above average at 154 and 140 problems, respectively. There is no excuse for VW still to rank so low.

The EU Looms Big For Piëch's Plans

The European Union, in the spring of 2001, after having laid $100 million in fines onto VW for price fixing on the Passat in Europe, was also taking a hard look at the antique corporate structure of VW that dates back to when Heinz Nordhoff was running the company.

Not only does the government of Lower Saxony own 20 percent of the company, but the company's charter says no other entity can own more than 20 percent. This has served as a baked-in poison pill, protecting Piëch and his predecessors from unwanted suitors such as Ford, Renault, GM, or Toyota. But the EU doesn't see why VW should have such protected status. If the EU orders the charter changed, which it is likely to do, that leaves VW suddenly very vulnerable because, as of June 2001, it would take less than $20 billion to acquire Europe's leading carmaker.

The EU is examining whether Lower Saxony's influence might interfere with the free movement of capital guaranteed under European Union rules. The Commission is concerned that a public authority, which does not own a majority of equity, can exert influence on the way the company is run. The current rule limits interest from foreign investors because a foreign investor will say, "What is the point of investing if locals might veto what I want to do?" A Commission ruling against the law would not necessarily force Lower Saxony to sell its stake in the group, but it would make the company more attractive to potential investors by diluting the influence of the state.

The investigation into VW came as the European Union was seeking to finalize a proposed new code that would harmonize takeover rules across the 15-member bloc. To replace the poison pill that has been in place, Piëch, as of this writing, is considering a restructuring of the company that would break it into two main parts, with VW, SEAT, and Skoda on one side, and Audi, Bentley, Bugatti, and Lamborghini on the other. Other parts of the companies, such as research and development, VW's finance division, its heavy truck operation, and other pieces would become a web of corporate subsidiaries in the style that

Japanese companies adopted long ago so that acquiring the company is more difficult and costly.

Whether these changes force Piëch's successor to alter some of the strategy set in place by the corporate scion remains to be seen. What seems certain, though, is that for the 6 years Piëch is chairman of the supervisory board, the next VW chairman is going to be caught between an investment community that will have to be taken far more seriously than in the past and a board chairman who has been one of the most willful and arrogant in German corporate history. It could be, as one news report in May 2001 stated, a "poisoned chalice for Piëch's successor."

Reflection

Ferdinand Piëch, Jens Neumann, Helmut Warkuss, Freeman Thomas, J Mays, Steve Wilhite, Bill Young, Clive Warrilow, Liz Vanzura, Steve Keyes, Tony Fouladpour, Ed Eskandarian, Ron Lawner, Lance Jensen, Alan Pafenbach, and Jon Castle—all played prominent roles in engineering a comeback for VW in America. Some have exerted more influence than others, but they, and many more not mentioned here, have contributed greatly to the resurgence of VW.

How close VW came to actually leaving the United States in the early 1990s is hard to measure. Certainly, it was not out of the question. The United States has become a fiercely competitive market for automobiles, and it has claimed its casualties—not only imports such as Fiat, Peugeot, Renault, and MG, but U.S. brands such as American Motor, Oldsmobile, and Plymouth.

Those brands that have left and that are leaving the new-car marketplace as the twenty-first century begins have their fans and enthusiasts. Perhaps because of its dramatic beginnings, though, I think VW is a bit more special. Conceived by a lunatic who wanted to use an inexpensive automobile to help win over the masses of Germany in the mid-1930s, the car, the brand, somehow climbed out of that misery and evil as if it was not even a part of the horror that took place. Victims used the car to rebuild their lives, feed their families, and reenter the daylight. It was literally a good that had come from an evil. Only then did it become a real people's car and live up to its name. It was much more, as later advertising would convey, than a way to get from point A to point B.

Many Americans who first greeted the Beetle in the early 1950s dismissed it as Hitler's car. While you couldn't ignore the troubled origins, it was, and always would be, the people's car. The company and the lineup of cars being hatched by Ferdinand Porsche's grandson in the twenty-first century are a far cry from what Heinz Nordhoff could have imagined in 1968 when he was only just seeing the beginnings of VW's foray into front-wheel-drive cars. The journey from being a one-car company in the early 1970s to the company of today was painful and full of wrong turns and dead ends. However, car companies, like sharks, die if they stop moving forward.

It seems a good bet that VW will continue to move forward in the United States for many years to come, and that the story will continue—to our surprise and delight.

Notes

Introduction

1. "Can VW Survive?," *Adweek's Marketing Week*, May 1, 1989.

Chapter One

Footnotes

1. Jim Mateja, *The Chicago Tribune*, February 13, 1994.
2. Shell Tomlin, Associated Press, January 1994.
3. VW Press release, November 28, 1994.
4. Ferdinand Piëch prepared remarks and subsequent interview, January 1998.

Interview and Source Notes

Remarks of Ullie Seiffert at the press conference.

Freeman Thomas interview, January 2001.

J Mays interview at January 1998 Auto Show.

Bill Young interviews, January 2001.

Donny Deutsch interview, April 1998.

Dave Huyett interview, February 2001.

Ferdinand Piëch prepared remarks and subsequent interview, January 1998.

Dr. Neumann interviews, September 2000 and January 2001.

Tony Fouladpour, February 2001.

Matt DeLorenzo, *The New Beetle*, MBI Publishing, 1998.

Chapter Two
Footnotes

1. Allan Nevins and Frank Ernest Hill, *Ford: The Times, the Man, the Company*, Charles Scribner's Sons, 1954.
2. Walter Henry Nelson, *Small Wonder*. Little Brown, 1970.
3. Adolf Hitler, *Mein Kampf*, CPA Books, English Translation, 1990.
4. Speech by Adolf Hitler, 1934 Berlin Auto Show, VW archive.
5. Ibid.
6. Walter Henry Nelson, *Small Wonder*. Little Brown, 1970.
7. Ibid.
8. Ibid.
9. Ibid.
10. Speech by Adolf Hitler at the laying of the cornerstone, KdF Factory, VW archive.
11. Robert W. Nitske, *The Amazing Porsche and Volkswagen Story*, Comet Press Books, 1958.
12. Ibid.
13. Ibid.
14. Karl Ludvigsen, *Battle for the Beetle*, Bentley Publishers, 2000.
15. Ibid.
16. *Volkswagen: Learning from History*, published by Volkswagen AG, 2000.
17. *The Volkswagen Factory and Its Workers in the Third Reich*, published by Volkswagen AG, 2000.
18. Ibid.
19. Ibid.
20. Ferry Porsche, *Cars Are My Life*, 1990, Motorbooks International.

21. *The Volkswagen Factory and Its Workers in the Third Reich,* pu[b]lished by Volkswagen AG, 2000.

Chapter Three
Footnotes

1. Ludvigsen, *Battle for the Beetle.*
2. Ibid.
3. Ibid.
4. *The Jersey Journal, The New York Times,* various issues, 1948.
5. *Stern,* December 12, 1948.
6. Graham Robson and the Auto Editors of Consumer Guid[e] *Road & Track, Motor Trend,* and *Mechanix Illustrated* cites fro[m] *VW Chronicle,* Publications International, 1996.
7. "The Story of a Motor Car, Biography of Volkswagen[,]" William Bittorf, ed., *Der Spiegel,* publication date NA.
8. Ibid.
9. Ibid.
10. Ibid.
11. Grace Glueck, *The New York Times,* January 30, 1955.
12. Graham Robson and the Auto Editors of Consumer Guid[e] *Road & Track, Motor Trend,* and *Mechanix Illustrated* cites fro[m] *VW Chronicle.* Publications International, 1996.
13. Nelson, *Small Wonder.*
14. Ibid.
15. Graham Robson and the Auto Editors of Consumer Guid[e] *Road & Track, Motor Trend,* and *Mechanix Illustrated* cites fro[m] *VW Chronicle.* Publications International, 1996.

Chapter Four
Footnotes

1. Nelson, *Small Wonder.*
2. *Sales Management,* March 1959.
3. Frank Rowsome, Jr., *Think Small,* Ballantine Books, 1970.
4. "The Story of a Motor Car, Biography of Volkswagen," *D[er] Spiegel,* date unknown.

ice Kanner, *100 Best TV Commercials: And Why They eed,* Times Books, 1999.

id Ogilvy, *Ogilvy on Advertising,* HarperCollins, 1987.

ria Steinem, VW Infomercial, 1993.

ham Robson and the Auto Editors of Consumer Guide, *d & Track, Motor Trend,* and *Mechanix Illustrated* cites from *Chronicle.* Publications International, 1996.

and Source Notes

Krone interview, 1999.

ce interview, February 2001.

erkins interview, February 2001.

ven interview, 1998.

ve

s

son, *Road & Track* cite from *Volkswagen Chronicle,*

yann Keller, *Collision: GM, Toyota, Volkswagen and the Race to the 21st Century,* William Morrow.

s Group memo, February 14, 1980, Porche-Audi-kswagen.

bit *Action Group Report,* August 1981, Porche-Audi-kswagen.

& Driver, November 1982.

es, January 28, 1985.

ew and Source Notes

Huyett interview, February 2001.

McLernon interview, February 2001.

ung interviews, January 2001.

laven interviews in 1997 and 1998.

Charlie Hughes interview, March 2001.

John Bulcroft interview, January 2001.

Dave Power interview, January 2001.

Car and Driver, May 1984.

Ibid., March 1985.

Ibid., August 1986.

Ibid., June 1985.

Ibid., February 1987.

Ibid., August 1987.

Ibid., May 1988.

Ibid., October 29, 1990.

Ibid., April 3, 1989.

Ibid., December 2, 1985.

Ibid., August 17, 1981.

Fortune, August 3, 1987.

Fortune, March 31, 1986.

Businessweek, December 7, 1987.

Ibid., June 22, 1987.

Ibid., January 27, 1986.

Ibid., July 15, 1985.

Ibid., July 11, 1983.

Ibid., April 14, 1980.

Ibid., October 5, 1981.

Ibid., November 16, 1981.

Ibid., March 3, 1980.

Ibid., August 2, 1982.

Ibid., October 25, 1982.

Ibid., April 25, 1983.

Ray Ketchledge interview, 1988, first published in *Adweek's Marketing Week*, May 1, 1988.

Roy Grace interview, February 2001.

Steve Keyes interview, December 2000.

Steve Wilhite interview, January 2001.

Dave Schembri interview, 1992.

Chapter Six

Footnote

1. *Forbes,* May 4, 1998.

Interview and Source Notes

Bill Young interviews, January 2001.
Steve Wilhite interviews, January 2001, February 2001.
Andy Berlin interviews, March 2000, May 1992.
Greg Staffen interview, March 1992.
Tony Wright interview, March 1992.
Dave Huyett interview, March 1992.
Mike Rogers interview, March 1992.
Chris von Berg interview, March 1992.
Clive Warrilow interviews, January 2001.
Dr. Neumann interviews, September 2000, January 2001.
Dr. Neumann speech transcript, VW dealer meeting, 1994.
Adam Green interview, February 2001.

Chapter Seven

Footnotes

1. Excerpt from T.S. Eliot, *Little Gidding V, Four Quartets.* Found on a single sheet of paper in a VW file folder containing documents pertaining to the advertising review.
2. *USA Today,* March 28, 1995.
3. *Adweek,* February 2, 2000.

Interview and Source Notes

Steve Wilhite interviews, January 2001.
Dave Huyett interview, February 2001.
Stan Richards interview, February 2001.
Ron Lawner interview, December 2000.
Kristin Volk interview, January 2001.
Fran Kelly interview, December 2000.
John Gaffney interview, December 2000.
Peter Dracoulius interview, February 2001.

Donny Deutsch interviews, 1995, 1996.

Ed Eskandarian interview, December 2000.

Liz Vanzura interview, March 2001.

Dr. Jens Neumann interviews, September 2000, January 2001.

Jon Castle interview, December 2000.

Ron Silagi interview, December 2000.

Lance Jensen interview, March 2001.

Chapter Eight

Footnotes

1. *USA Today,* July 23, 1997.
2. *Automobile* magazine, March 1998.
3. *USA Today,* November 20, 1998.
3. *Adweek,* January 24, 2000.

Interview and Source Notes

Steve Wilhite interview, January 2001.

John Gaffney interview, December 2000.

Ron Lawner interview, December 2000.

Dr. Neumann interviews, September 2000, January 2001.

Jon Castle interview, December 2000.

Steve Keyes interview, December 2000.

Liz Vanzura interview, March 2001.

Dennis Keene interview, May 2000.

Fran Kelly interview, December 2000.

Lance Jensen interview, February 2001.

Clive Warrilow interview, January 2001.

Adam Green interview, March 2001.

Dave Huyett interview, March 2000.

Ron Silagi interview, December 2000.

Kristin Volk interview, March 2001.

Chapter Nine

Footnotes

1. Piëch interviews, January 1994, January 1998.
2. *Manager Magazin* (German), April 1998.

3. *Businessweek*, October 5, 1998.

4. *Manager Magazin*, April 1998.

5. Ferry Porsche, *Cars Are My Life*, Motorbooks International, 1990.

6. *Newsweek*, January 12, 1998.

6. *Automotive News*, February 12, 2000.

8. Paris Auto Show post speech remarks, September 2000.

Interview and Source Notes

Dr. Neumann interviews, September 2000, January 2001.

Ed Eskandarian interview, December 2000.

Gerd Klauss interview, February 2001.

Piëch speech, Geneva Car Show, March 1997.

Piëch speech, Palm Springs, CA, November 1998.

Businessweek, January 11, 1999.

The Toronto Star, November 21, 1998.

Piëch speech, Detroit Auto Show, January 1997.

Investor's Business Daily, December 1, 1998.

Manager Magazin (German), April 1998.

Robb Report, October 1998.

Financial Times, January 6, 1998.

Newsweek, January 12, 1998.

Automotive Industries, March 1, 1998.

Chicago Tribune, January 7, 1999.

Businessweek, March 30, 1998.

Fortune, March 29, 1999.

Piëch interviews, January 1994, January 1998.

Videotape of Piëch, July 1993.

Clive Warrilow interviews, January 2001.

Steve Schroeder interview, August 2000.

John Slaven interview, 1994.

George Peterson interview, March 2001.

Car magazine, May 13, 1999.

Piëch speech, Atlanta, GA, February 1998.

Wall Street Journal, March 4, 1998.

Stern, February 28, 1998.

Ferry Porsche, *Cars Are My Life*, Motorbooks International, 1990.
Automotive News, February 12, 2000.
Newsweek, January 12, 1998.

Chapter Ten
Interview and Source Notes
Dr. Neumann interview, January 2001.
Gerd Klauss interview, February 2001.
Jon Castle interview, December 2000.
Ed Eskandarian interview, December 2000.
Steve Wilhite interview, January 2001.
Lance Jensen interview, February 2001.

Index